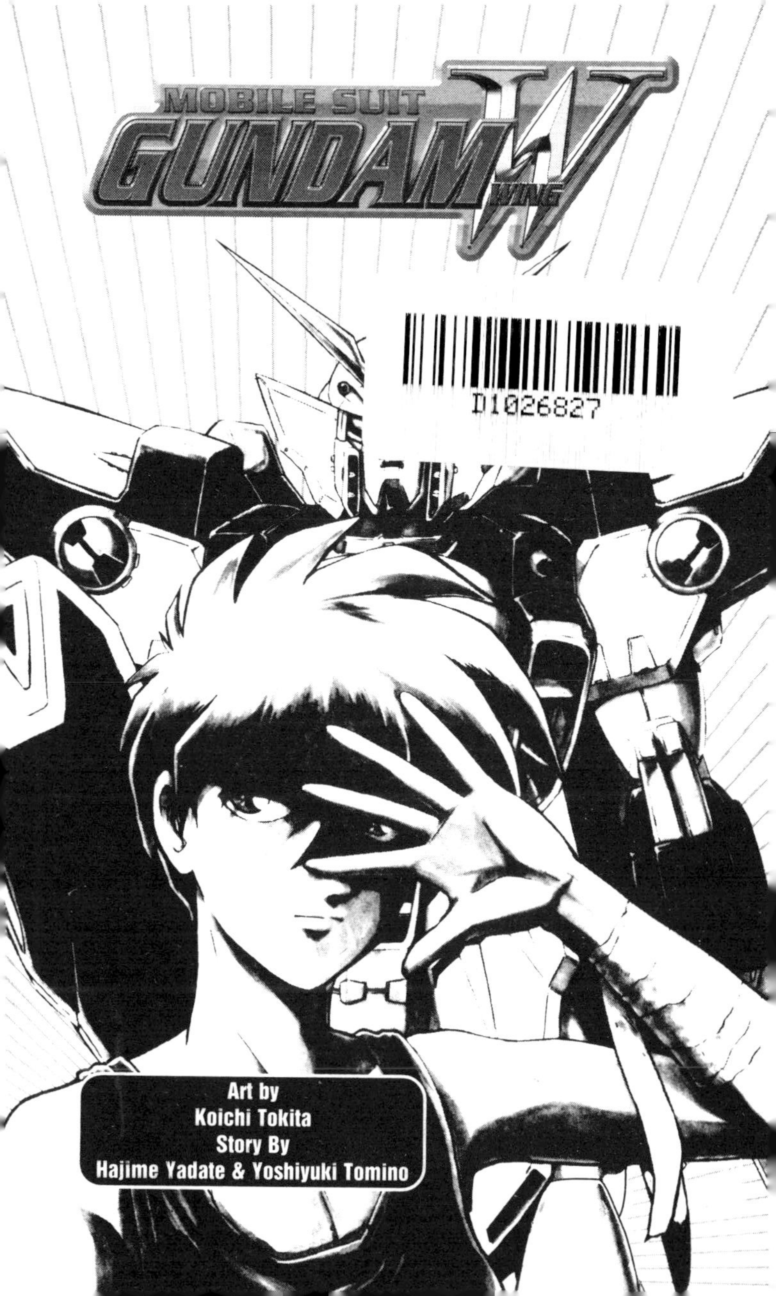
MOBILE SUIT
GUNDAM
WING
D1026827
Art by
Koichi Tokita
Story By
Hajime Yadate & Yoshiyuki Tomino

Mixx Entertainment Presents
Gundam Wing 1 by Koich Tokita
Mixx Manga Pocket Edition is an imprint of Mixx Entertainment, Inc.

ISBN: 1-892213-41-9
First Printing May 2000

10 9 8 7 6 5 4 3 2 1

Story originally appeared in Gundam Wing Mixx Manga No. 1 through No. 4 in its entirety.

Email: info@mixxonline.com
Come visit us at www.TOKYOPOP.com.

Mixx Entertainment, Inc.
Los Angeles - Tokyo

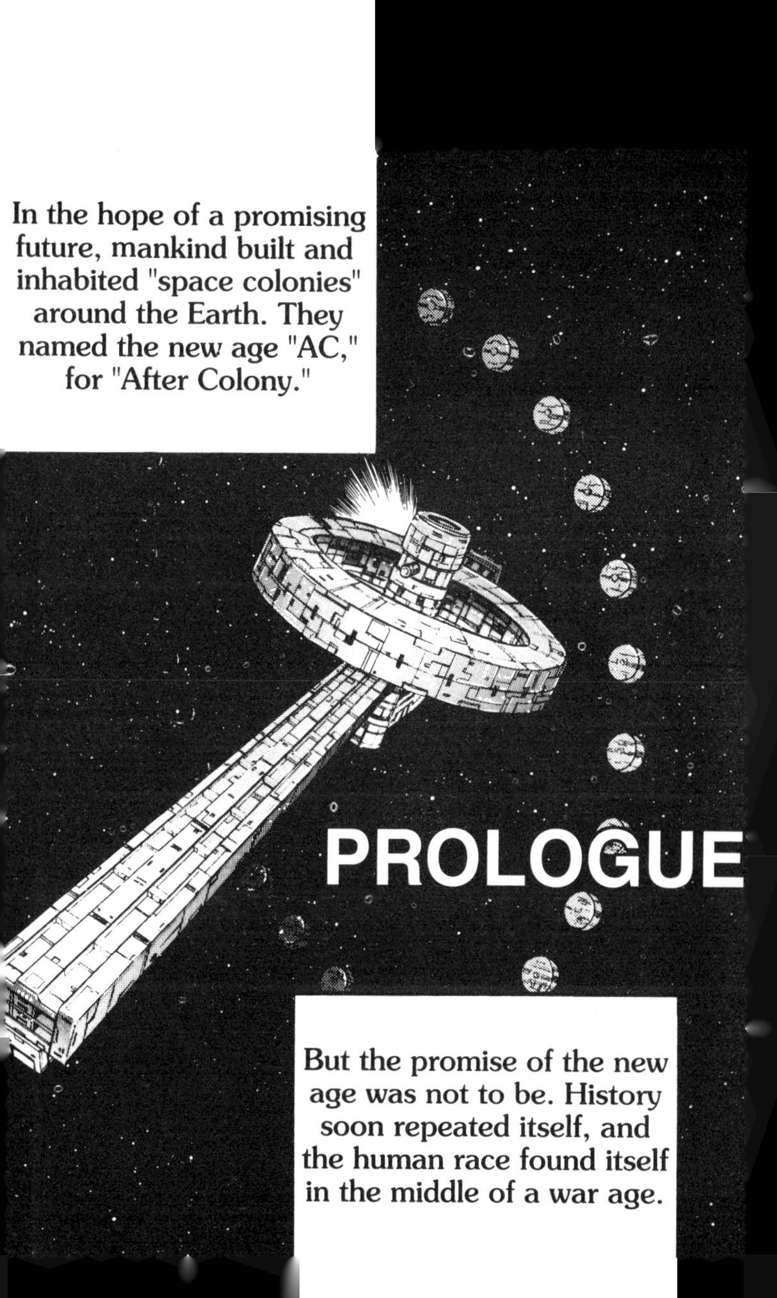
In the hope of a promising future, mankind built and inhabited "space colonies" around the Earth. They named the new age "AC," for "After Colony."
PROLOGUE
But the promise of the new age was not to be. History soon repeated itself, and the human race found itself in the middle of a war age.

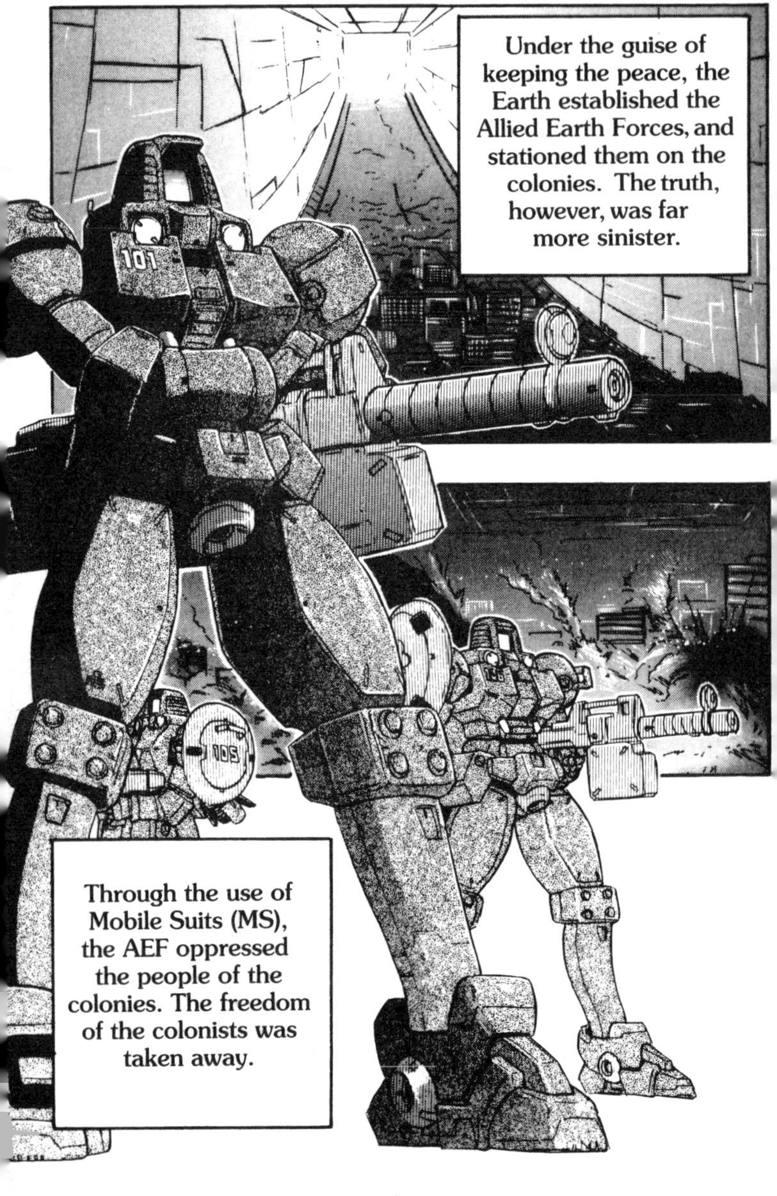
Under the guise of keeping the peace, the Earth established the Allied Earth Forces, and stationed them on the colonies. The truth, however, was far more sinister.
101
105
Through the use of Mobile Suits (MS), the AEF oppressed the people of the colonies. The freedom of the colonists was taken away.

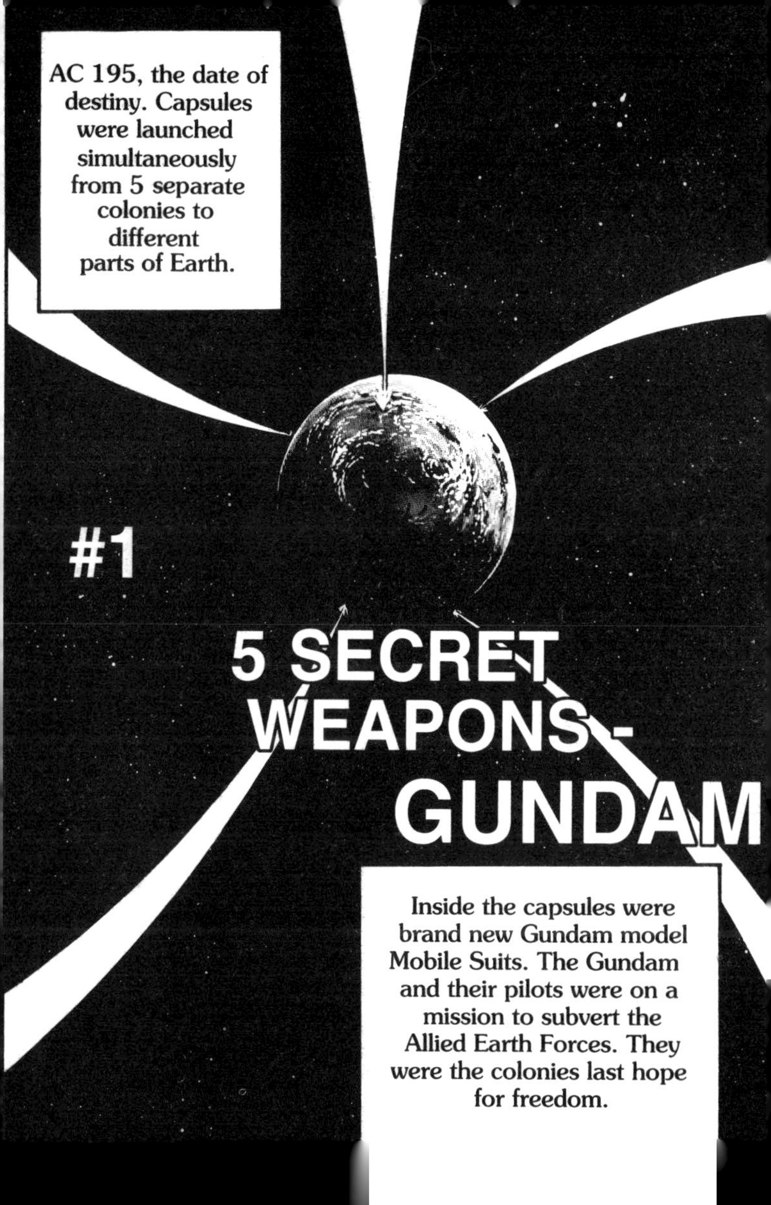
AC 195, the date of destiny. Capsules were launched simultaneously from 5 separate colonies to different parts of Earth.
#1
5 SECRET WEAPONS - GUNDAM
Inside the capsules were brand new Gundam model Mobile Suits. The Gundam and their pilots were on a mission to subvert the Allied Earth Forces. They were the colonies last hope for freedom.

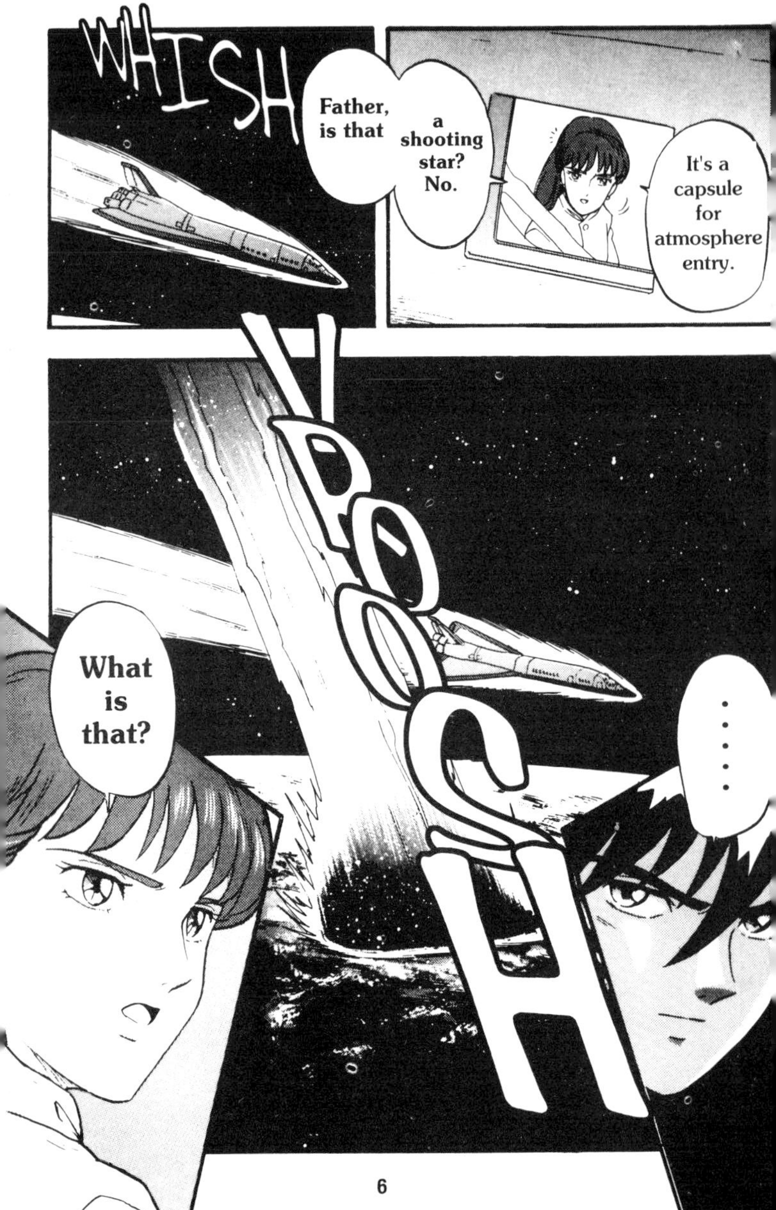
WHISH
Father, is that
a shooting star? No.
It's a capsule for atmosphere entry.
VROO-OOSH
What is that?
.....

Special Lieutenant Zechs! We've located one of the capsules!

It should touch down in East Eurasia! It must be the capsule from Operation M. Go after it!

OZ TRANSPORT

VOOM

ZECHS MERQUISE, OZ SPECIAL LIEUTENANT

It's the Allies' attack transport.

PEEP

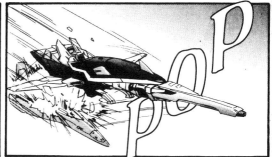

POP

VOOM

Whoever saw my ride has to die.

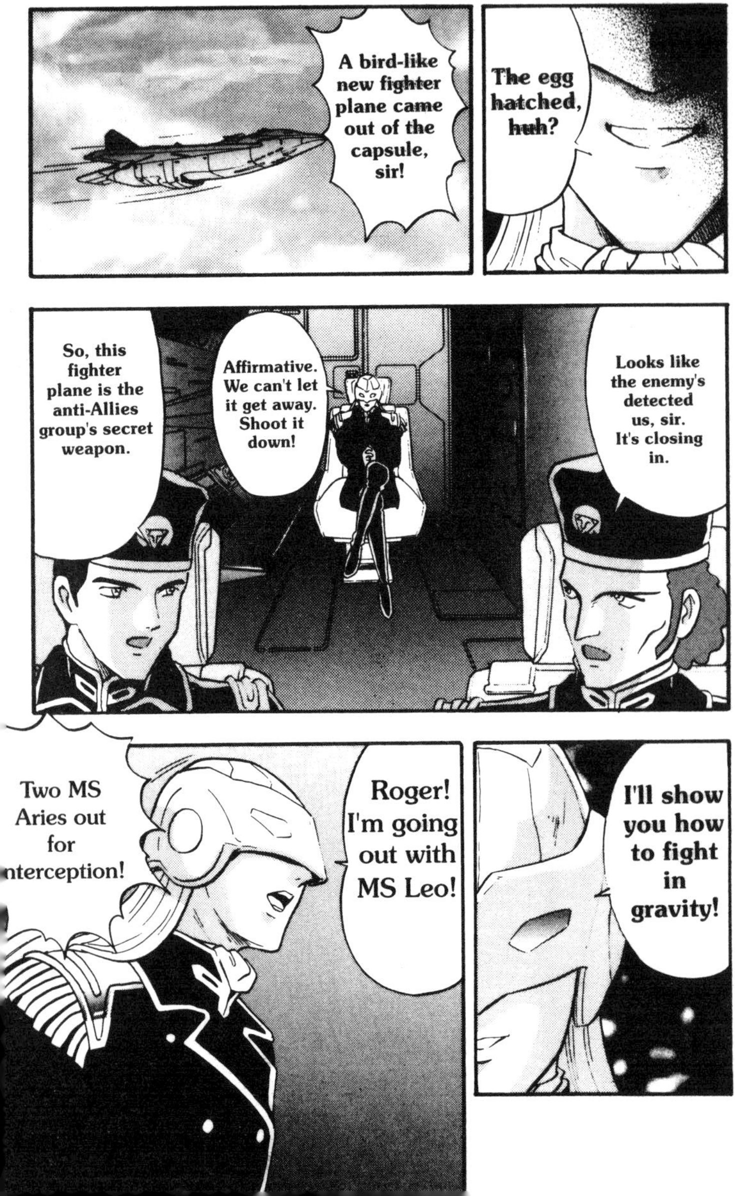
A bird-like new fighter plane came out of the capsule, sir!
The egg hatched, huh?
So, this fighter plane is the anti-Allies group's secret weapon.
Affirmative. We can't let it get away. Shoot it down!
Looks like the enemy's detected us, sir. It's closing in.
Two MS Aries out for nterception!
Roger! I'm going out with MS Leo!
I'll show you how to fight in gravity!

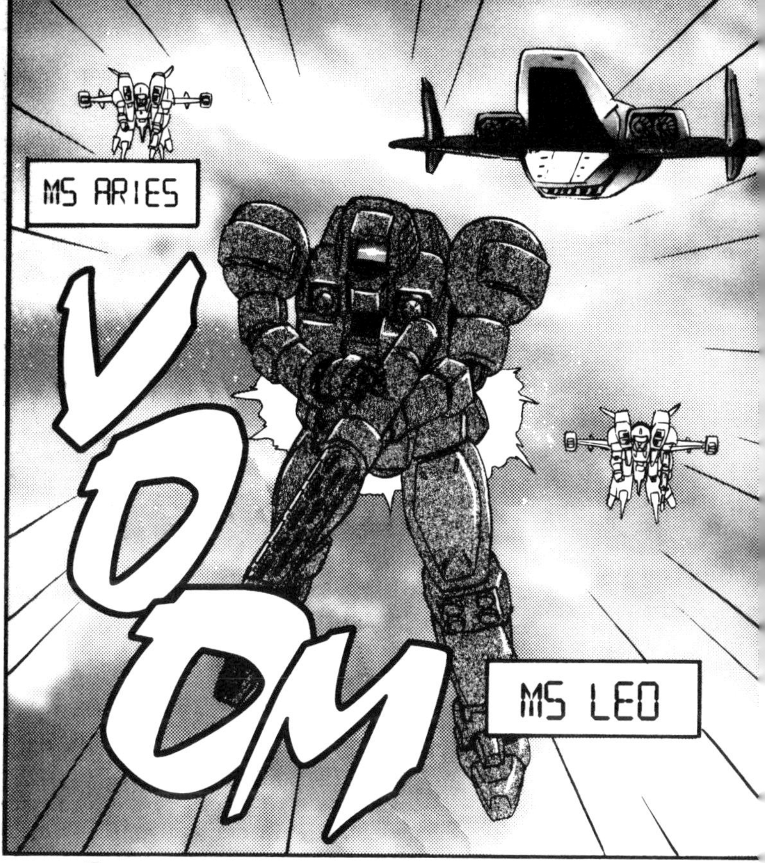
MS ARIES
VOOM
MS LEO

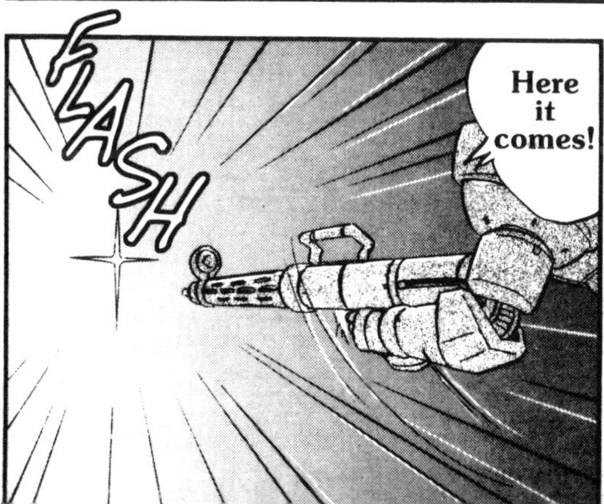
FLASH
Here it comes!

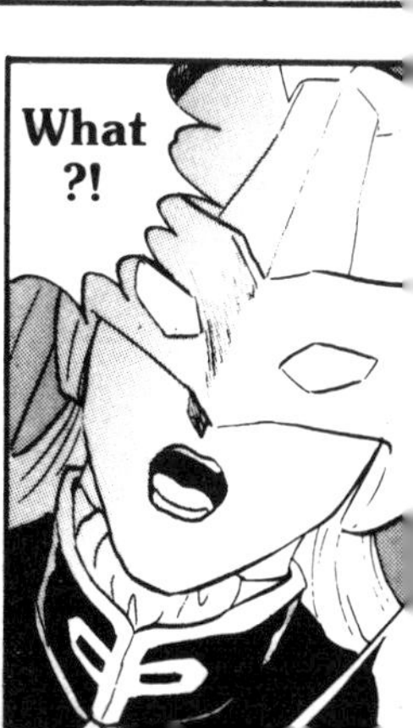
What ?!

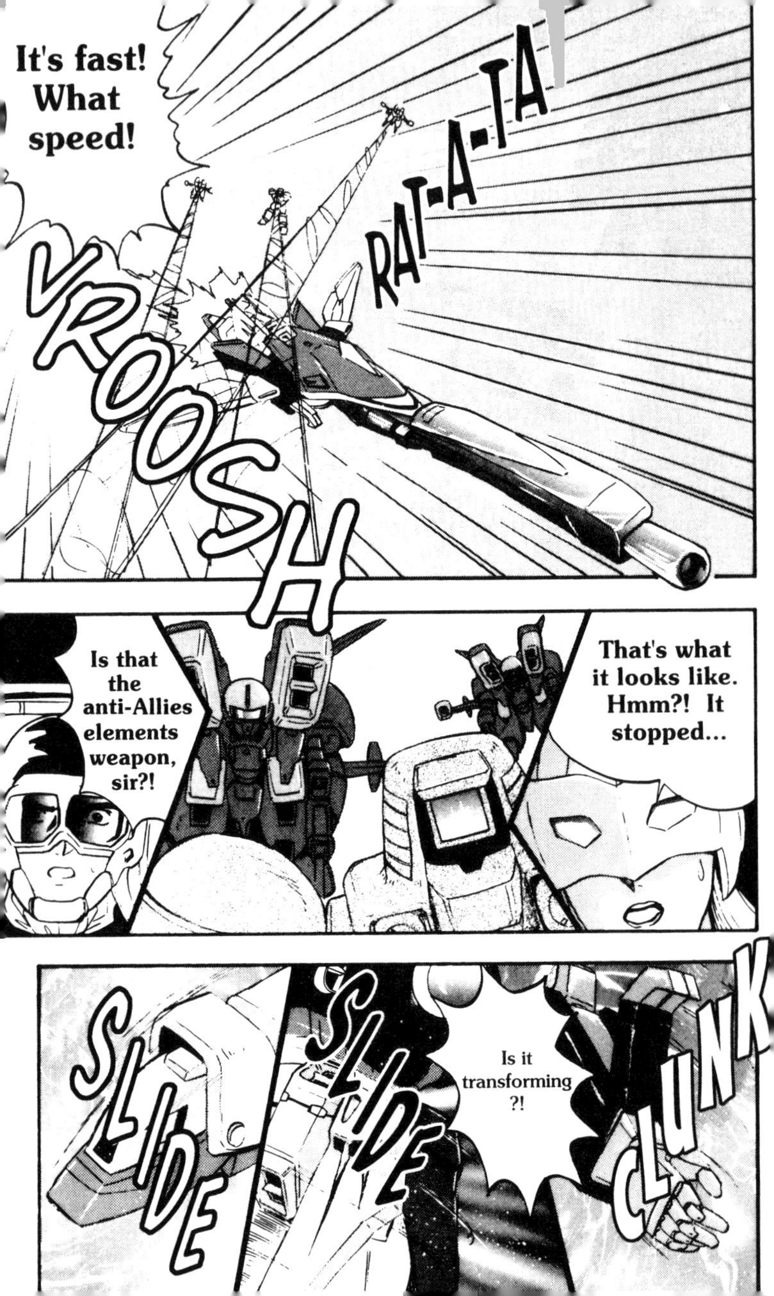
It's fast! What speed!
RAT-A-TA
VROOSH
Is that the anti-Allies elements weapon, sir?!
That's what it looks like. Hmm?! It stopped...
SLIDE
SLIDE
Is it transforming?!
CLUNK

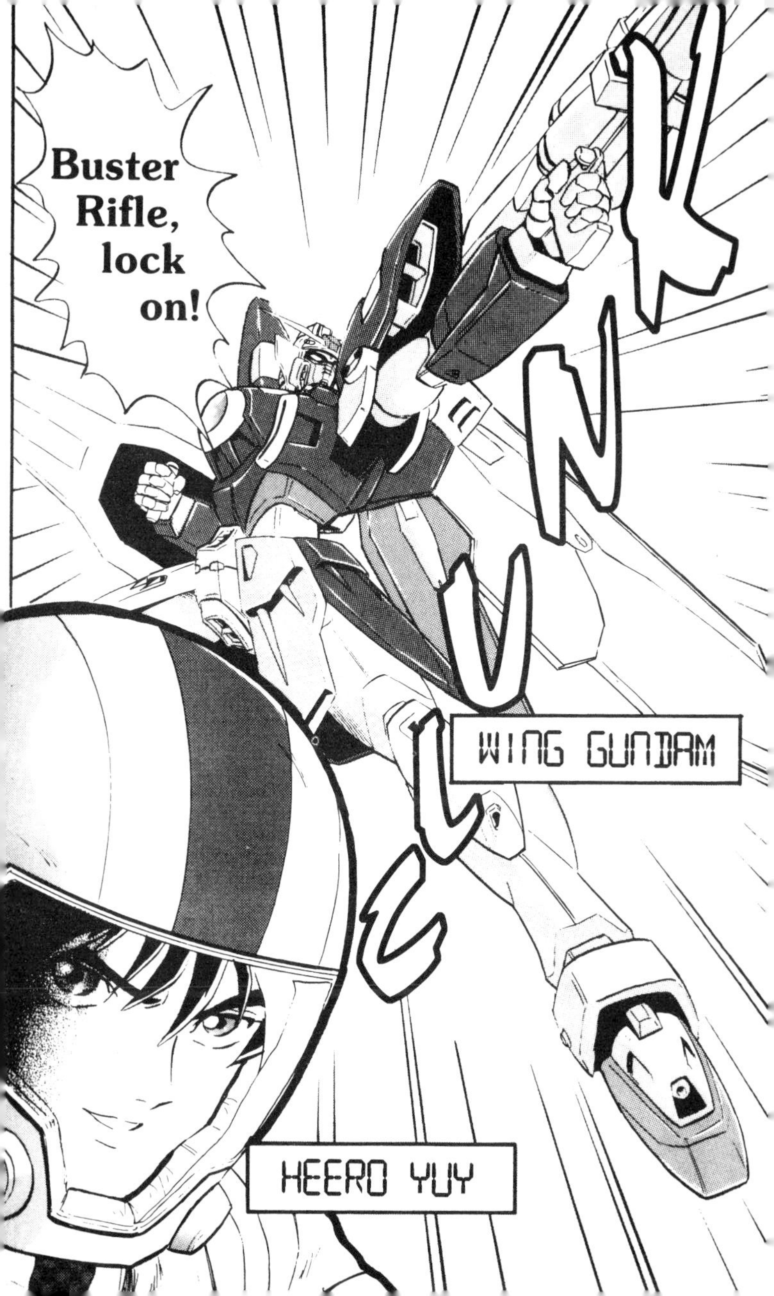
Buster Rifle, lock on!
CLUNK
WING GUNDAM
HEERO YUY

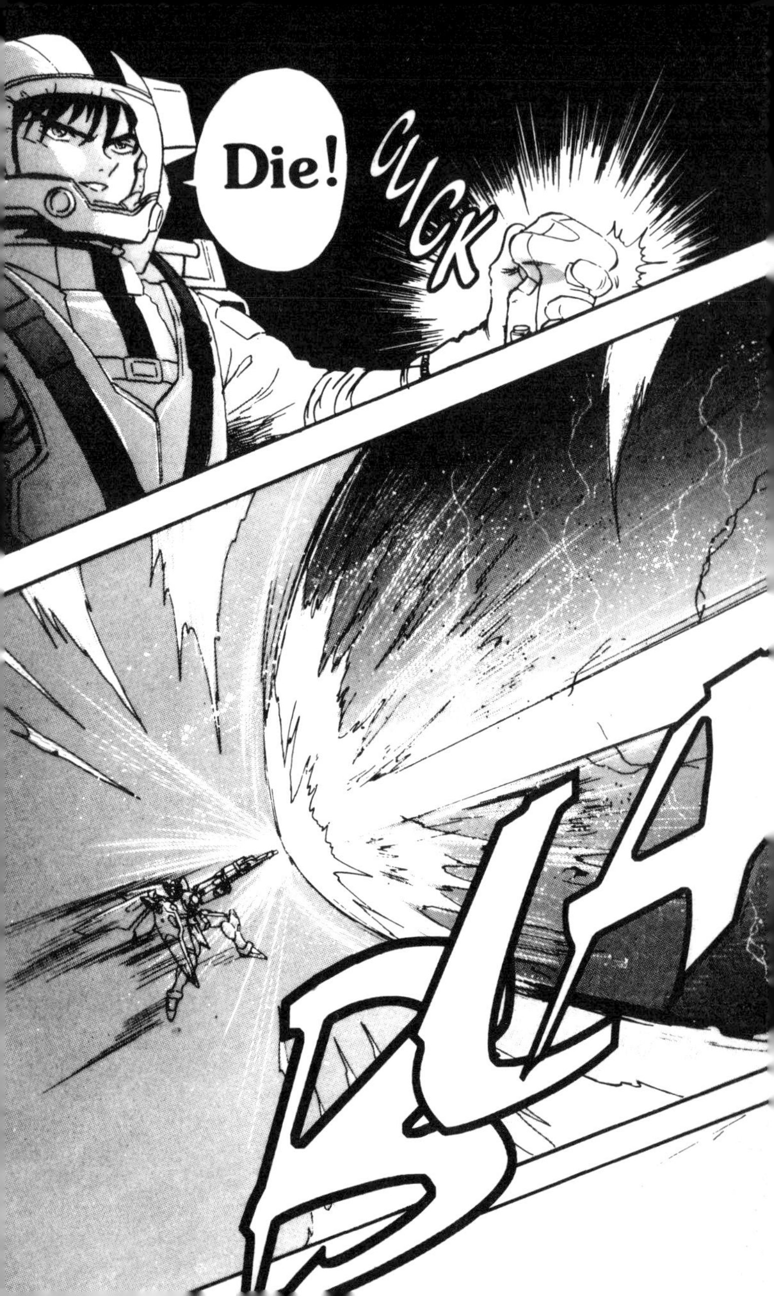
Die!
CLICK

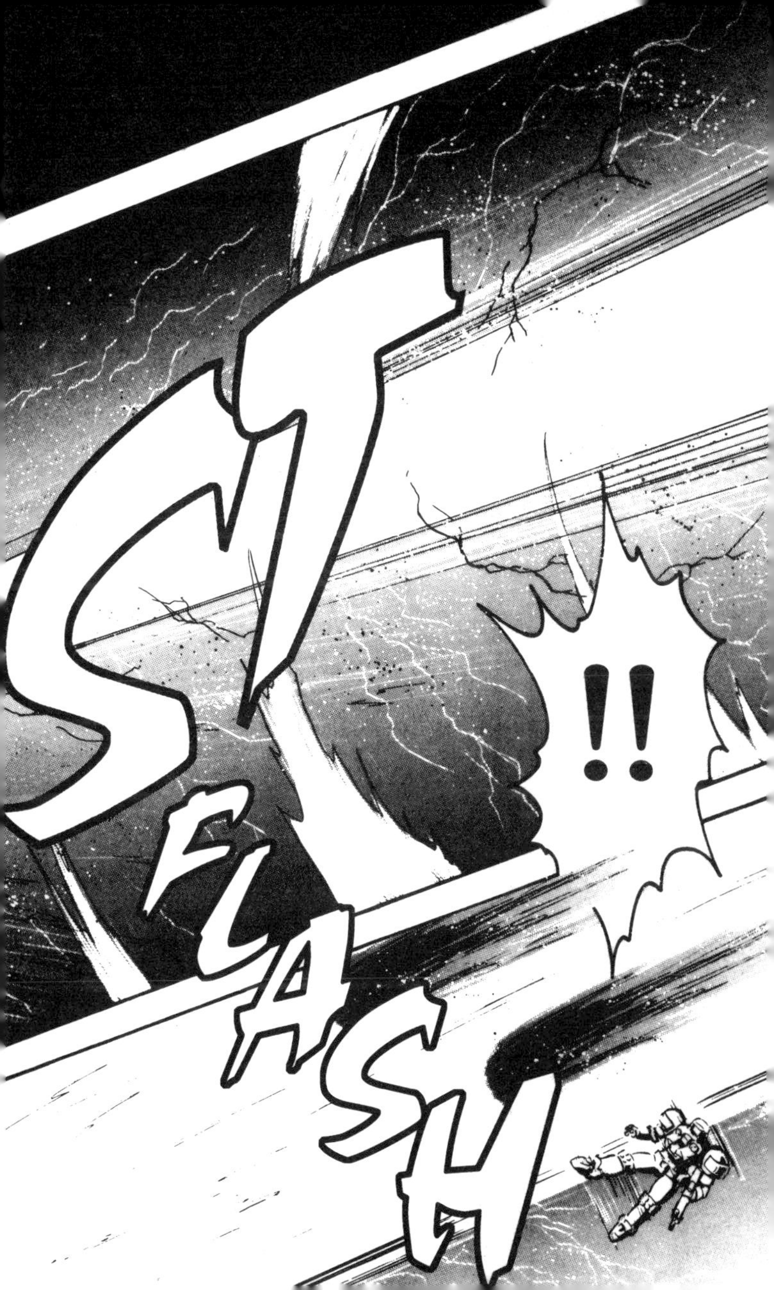

SFLASH
!!

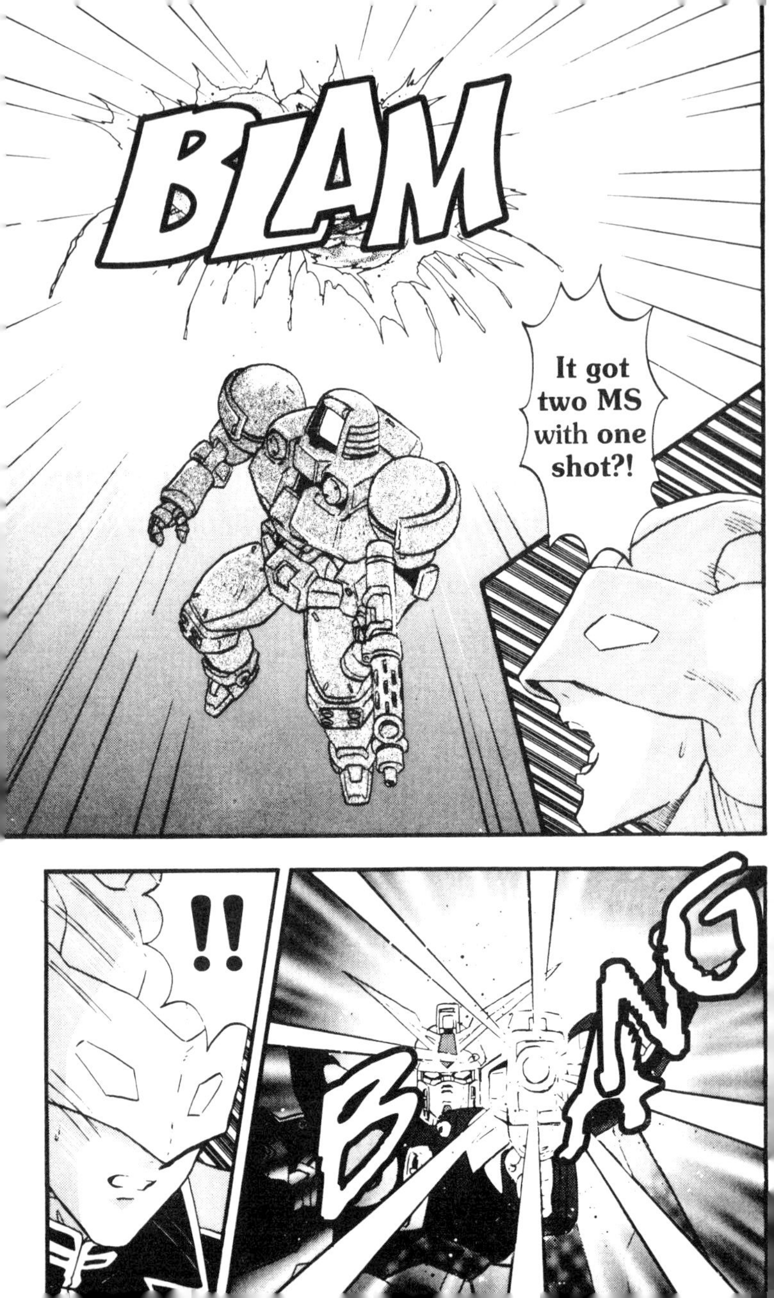
BLAM
It got two MS with one shot?!
!!
BANG

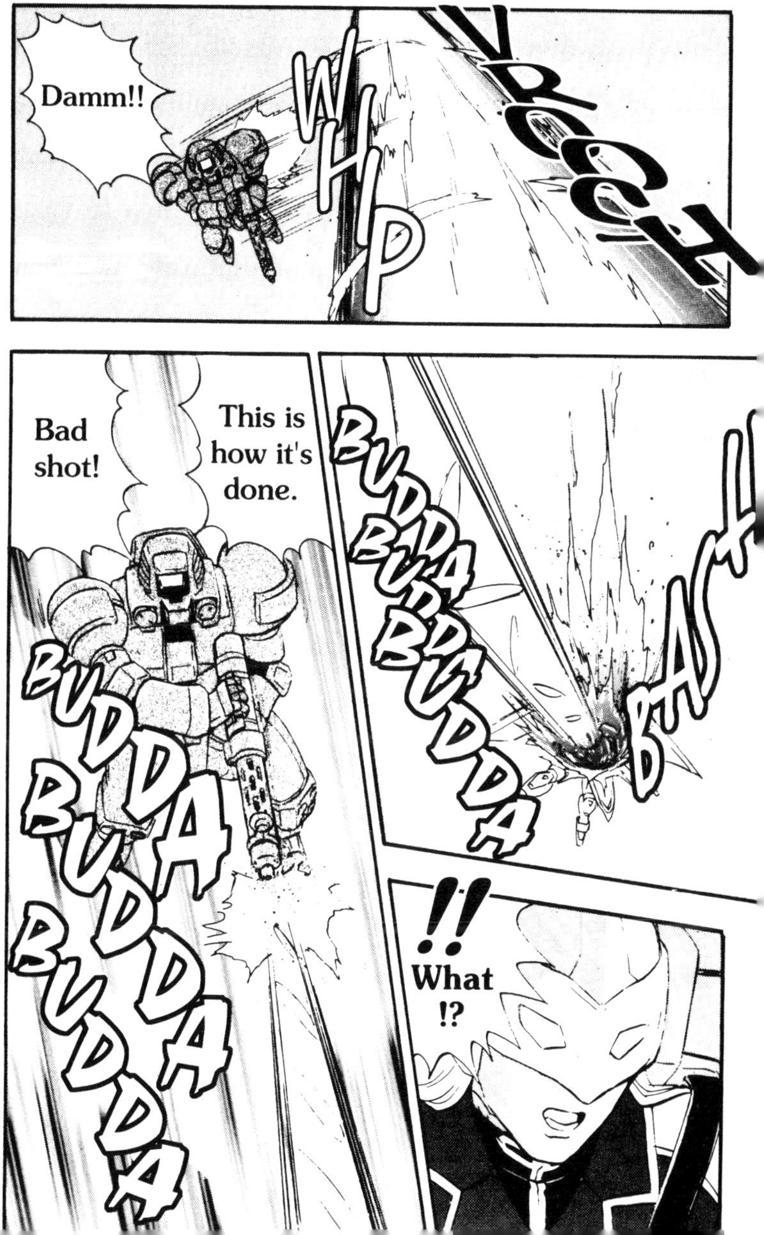
Damm!!
WHIP
VROOCH
Bad shot!
This is how it's done.
BUDDA BUDDA BUDDA BUDDA
BUDDA BUDDA BUDDA
BASH
!!
What !?

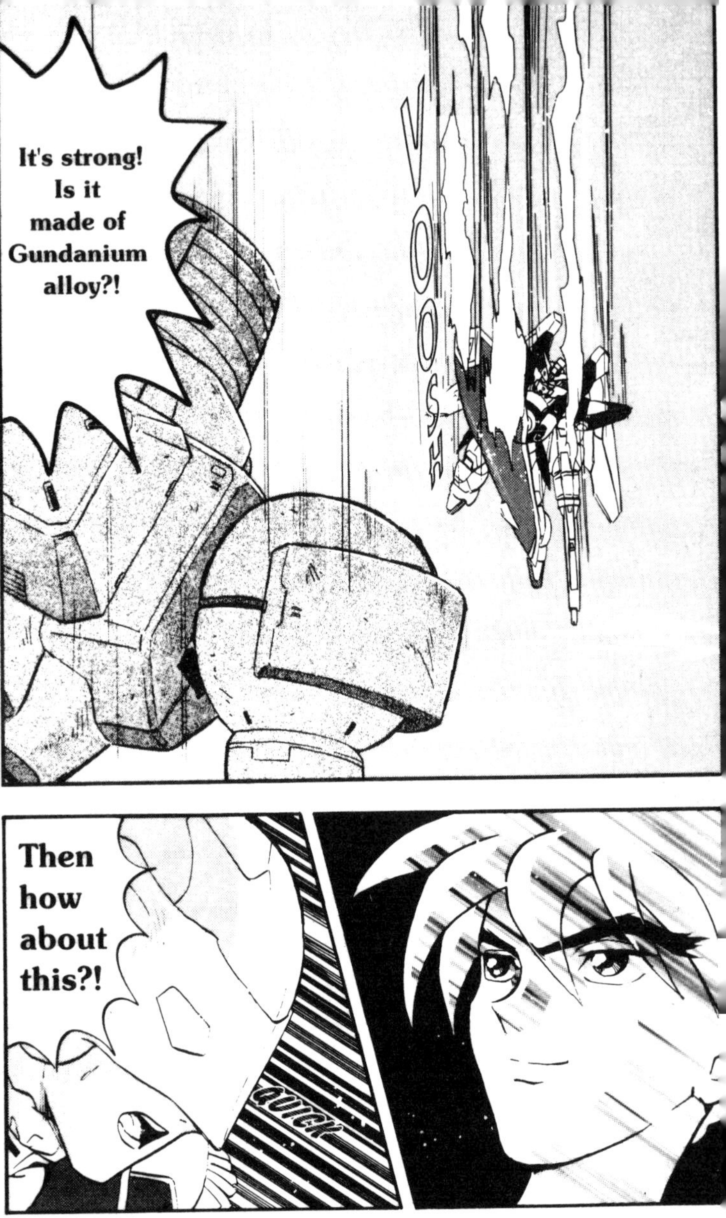
It's strong! Is it made of Gundanium alloy?!
VOOSH
Then how about this?!
QUICK

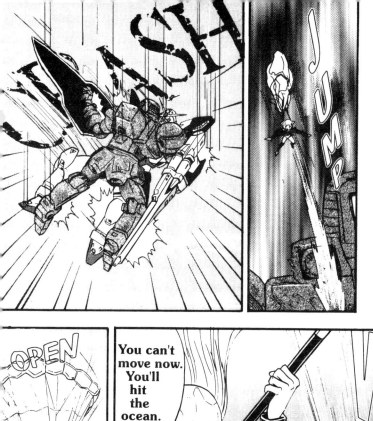

You can't move now. You'll hit the ocean.

The robot might survive, but not the pilot.

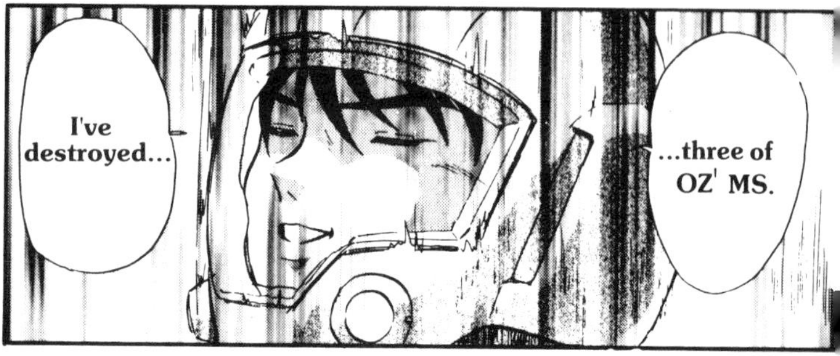
I've destroyed...
...three of OZ' MS.

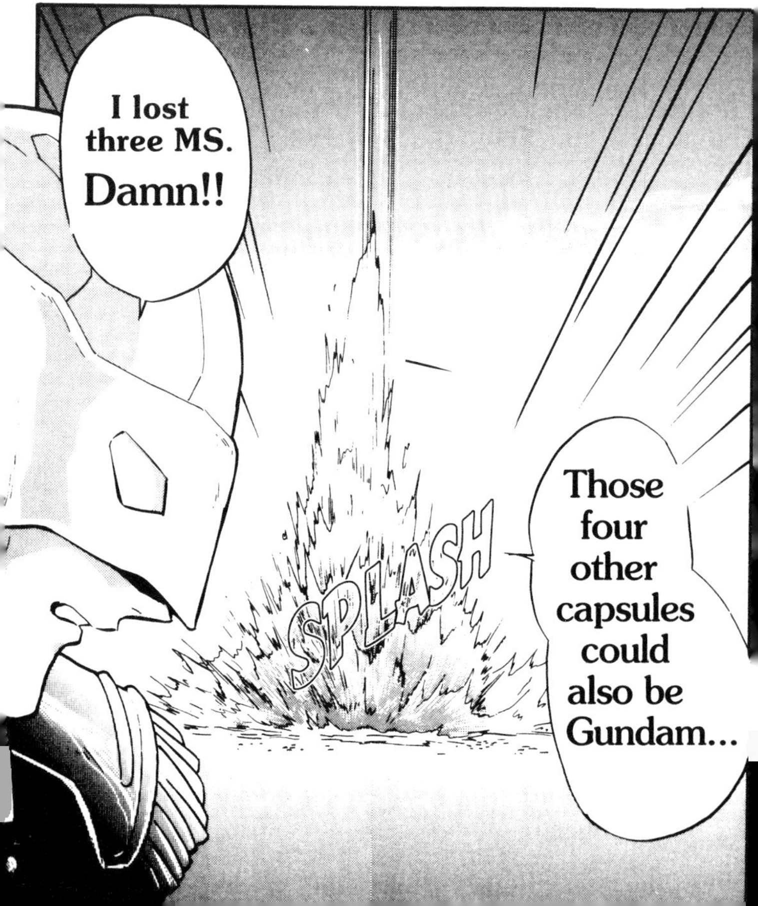
I lost three MS. Damn!!
SPLASH
Those four other capsules could also be Gundam...

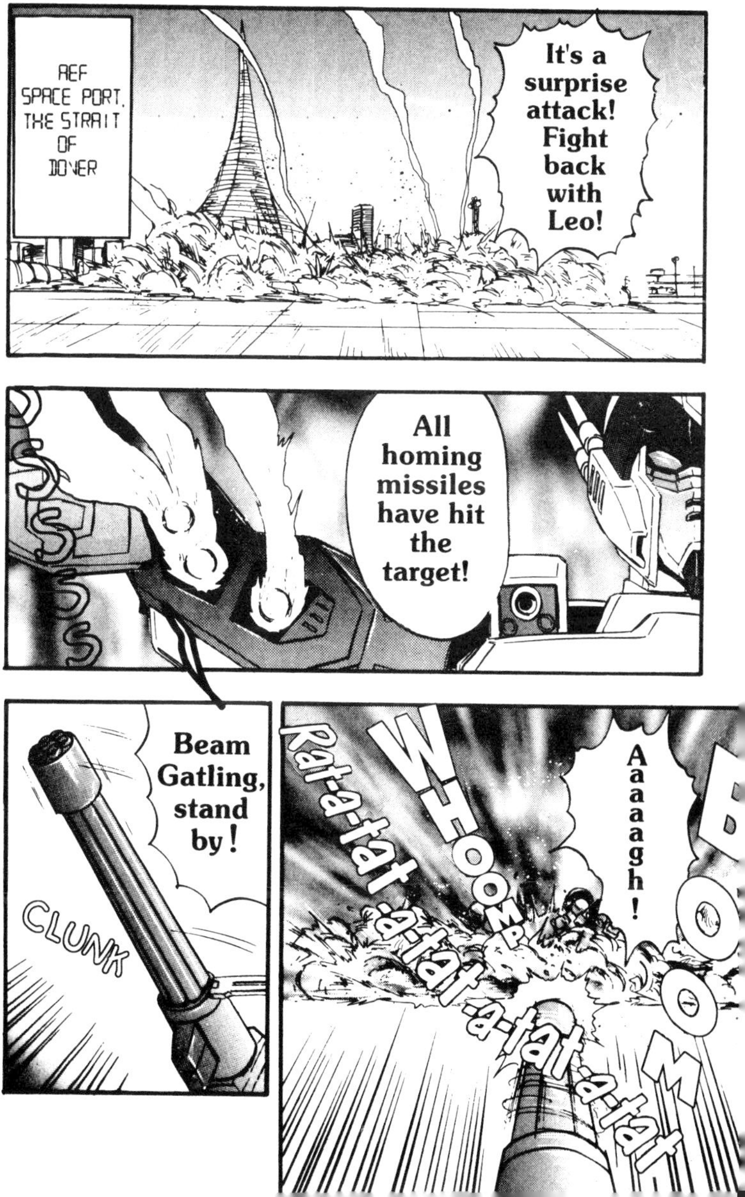
AEF
SPACE PORT,
THE STRAIT
OF
DOVER
It's a surprise attack! Fight back with Leo!
All homing missiles have hit the target!
Beam Gatling, stand by!
CLUNK
Rat-a-tat-a-tat-a-tat-a-tat-a-tat
WHOOMP
Aaaaagh!
BOOM

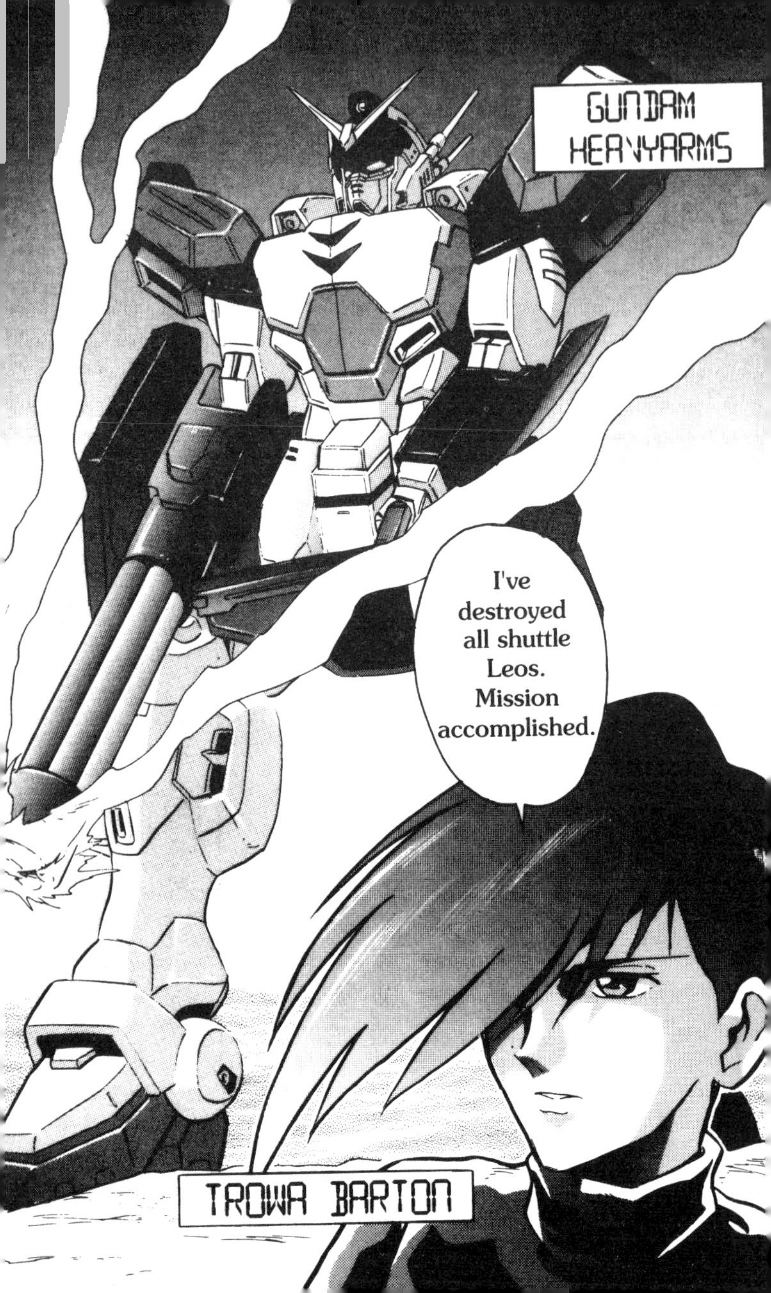
GUNDAM HEAVYARMS
I've destroyed all shuttle Leos. Mission accomplished.
TROWA BARTON

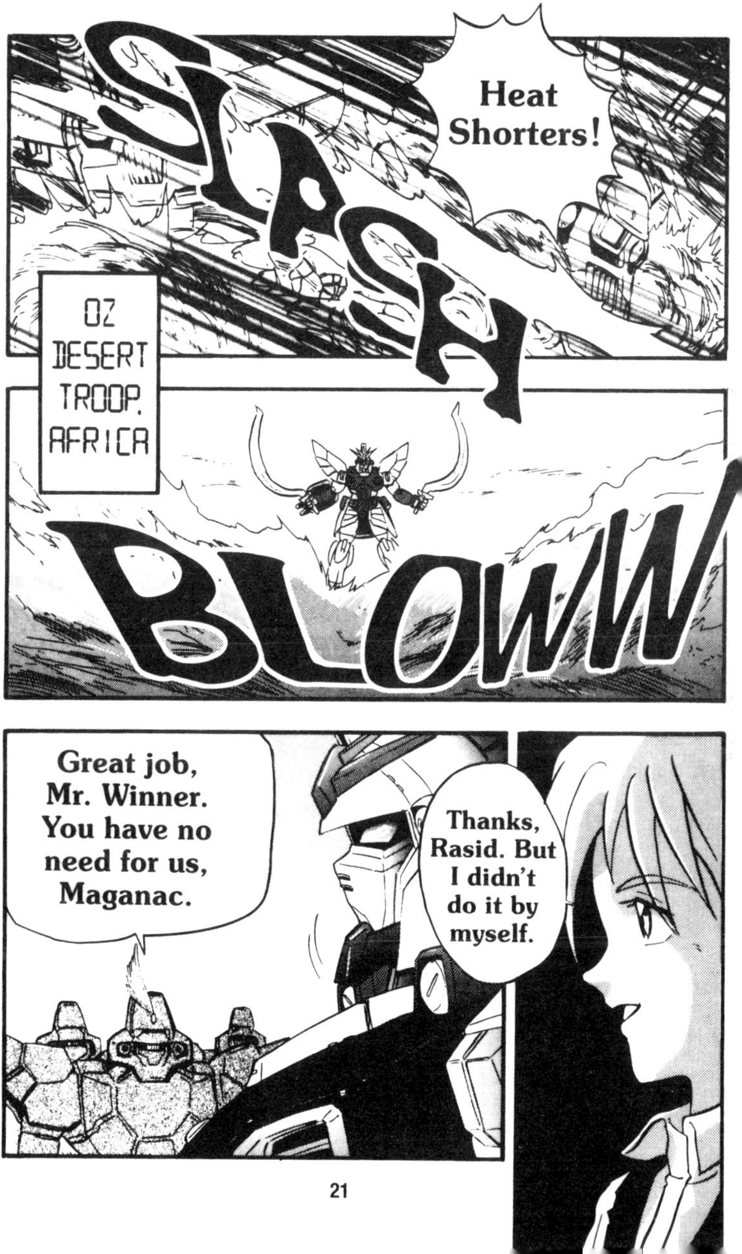
SLASH
Heat Shorters!
OZ DESERT TROOP, AFRICA
BLOWW
Great job, Mr. Winner. You have no need for us, Maganac.
Thanks, Rasid. But I didn't do it by myself.

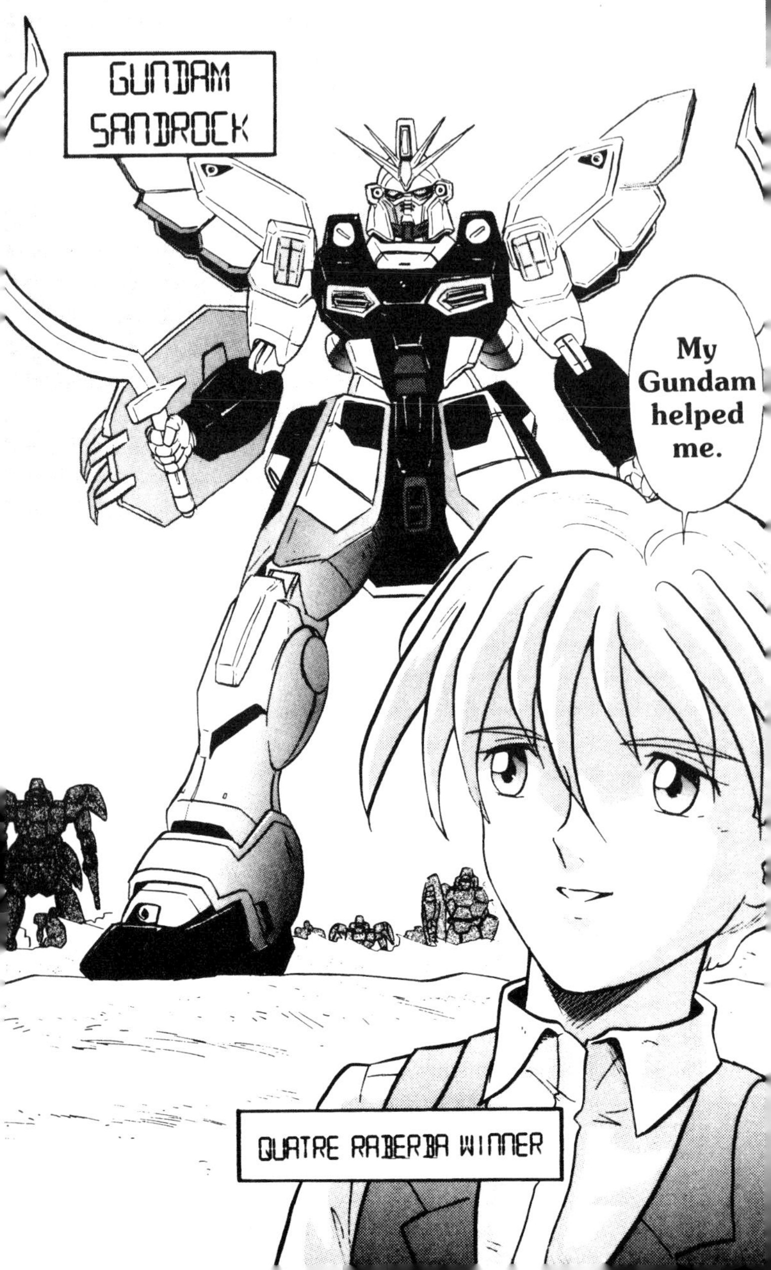
GUNDAM SANDROCK
My Gundam helped me.
QUATRE RABERBA WINNER

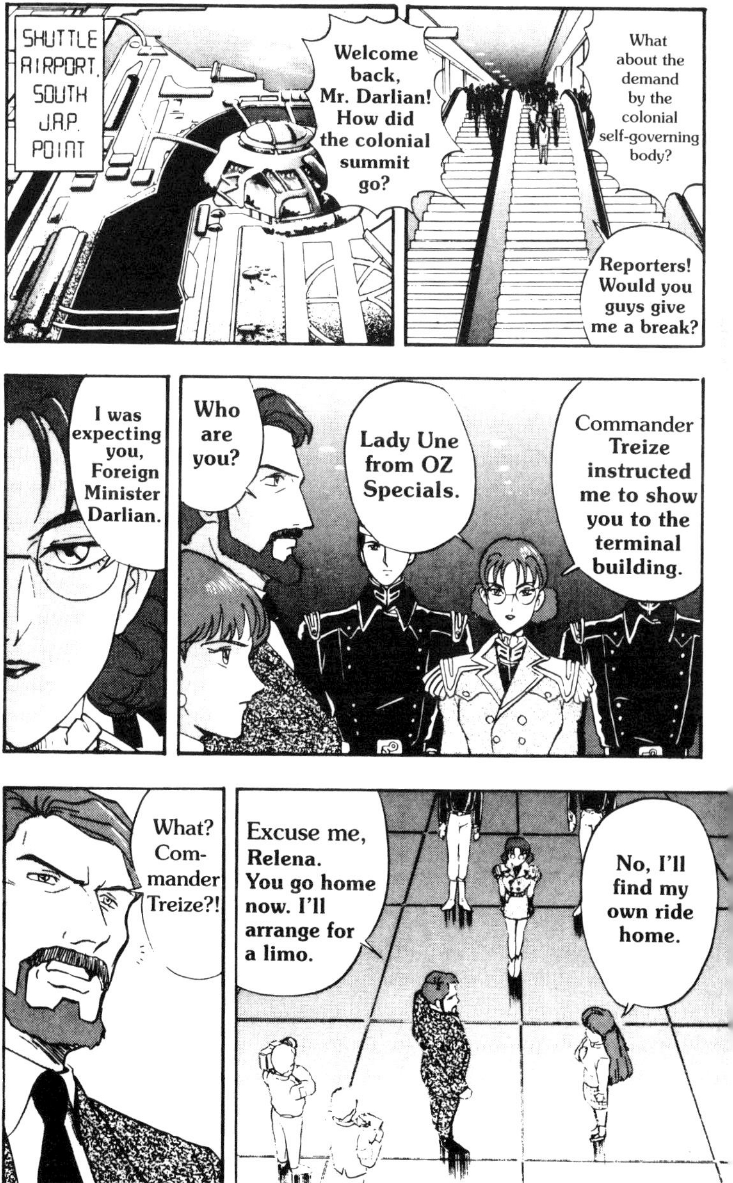
SHUTTLE AIRPORT, SOUTH J.A.P. POINT
Welcome back, Mr. Darlian! How did the colonial summit go?
What about the demand by the colonial self-governing body?
Reporters! Would you guys give me a break?
I was expecting you, Foreign Minister Darlian.
Who are you?
Lady Une from OZ Specials.
Commander Treize instructed me to show you to the terminal building.
What? Commander Treize?!
Excuse me, Relena. You go home now. I'll arrange for a limo.
No, I'll find my own ride home.

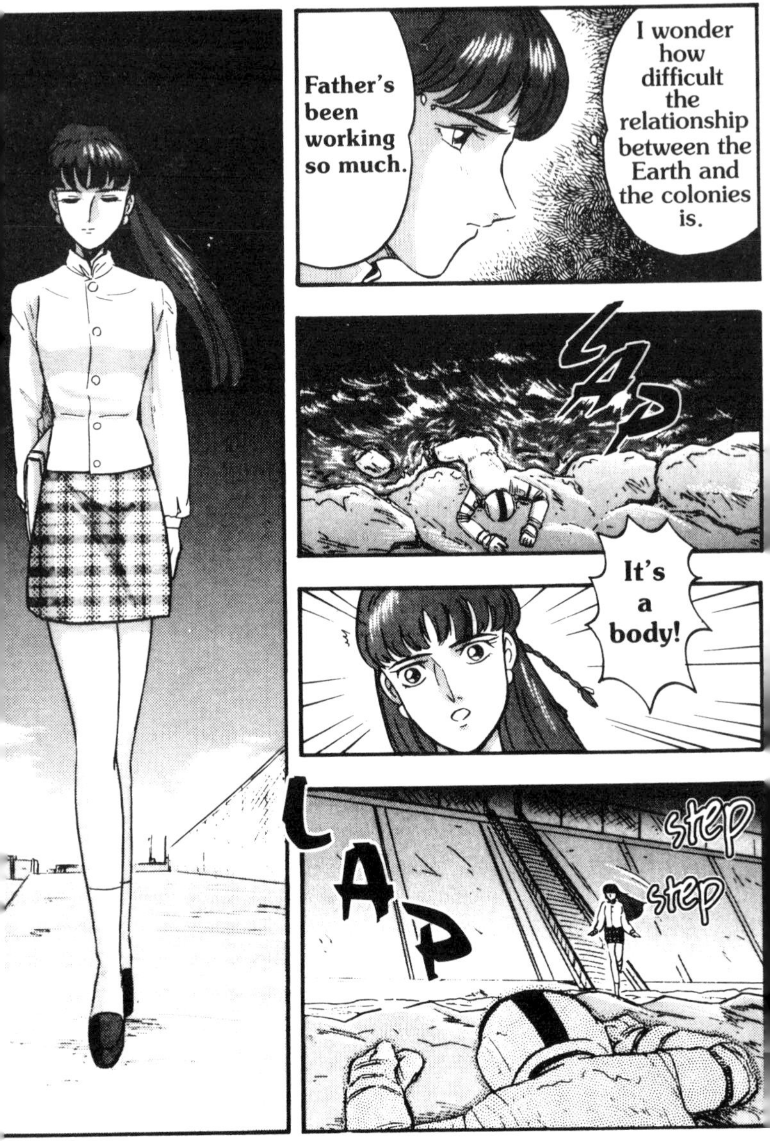
Father's been working so much.
I wonder how difficult the relationship between the Earth and the colonies is.
LAP
It's a body!
LAP
step
step

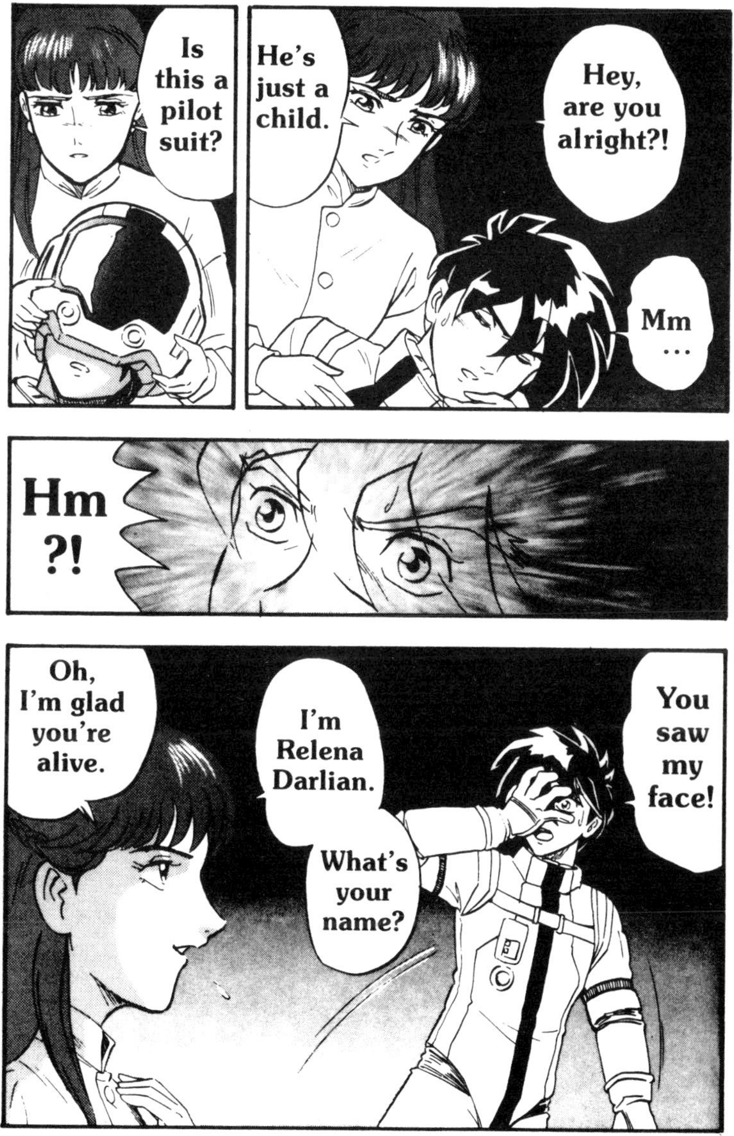

Is this a pilot suit?
He's just a child.
Hey, are you alright?!
Mm ...
Hm ?!
Oh, I'm glad you're alive.
I'm Relena Darlian.
What's your name?
You saw my face!

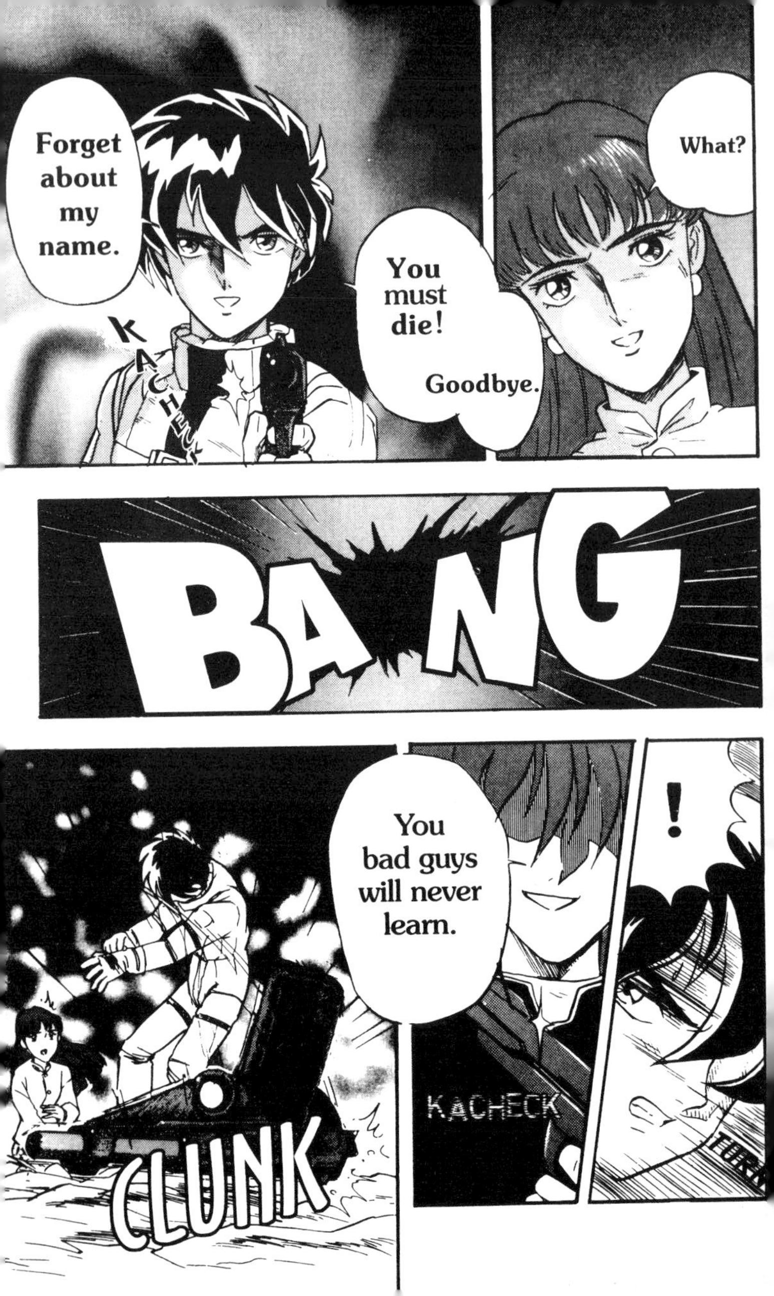
Forget about my name.
KACHEK
What?
You must die!
Goodbye.
BANG
CLUNK
You bad guys will never learn.
KACHECK
!
TUR

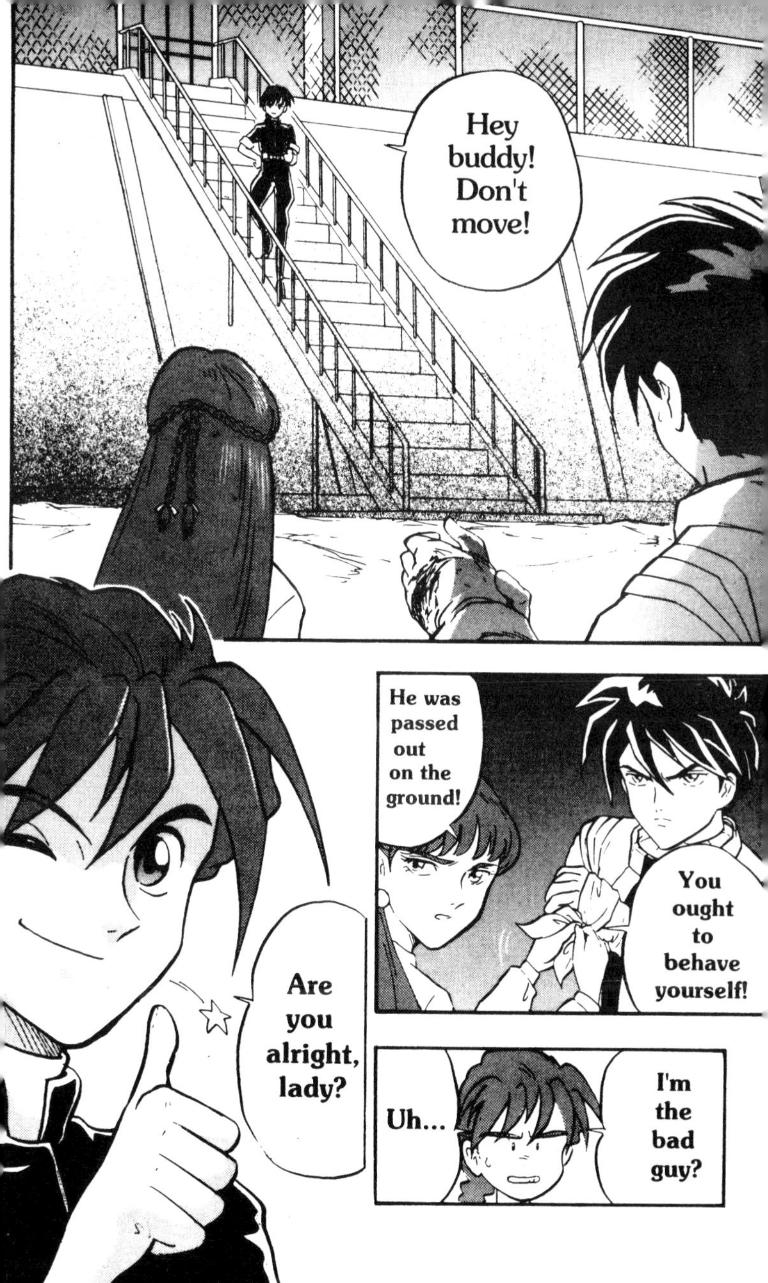

Hey buddy! Don't move!
Are you alright, lady?
He was passed out on the ground!
You ought to behave yourself!
Uh...
I'm the bad guy?

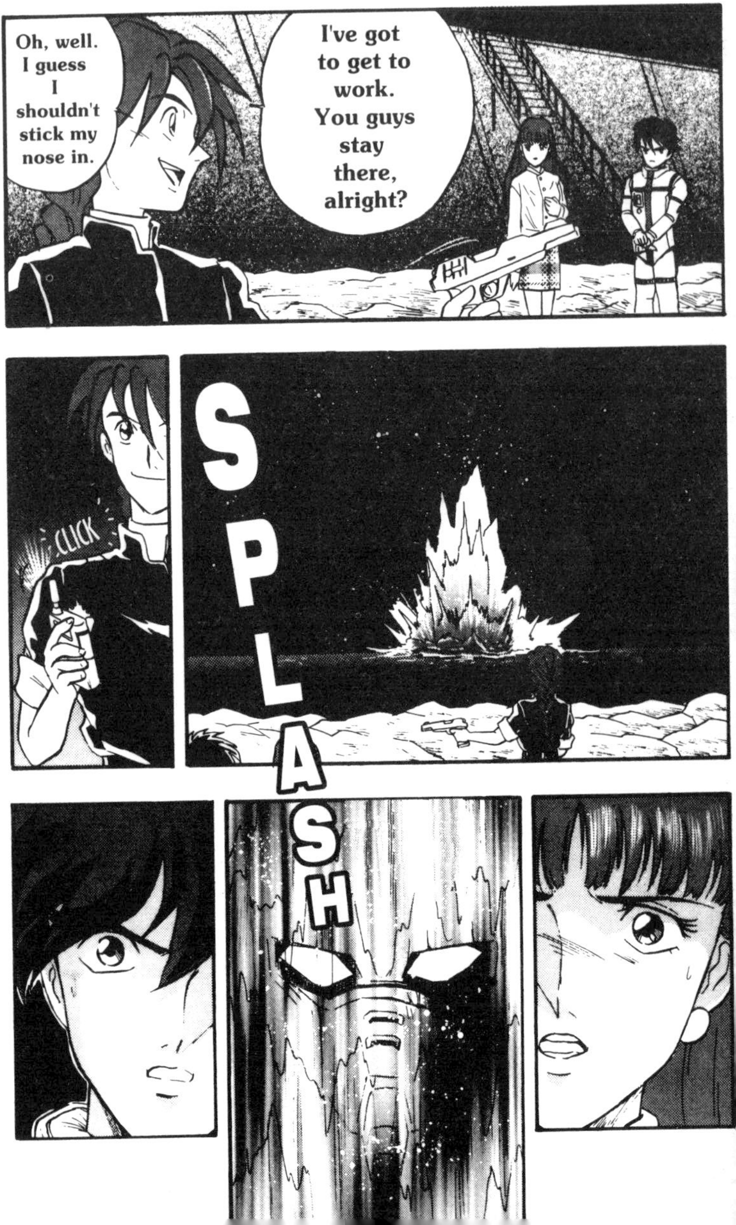
Oh, well. I guess I shouldn't stick my nose in.
I've got to get to work. You guys stay there, alright?
CLICK
SPLASH

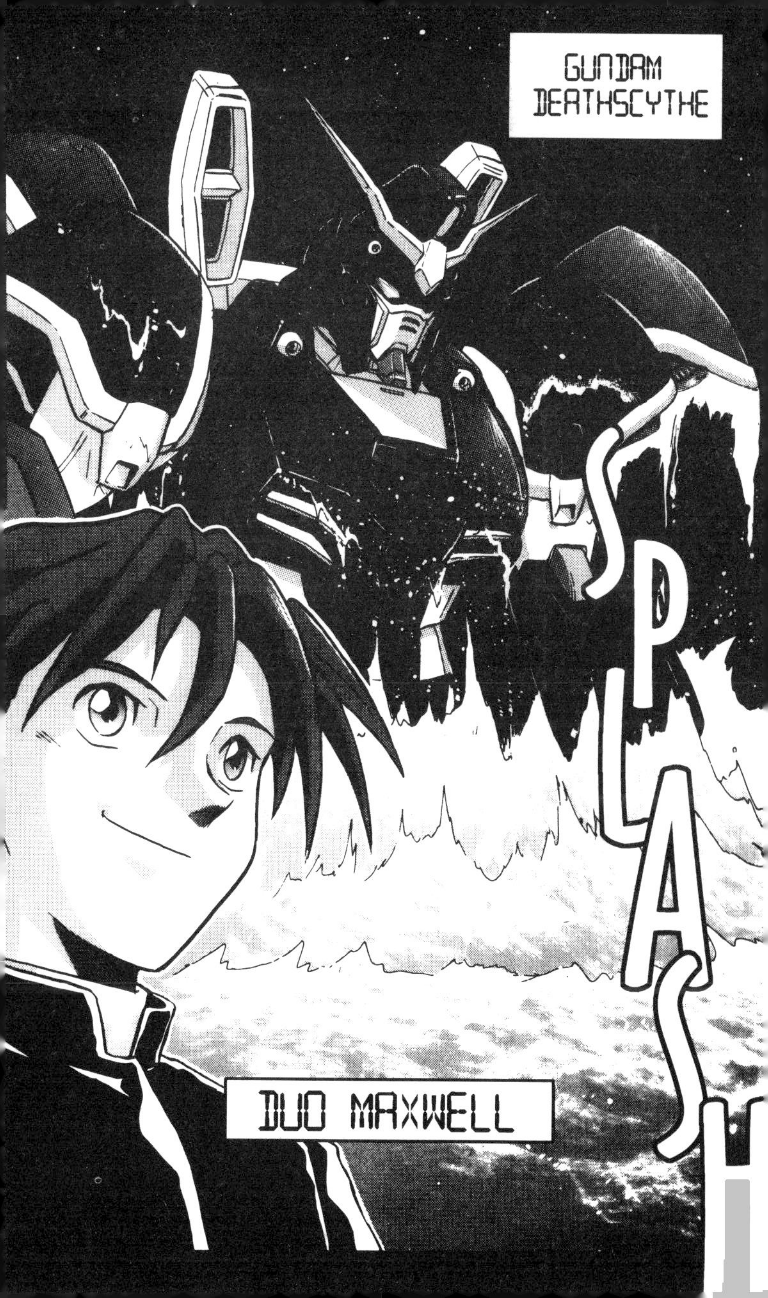
GUNDAM DEATHSCYTHE
SPLASH
DUO MAXWELL

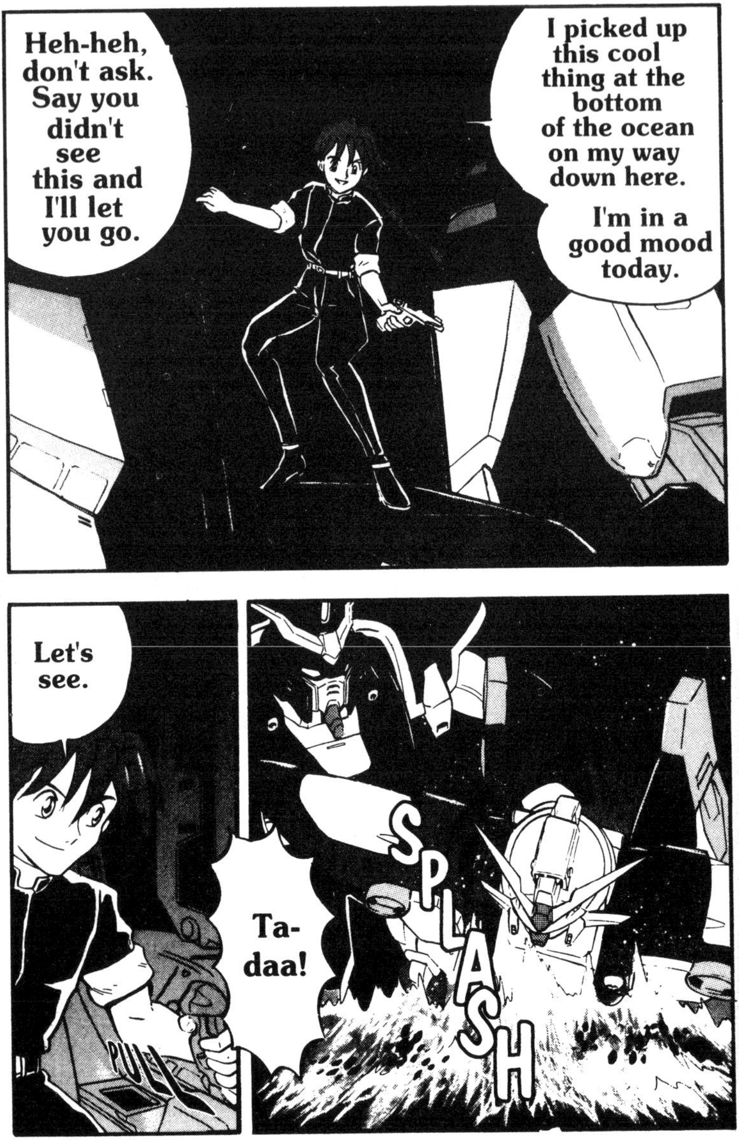
Heh-heh, don't ask. Say you didn't see this and I'll let you go.
I picked up this cool thing at the bottom of the ocean on my way down here.
I'm in a good mood today.
Let's see.
PULL
Ta-daa!
SPLASH

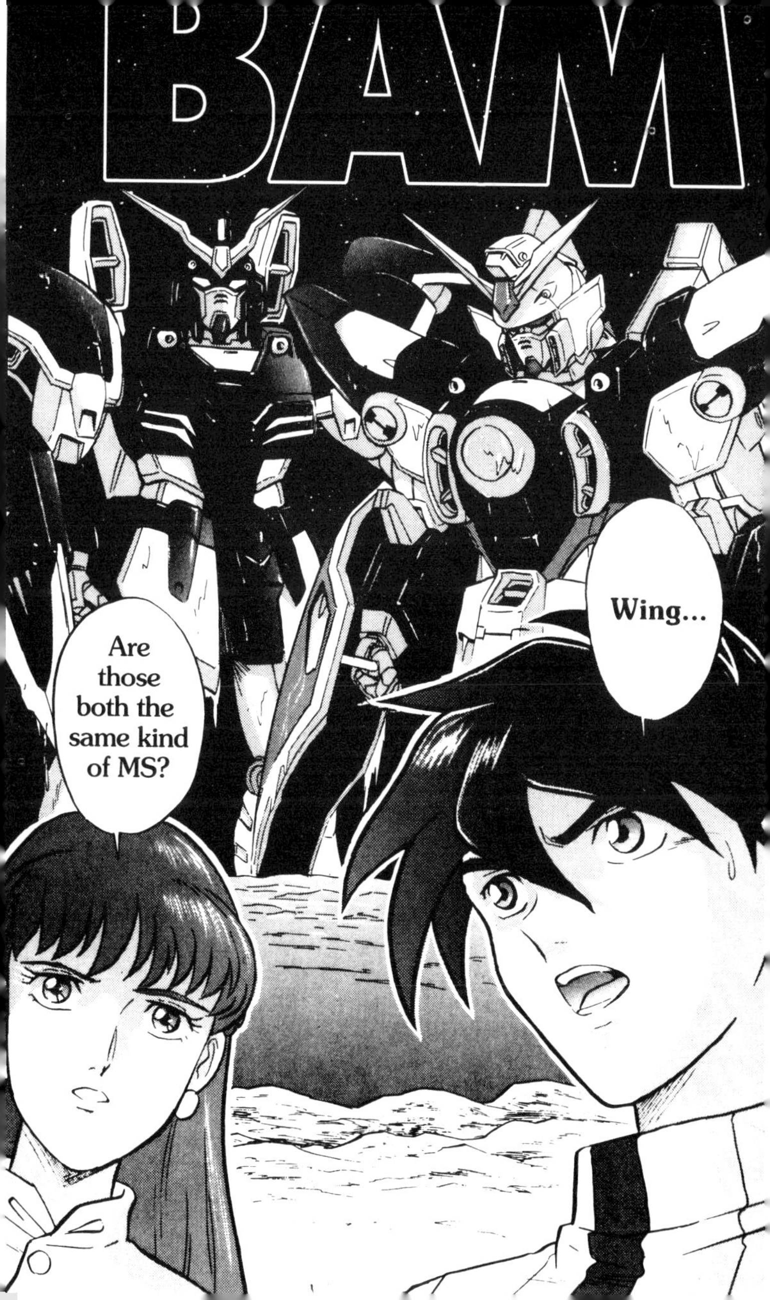
BAM
Are those both the same kind of MS?
Wing...

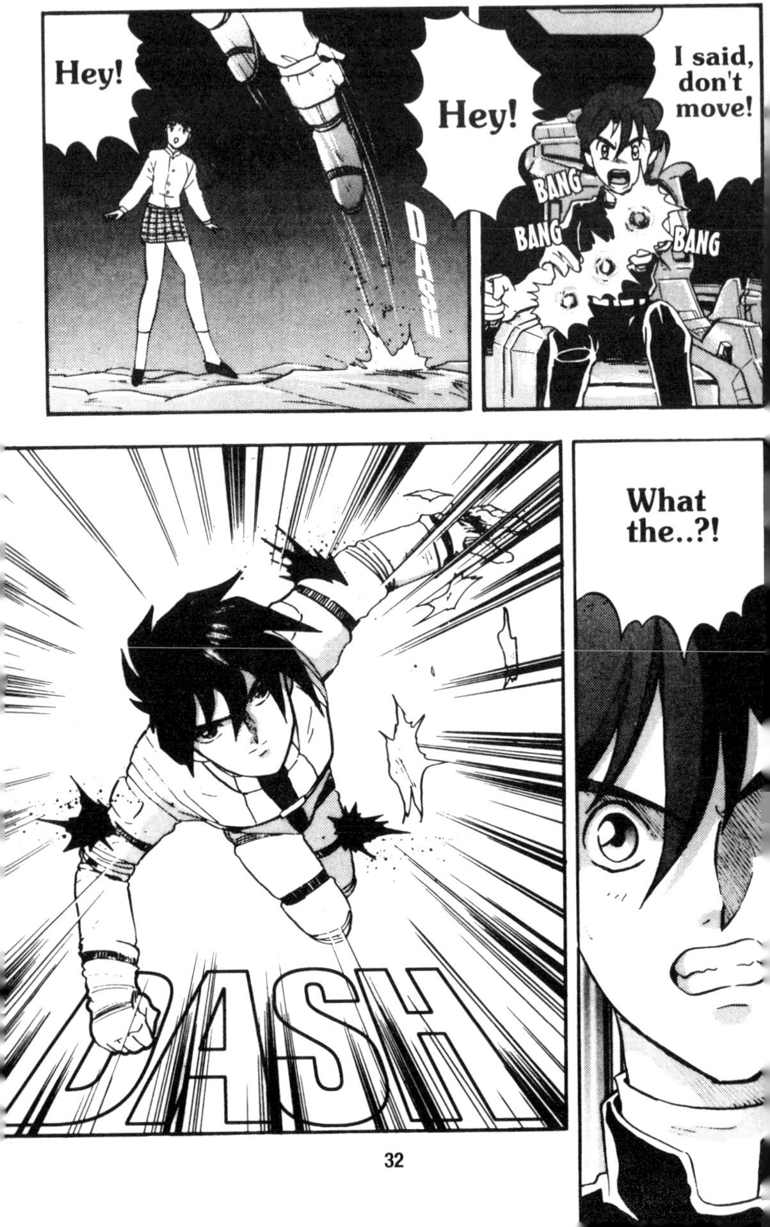

Hey!
DASSH
Hey!
I said, don't move!
BANG
BANG
BANG
DASH
What the..?!

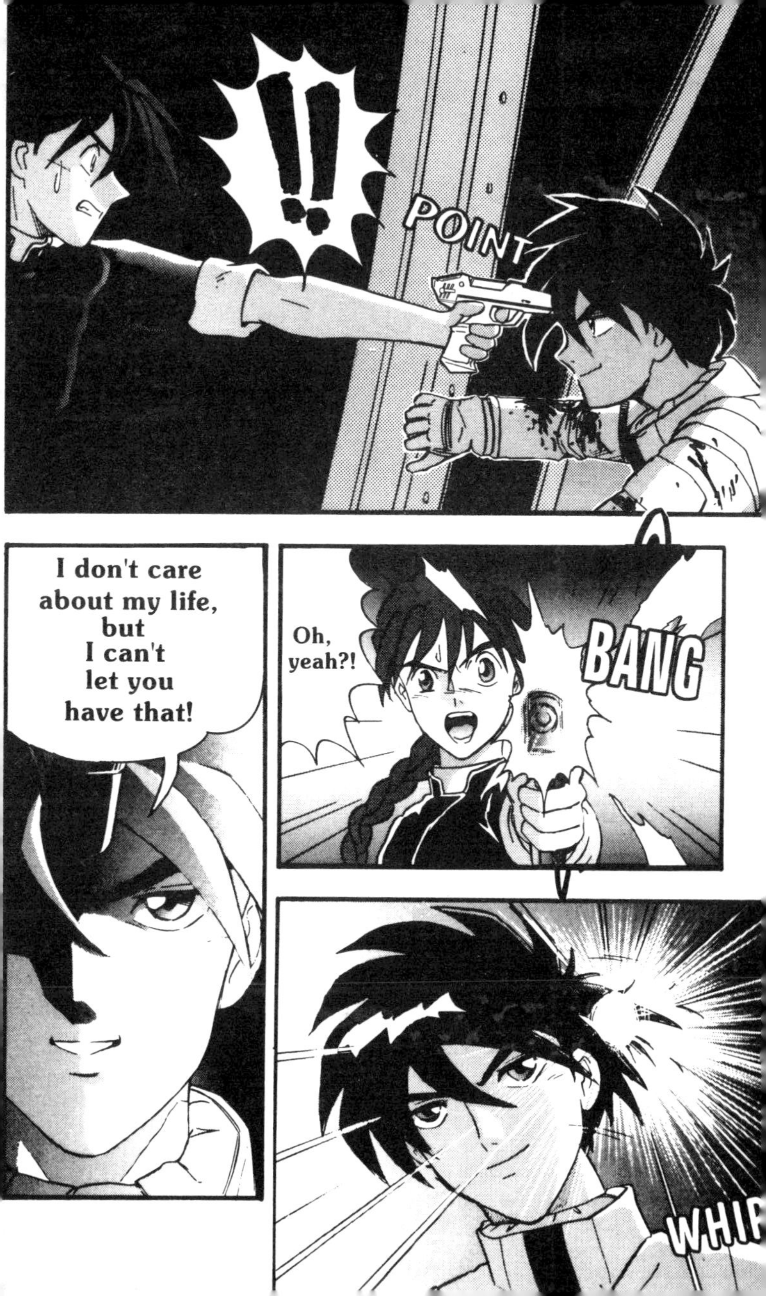
!!
POINT
I don't care about my life, but I can't let you have that!
Oh, yeah?!
BANG
WHIP

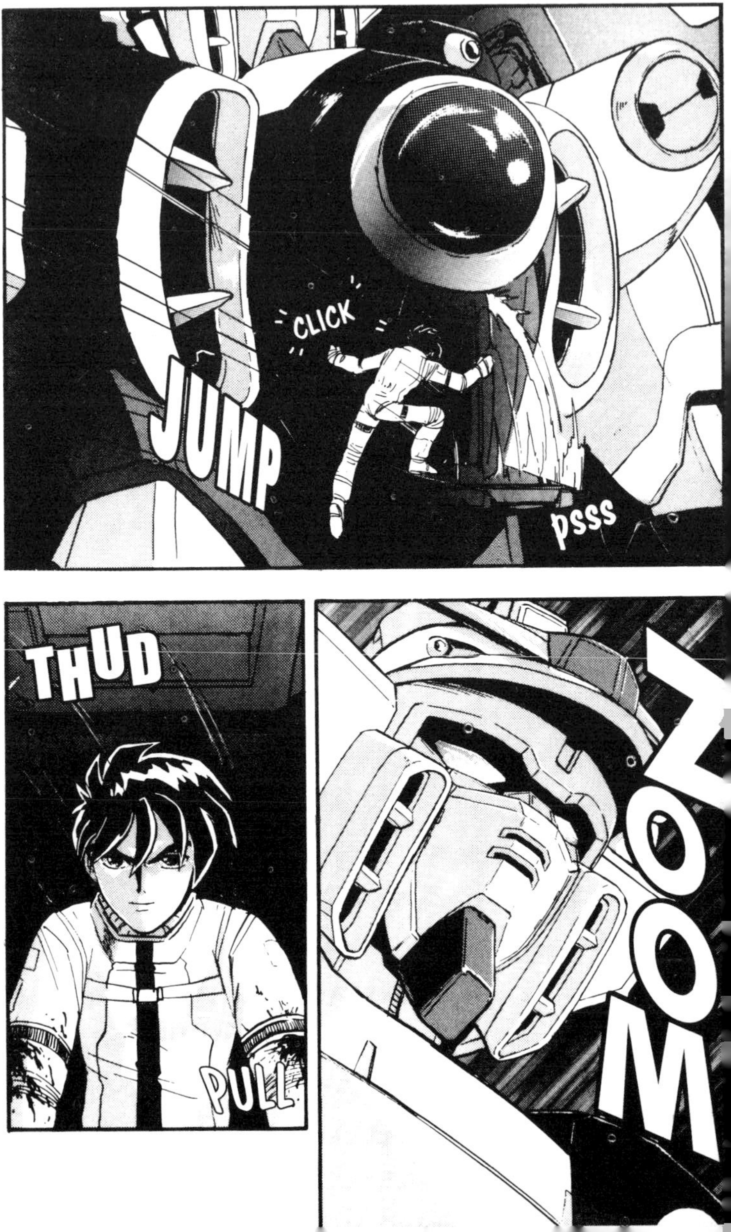
CLICK
JUMP
psss
THUD
PULL
VOOOM

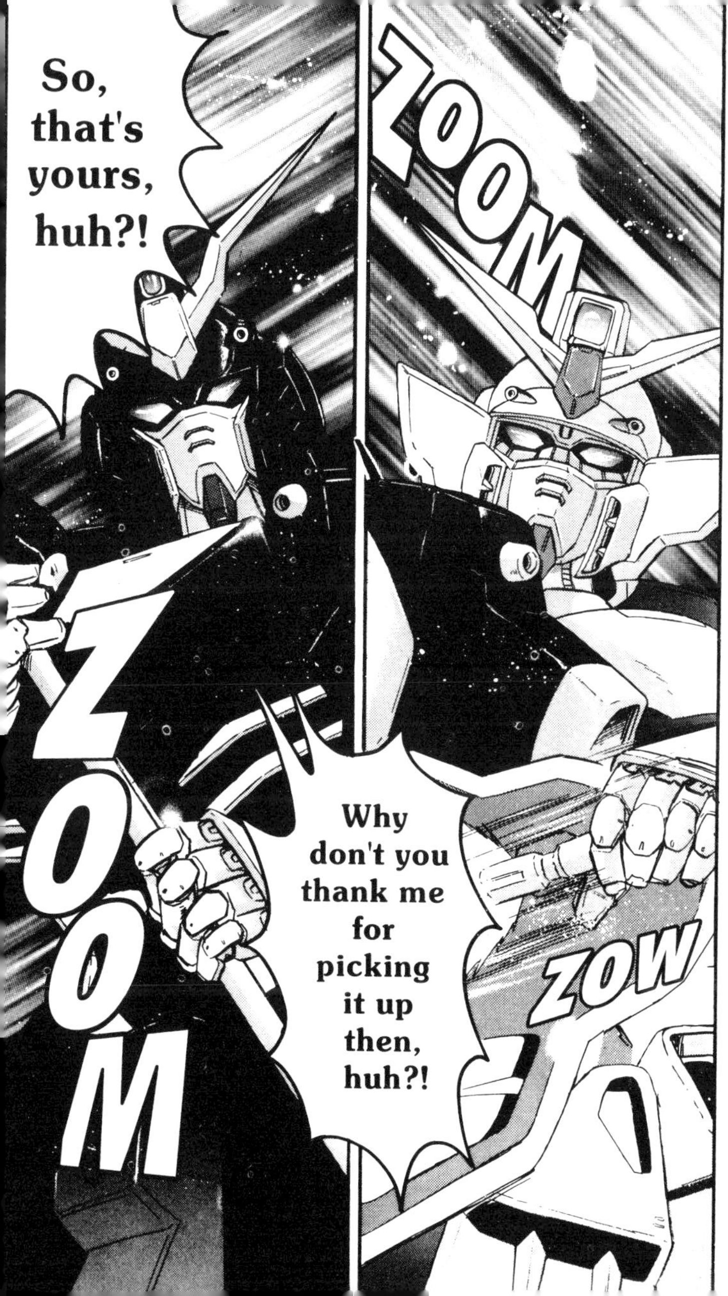
So, that's yours, huh?!
ZOOM
ZOOM
Why don't you thank me for picking it up then, huh?!
ZOW

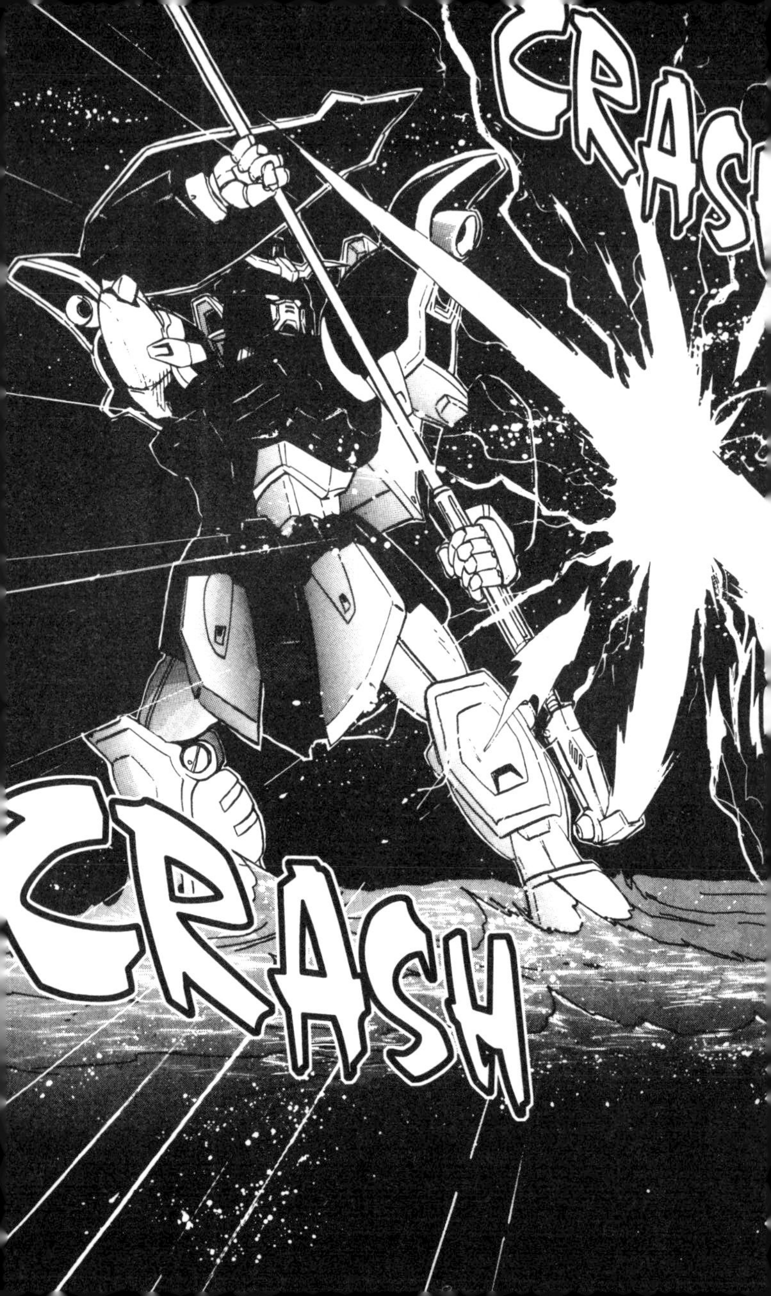
CRASH
CRASH

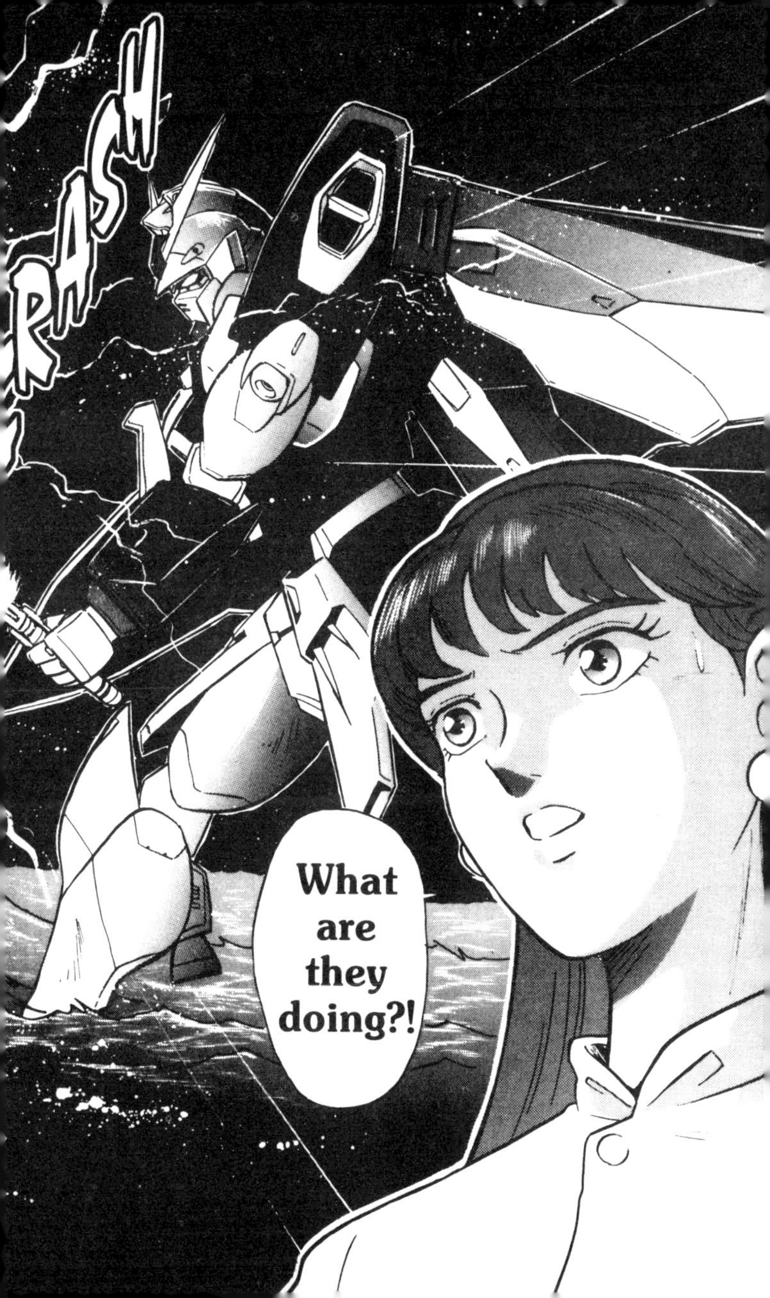
RASH
What are they doing?!

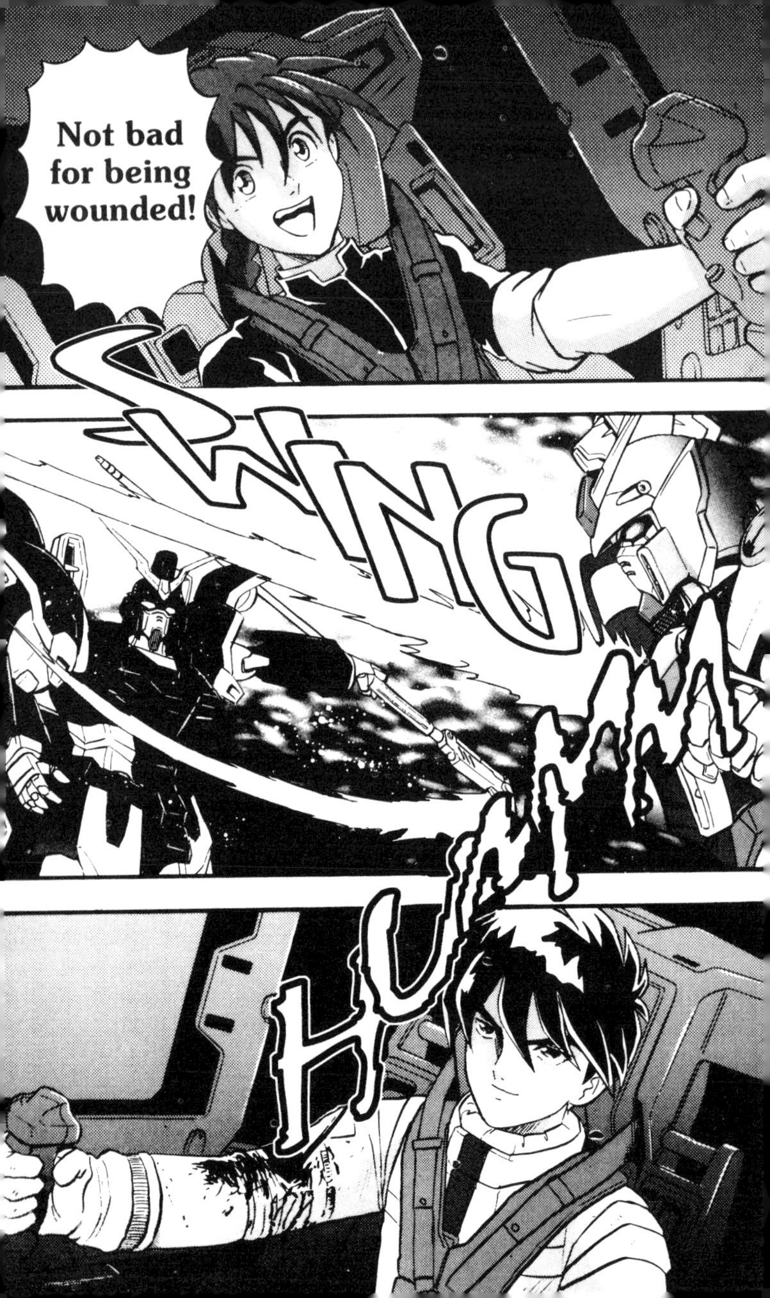
Not bad for being wounded!
SWING

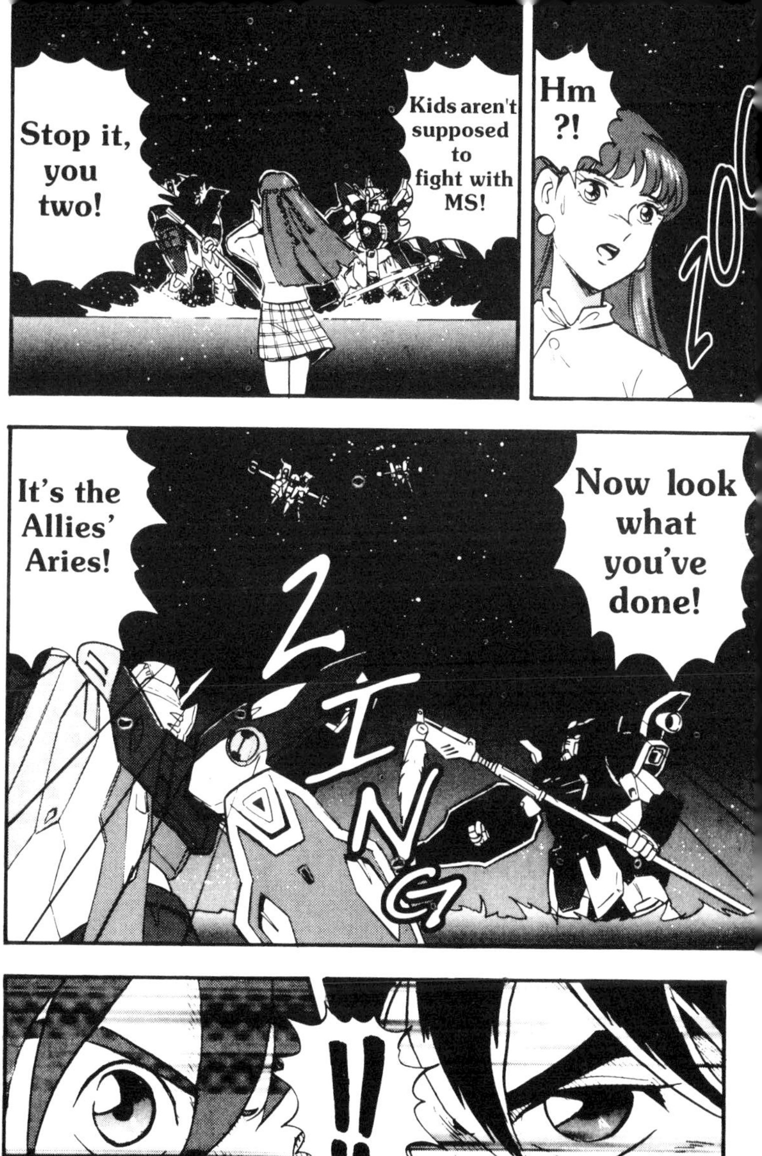
Stop it, you two!
Kids aren't supposed to fight with MS!
Hm ?!
ZOO
It's the Allies' Aries!
Now look what you've done!
ZING
!!

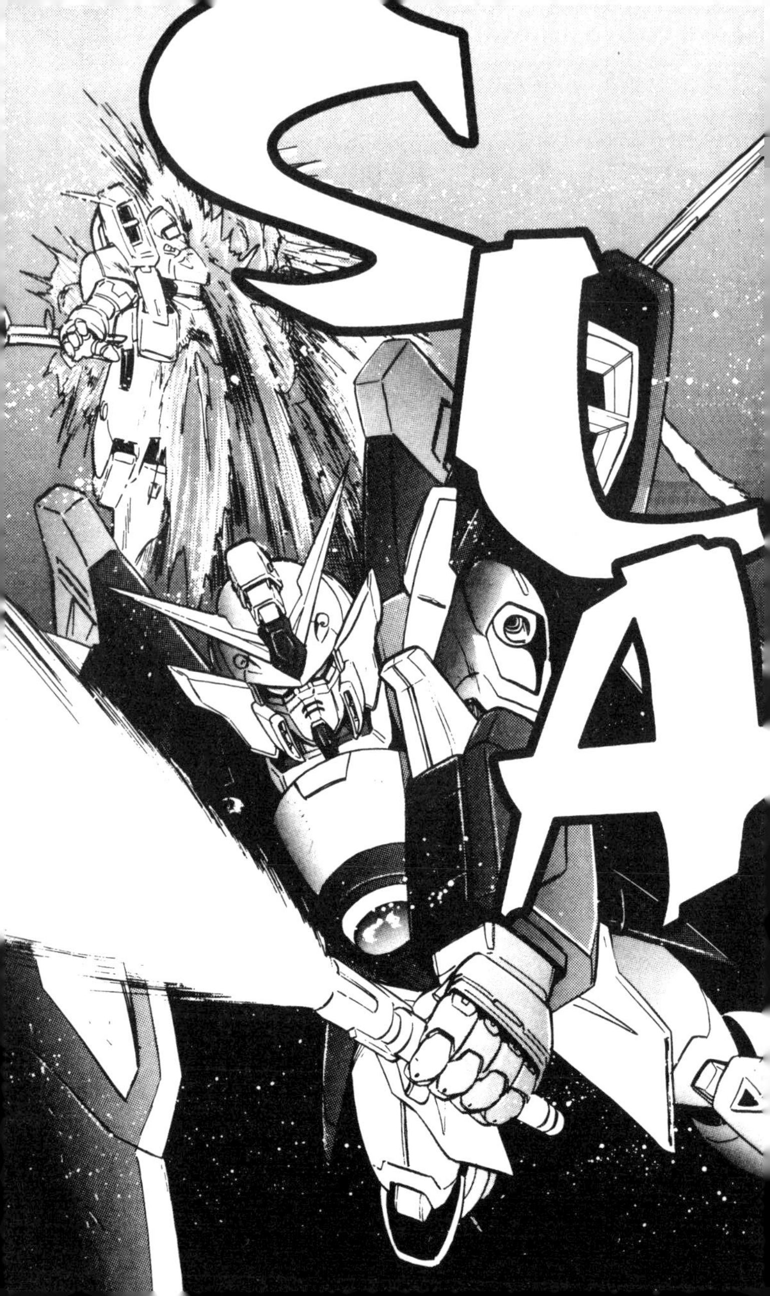

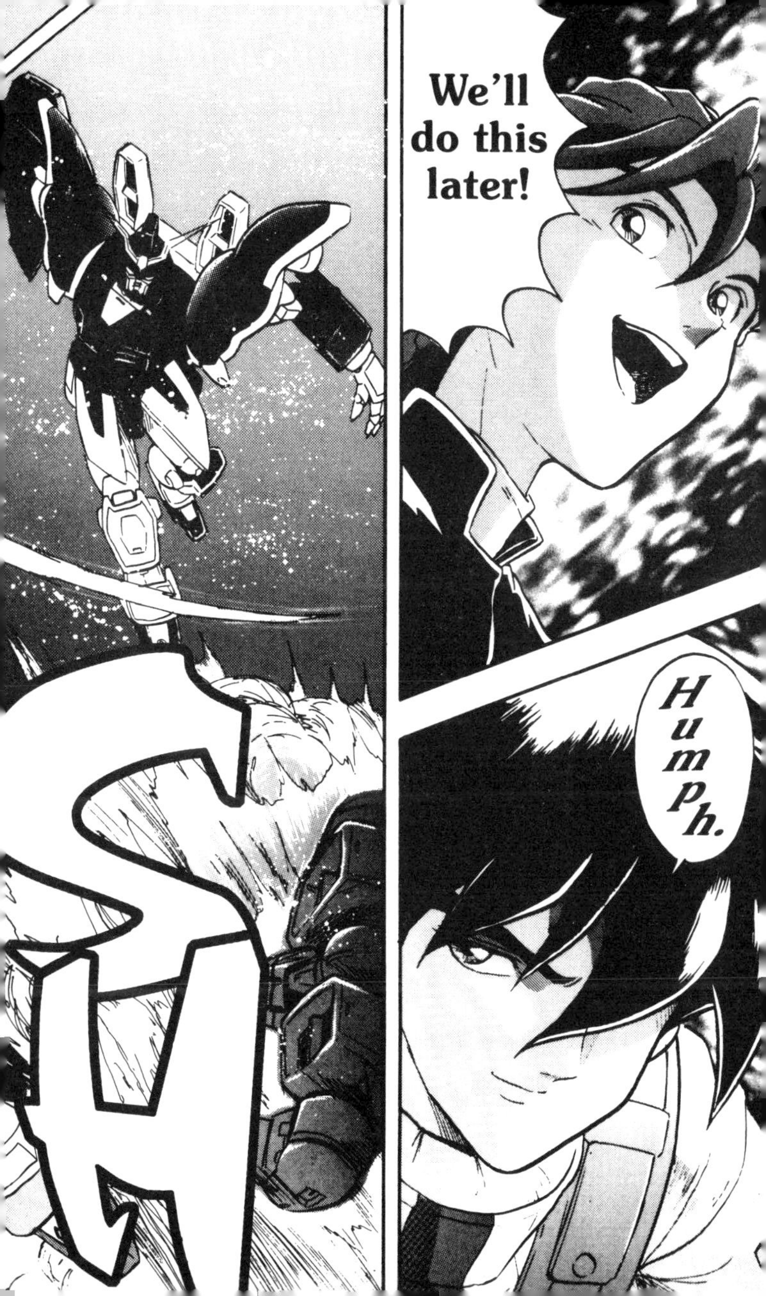
We'll do this later!
Humph.

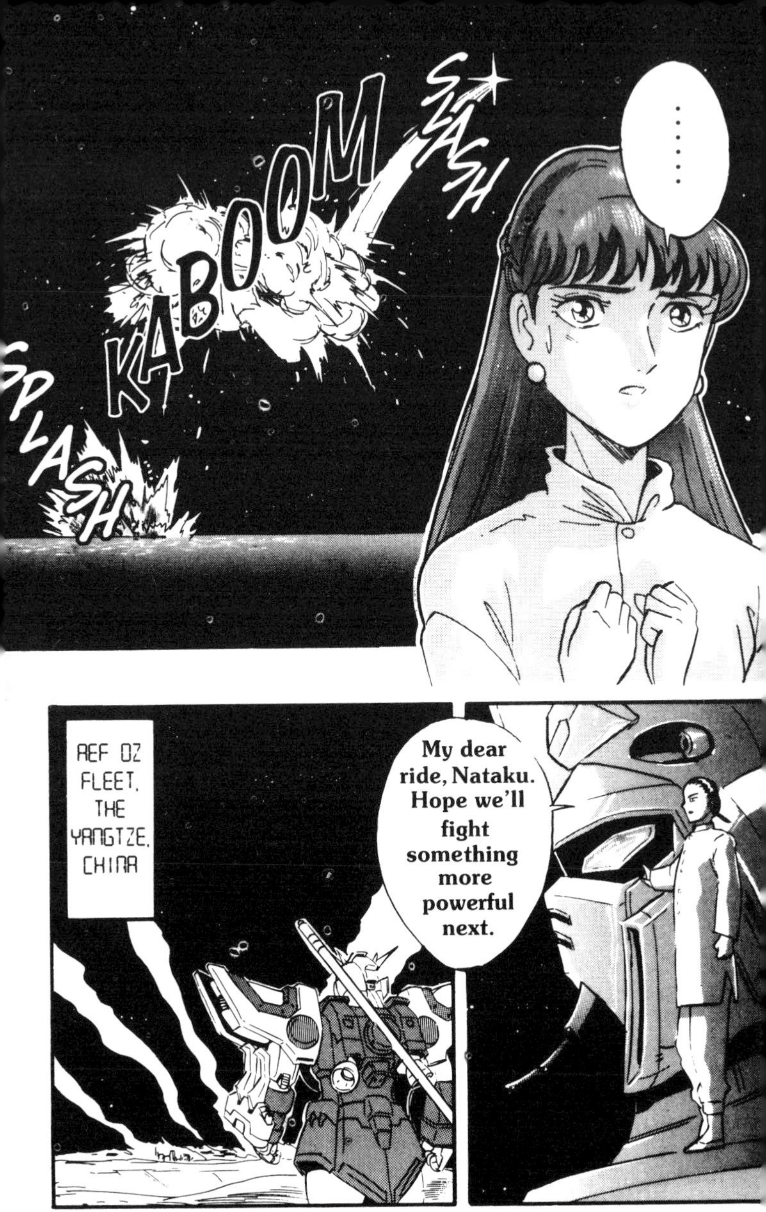
KABOOM
SLASH
......
SPLASH
AEF OZ FLEET, THE YANGTZE, CHINA
My dear ride, Nataku. Hope we'll fight something more powerful next.

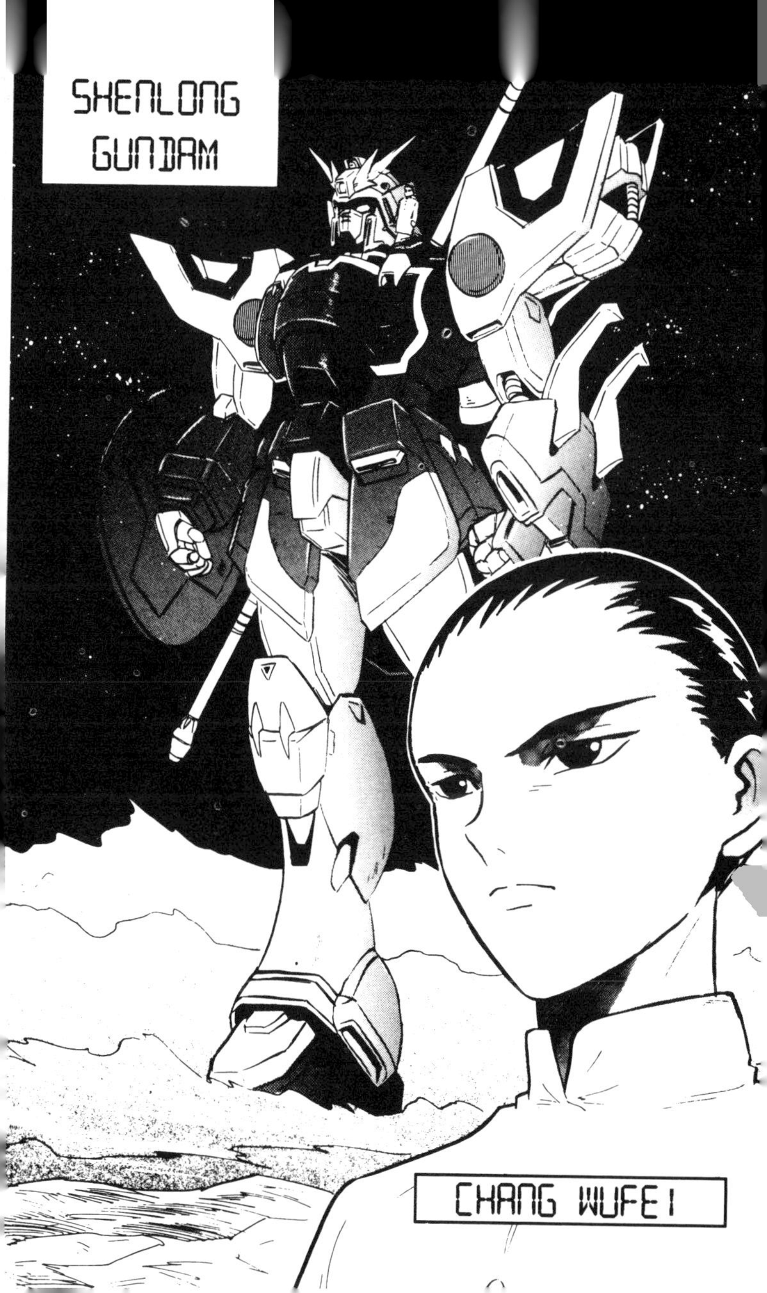
SHENLONG
GUNDAM
CHANG WUFEI

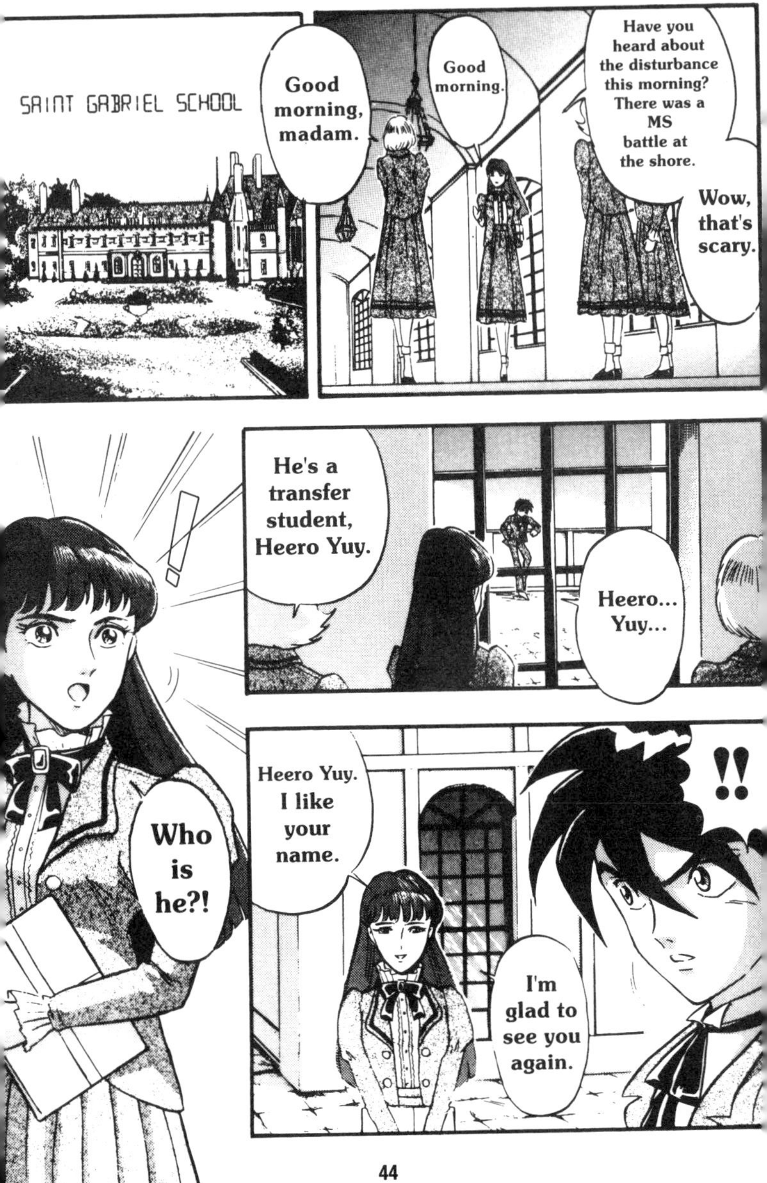
SAINT GABRIEL SCHOOL
Good morning, madam.
Good morning.
Have you heard about the disturbance this morning? There was a MS battle at the shore.
Wow, that's scary.
!
Who is he?!
He's a transfer student, Heero Yuy.
Heero... Yuy...
Heero Yuy. I like your name.
!!
I'm glad to see you again.

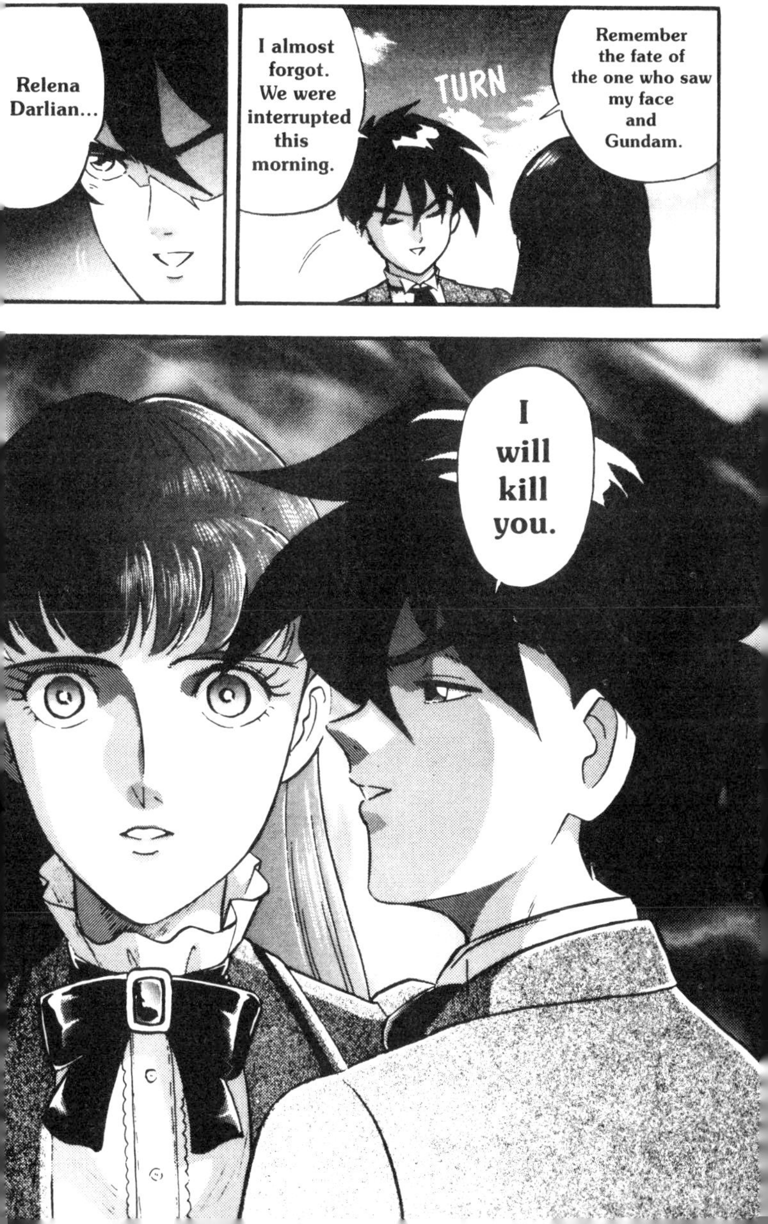
Relena Darlian...
I almost forgot. We were interrupted this morning.
TURN
Remember the fate of the one who saw my face and Gundam.
I will kill you.

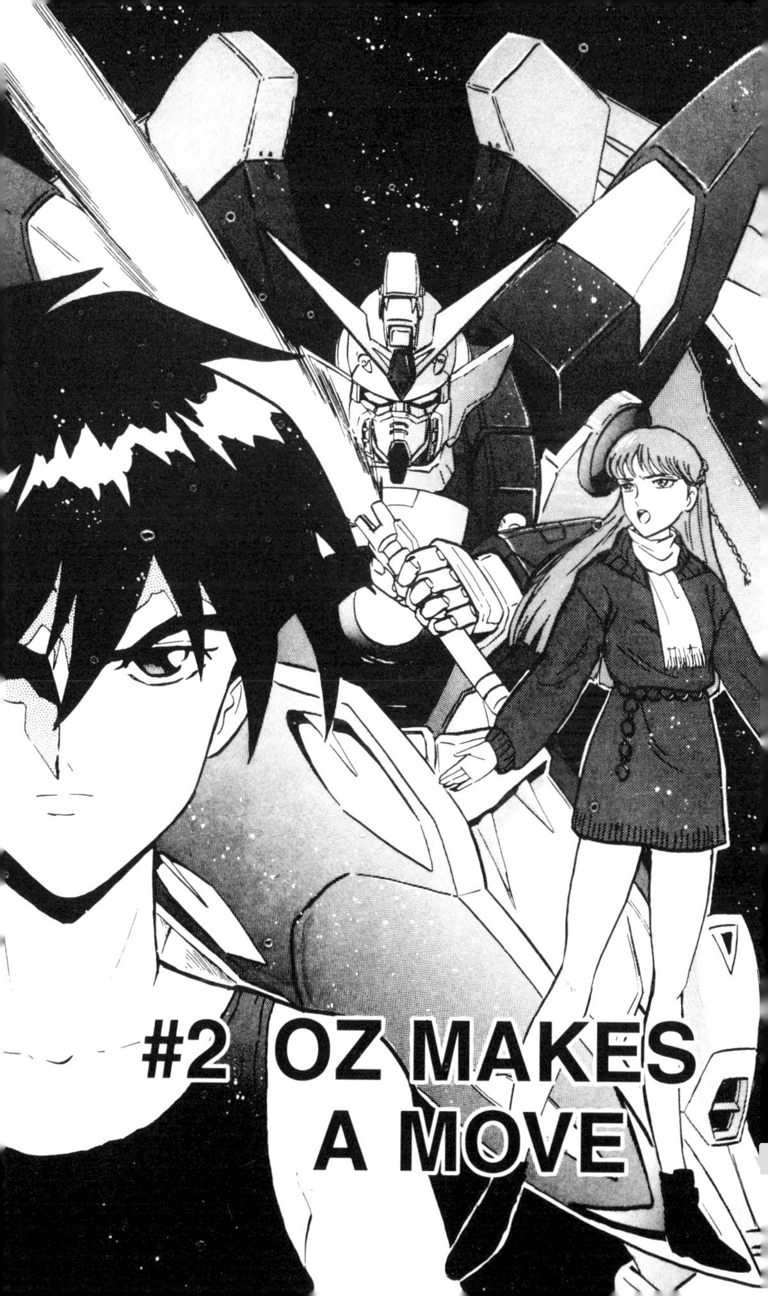
#2 OZ MAKES
A MOVE

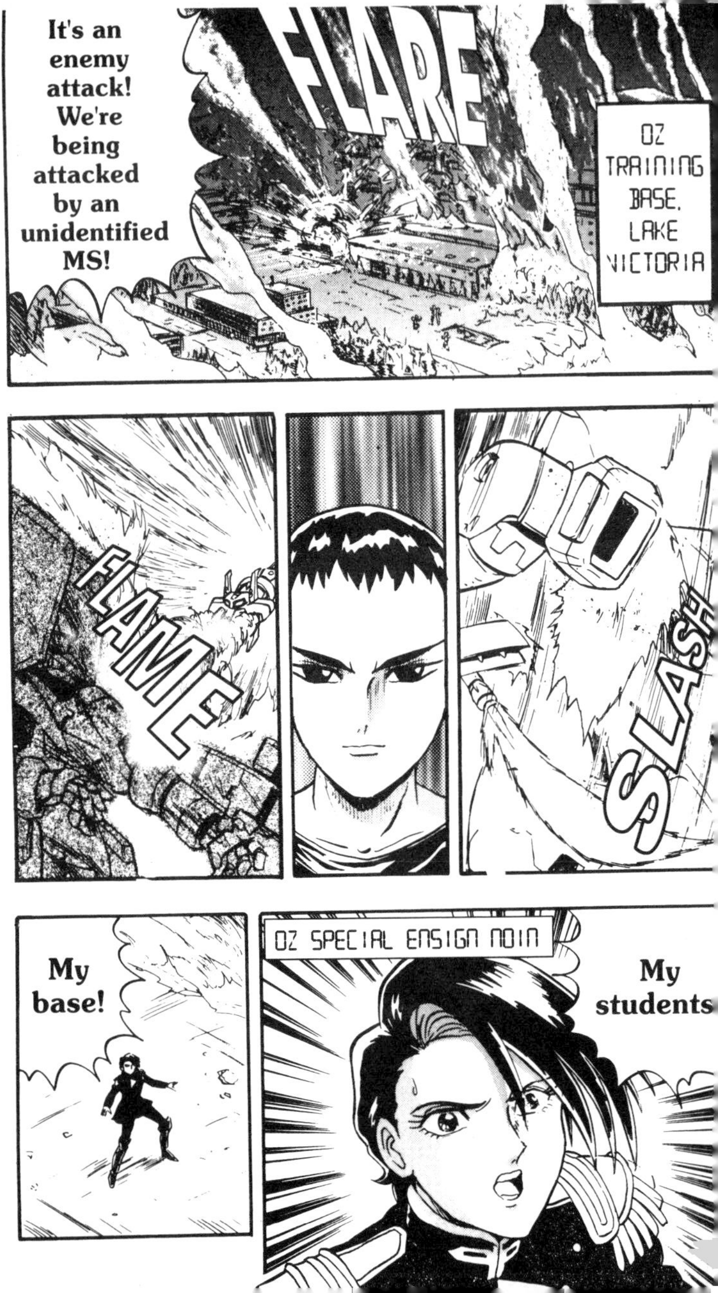
It's an enemy attack! We're being attacked by an unidentified MS!
FLARE
OZ TRAINING BASE, LAKE VICTORIA
FLAME
SLASH
My base!
OZ SPECIAL ENSIGN NOIN
My students

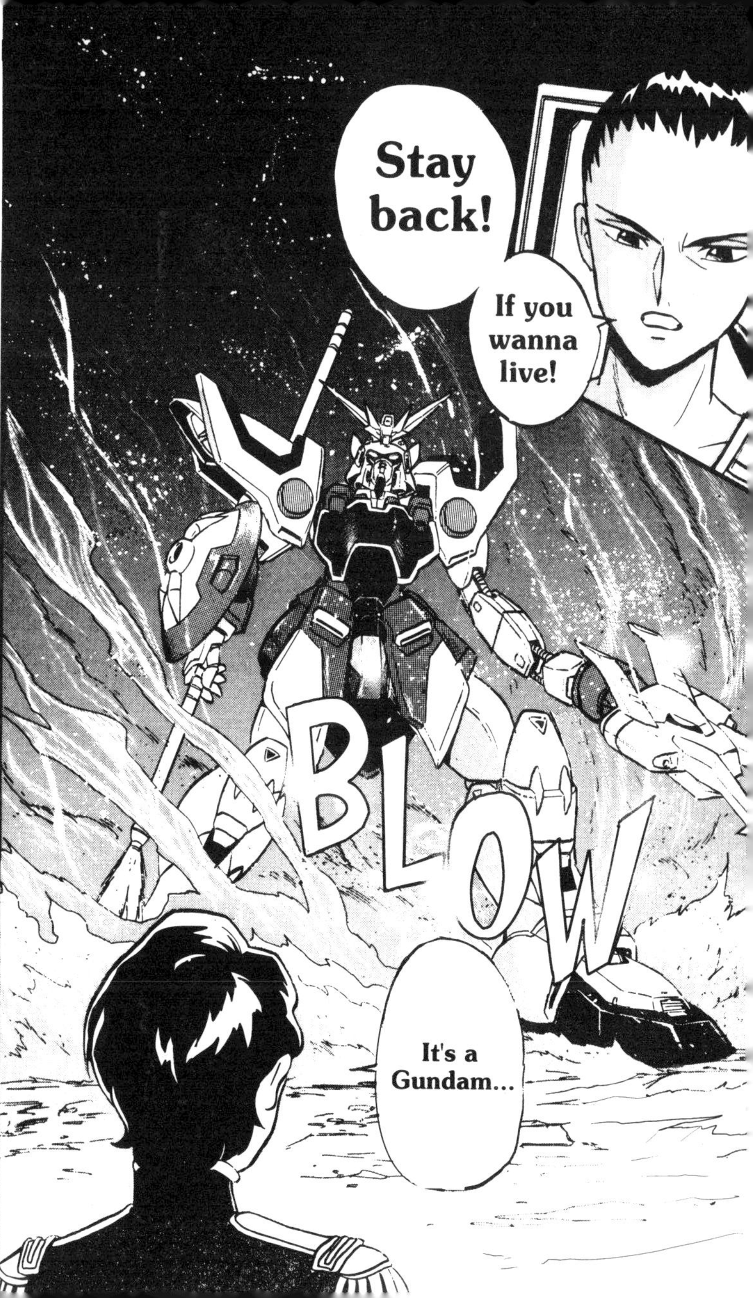
Stay back!
If you wanna live!
BLOW
It's a Gundam...

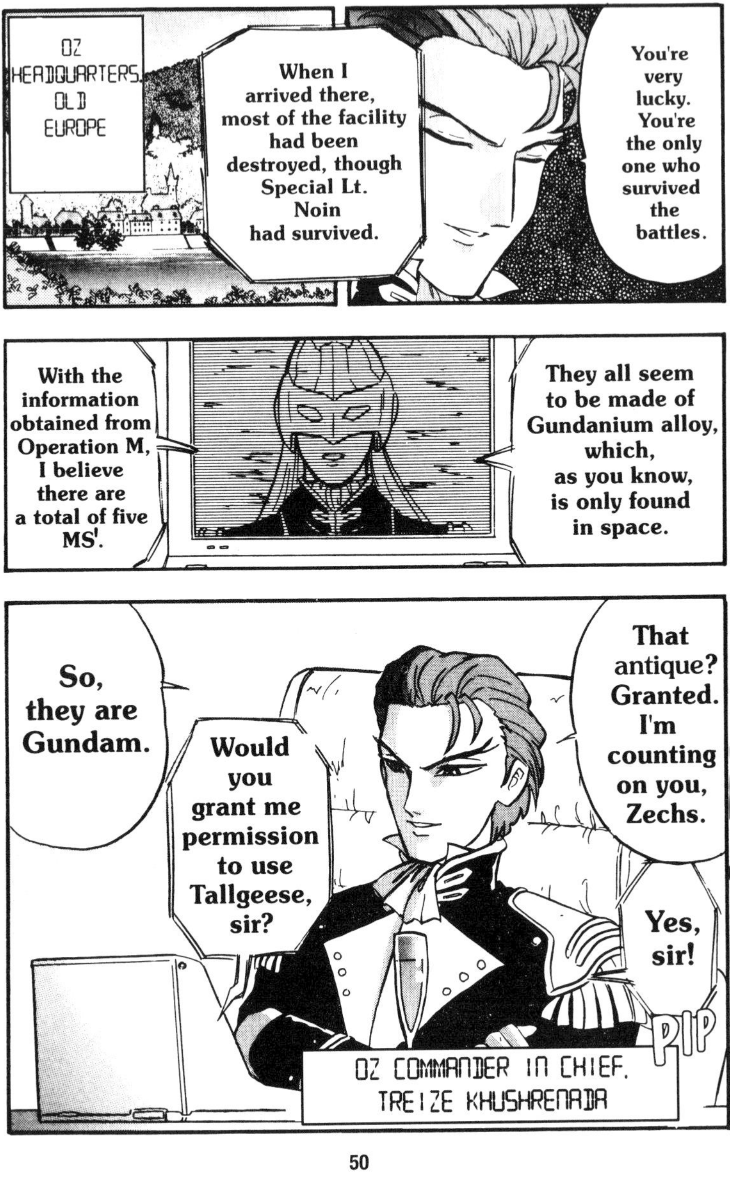
OZ HEADQUARTERS, OLD EUROPE
When I arrived there, most of the facility had been destroyed, though Special Lt. Noin had survived.
You're very lucky. You're the only one who survived the battles.
With the information obtained from Operation M, I believe there are a total of five MS'.
They all seem to be made of Gundanium alloy, which, as you know, is only found in space.
So, they are Gundam.
Would you grant me permission to use Tallgeese, sir?
That antique? Granted. I'm counting on you, Zechs.
Yes, sir!
PIP
OZ COMMANDER IN CHIEF, TREIZE KHUSHRENADA

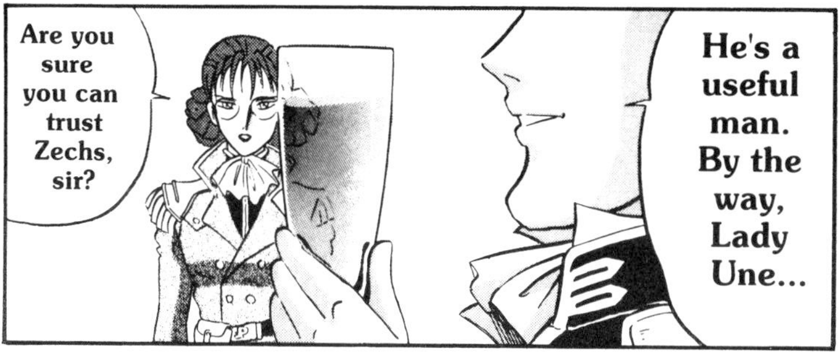
Are you sure you can trust Zechs, sir?
He's a useful man. By the way, Lady Une...
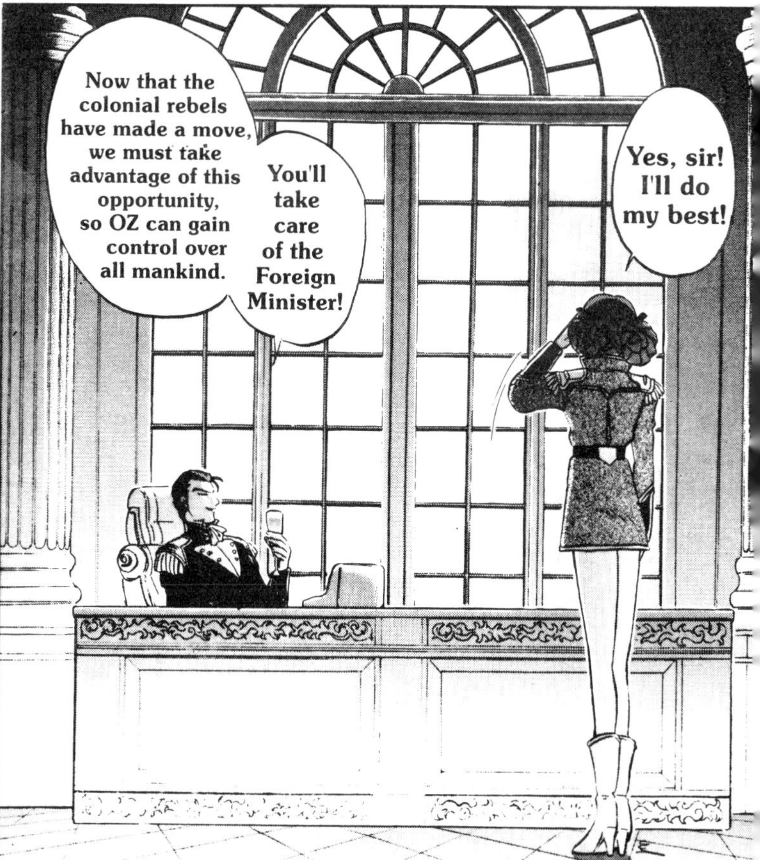
Now that the colonial rebels have made a move, we must take advantage of this opportunity, so OZ can gain control over all mankind.
You'll take care of the Foreign Minister!
Yes, sir! I'll do my best!

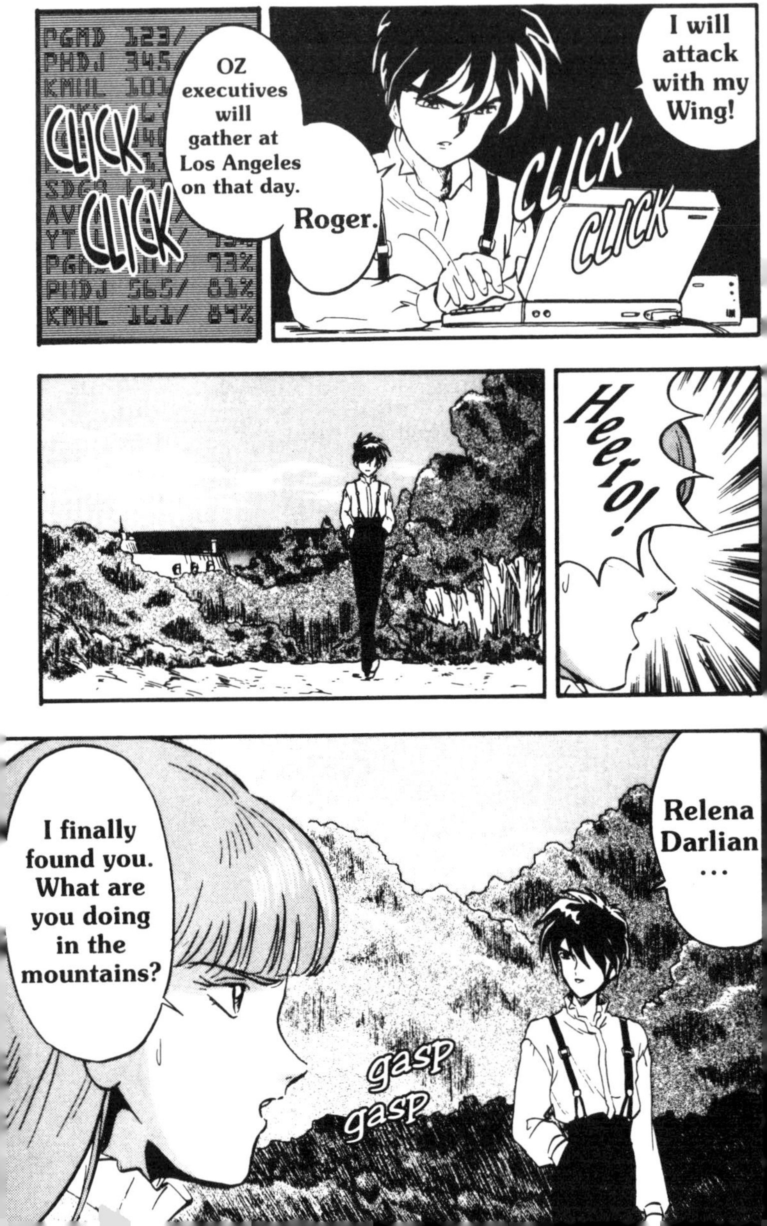
CLICK
CLICK
OZ executives will gather at Los Angeles on that day.
Roger.
I will attack with my Wing!
CLICK
CLICK
Heero!
I finally found you. What are you doing in the mountains?
gasp
gasp
Relena Darlian …

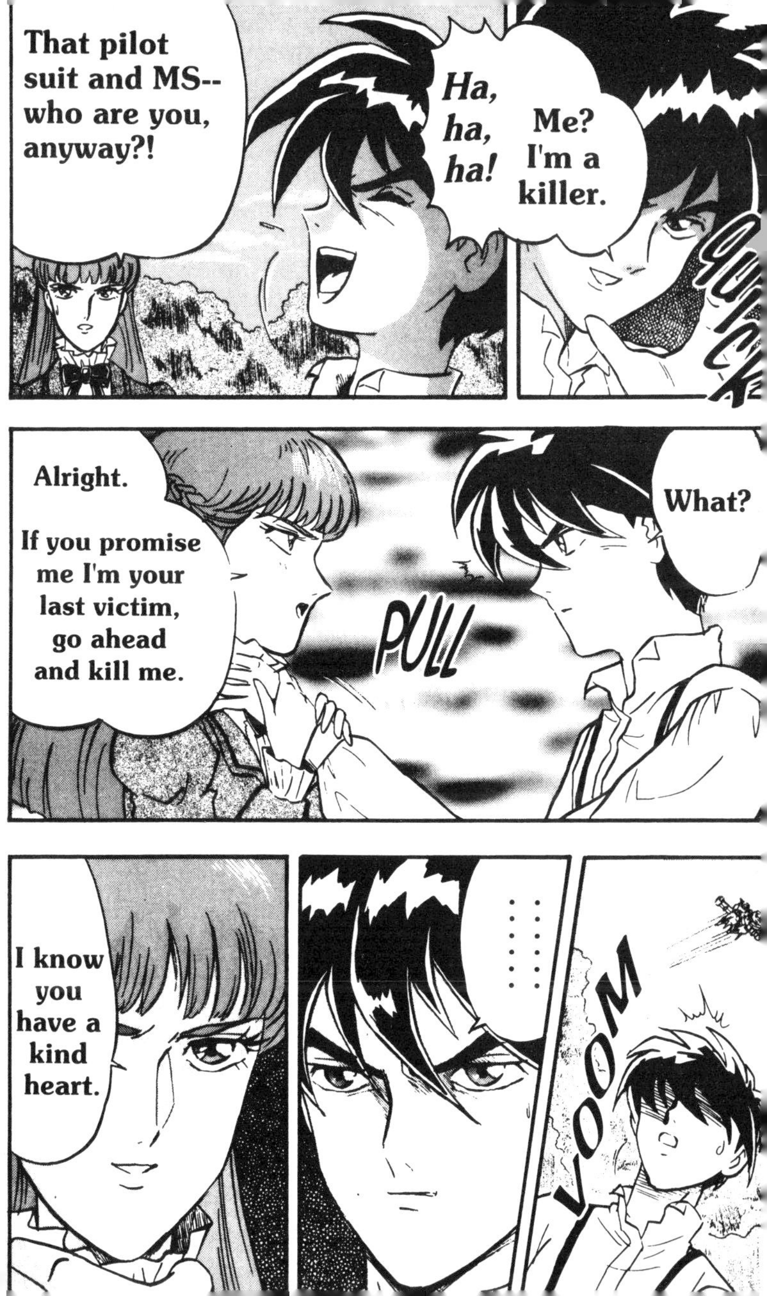
That pilot suit and MS-- who are you, anyway?!
Ha, ha, ha!
Me? I'm a killer.
QUICK
Alright.
If you promise me I'm your last victim, go ahead and kill me.
PULL
What?
I know you have a kind heart.
......
VOOM

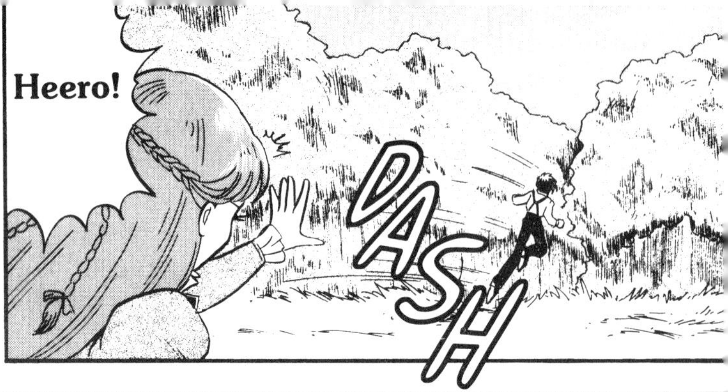
Heero!
DASH
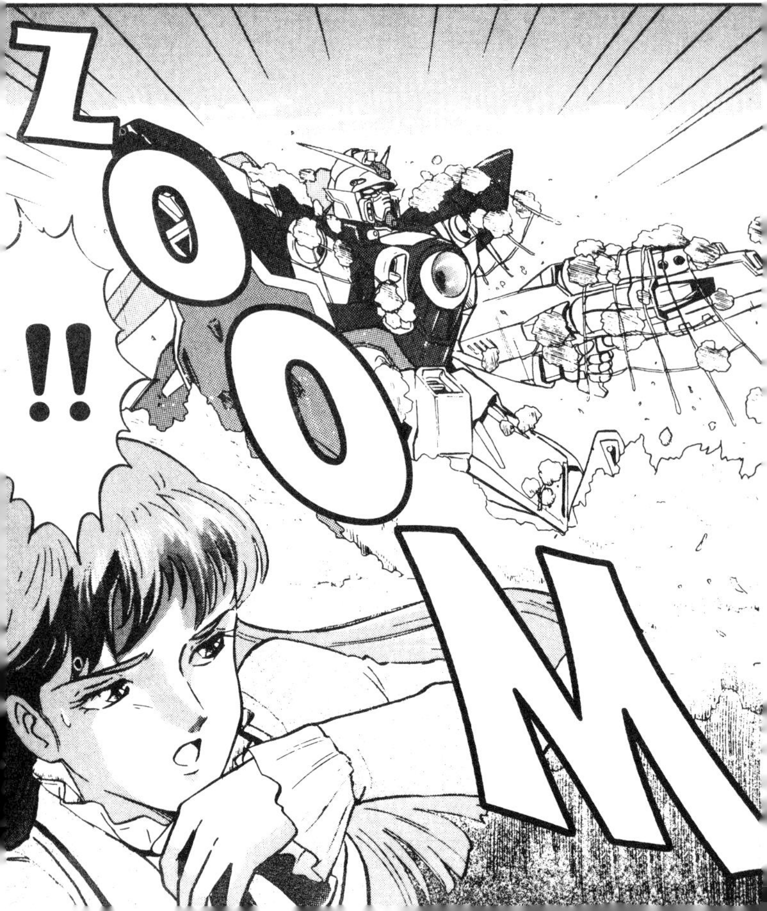
ZOOOM
!!

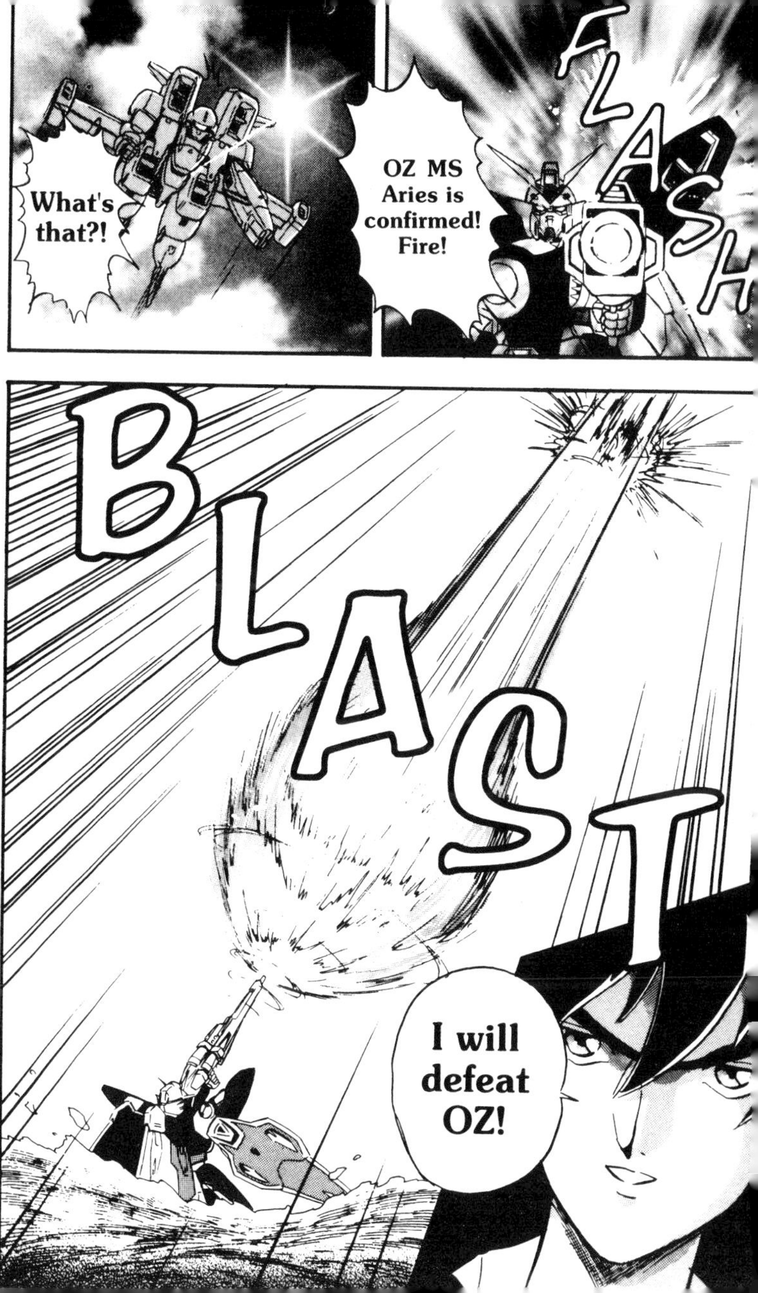
What's that?!
OZ MS Aries is confirmed! Fire!
FLASH
BLAST
I will defeat OZ!

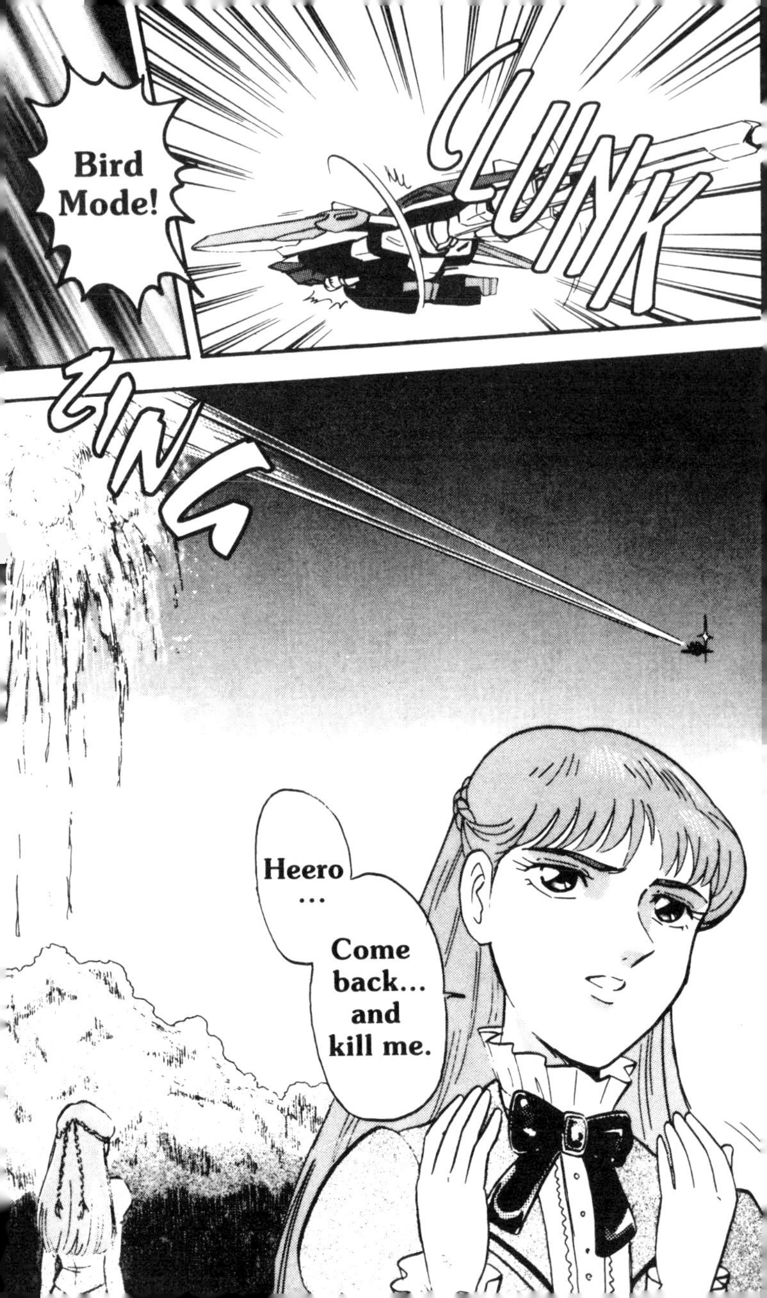
Bird Mode!
CLUNK
ZING
Heero ...
Come back... and kill me.

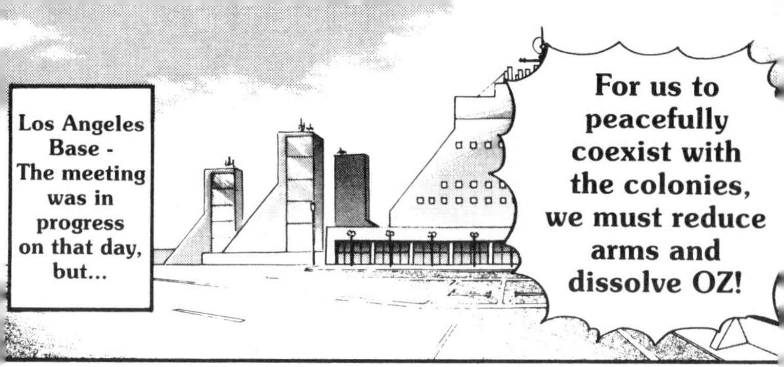

Los Angeles Base - The meeting was in progress on that day, but...
For us to peacefully coexist with the colonies, we must reduce arms and dissolve OZ!

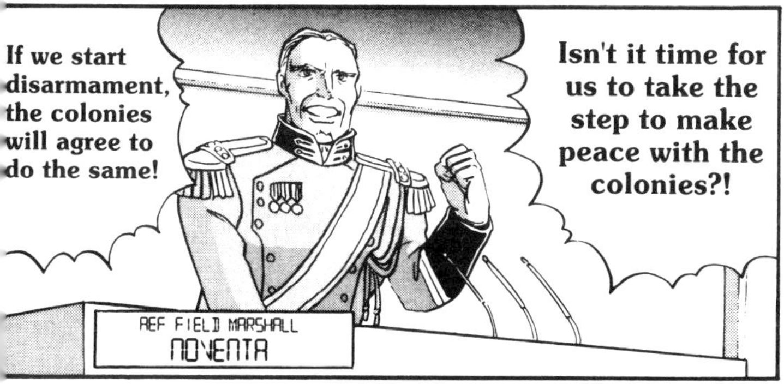

If we start disarmament, the colonies will agree to do the same!
Isn't it time for us to take the step to make peace with the colonies?!
AEF FIELD MARSHALL
NOVENTA

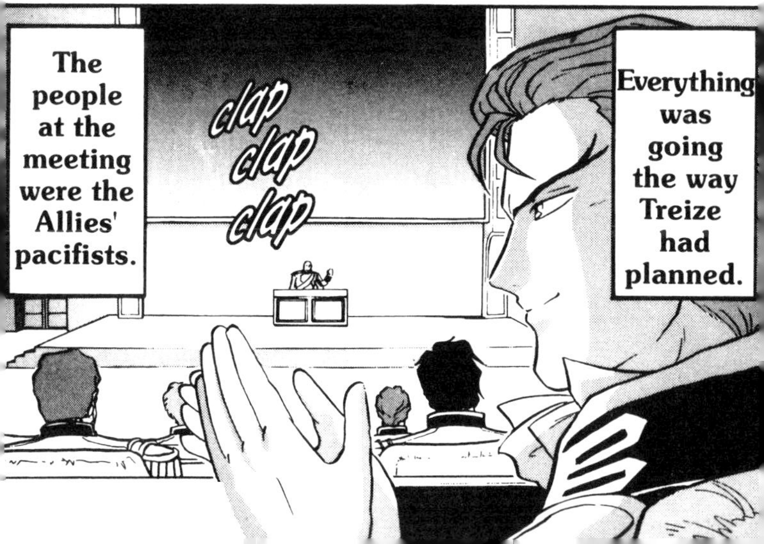

The people at the meeting were the Allies' pacifists.
clap
clap
clap
Everything was going the way Treize had planned.

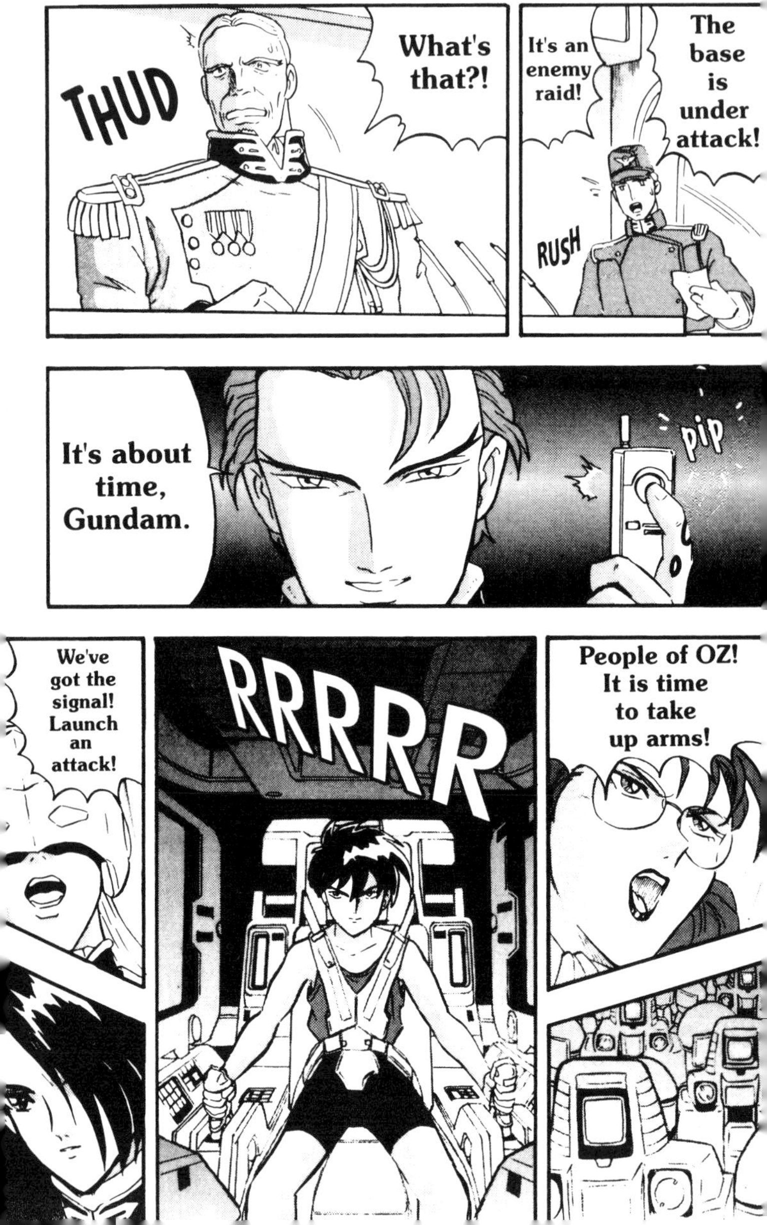
THUD
What's that?!
It's an enemy raid!
The base is under attack!
RUSH
It's about time, Gundam.
pip
We've got the signal! Launch an attack!
RRRRR
People of OZ! It is time to take up arms!

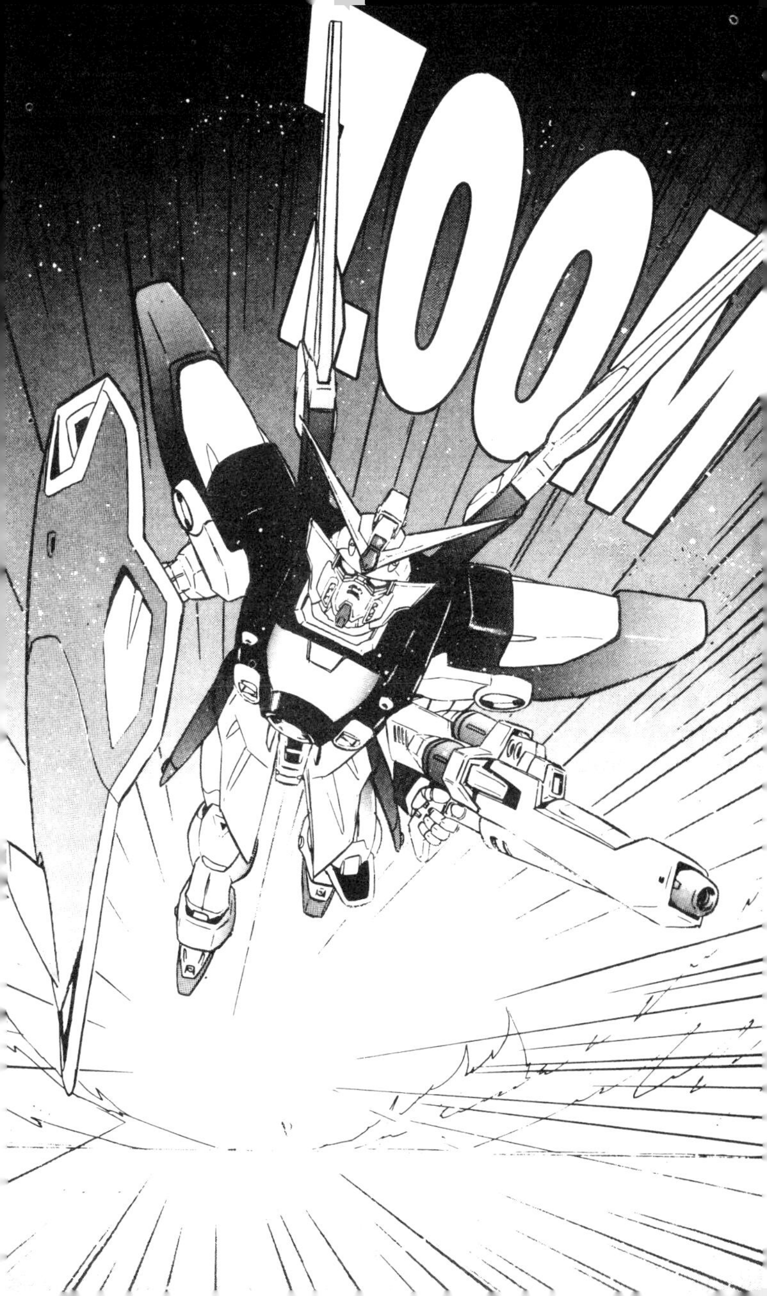
ZOOM

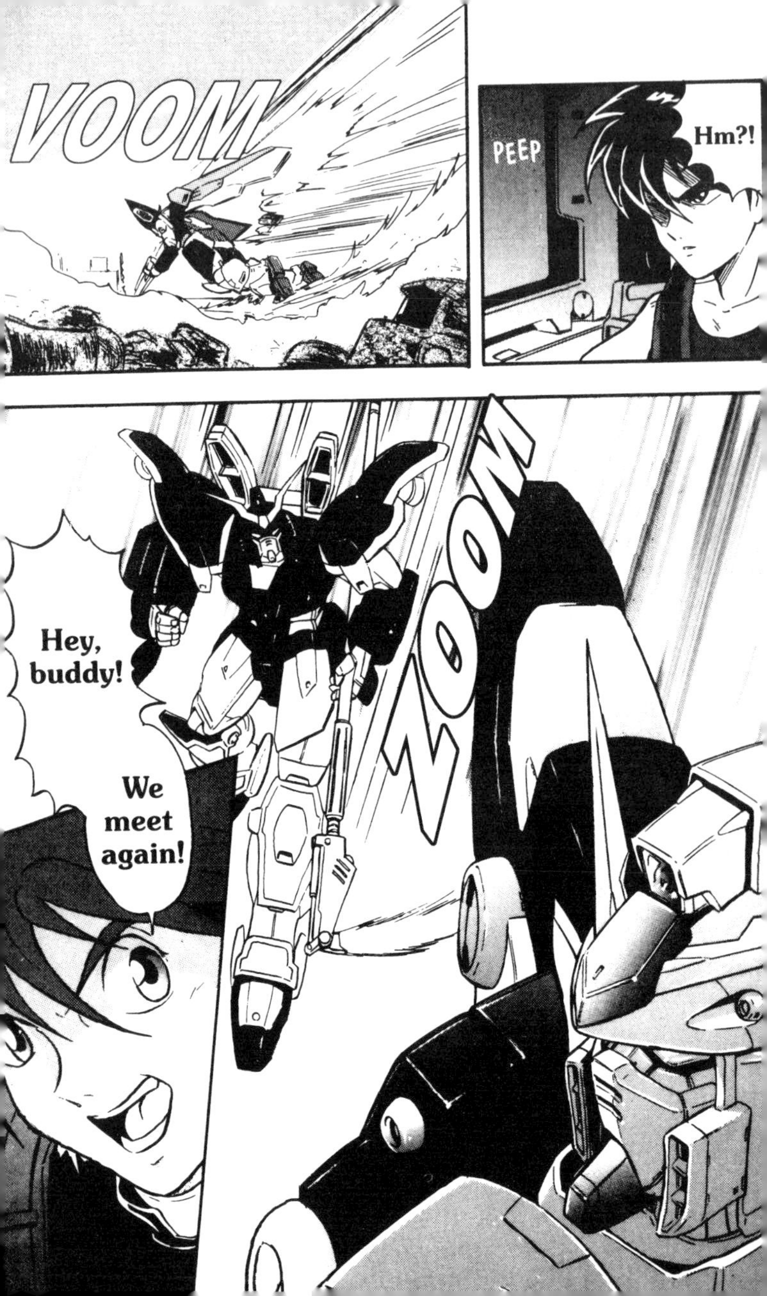
VOOM
PEEP
Hm?!
Hey, buddy!
We meet again!
ZOOM

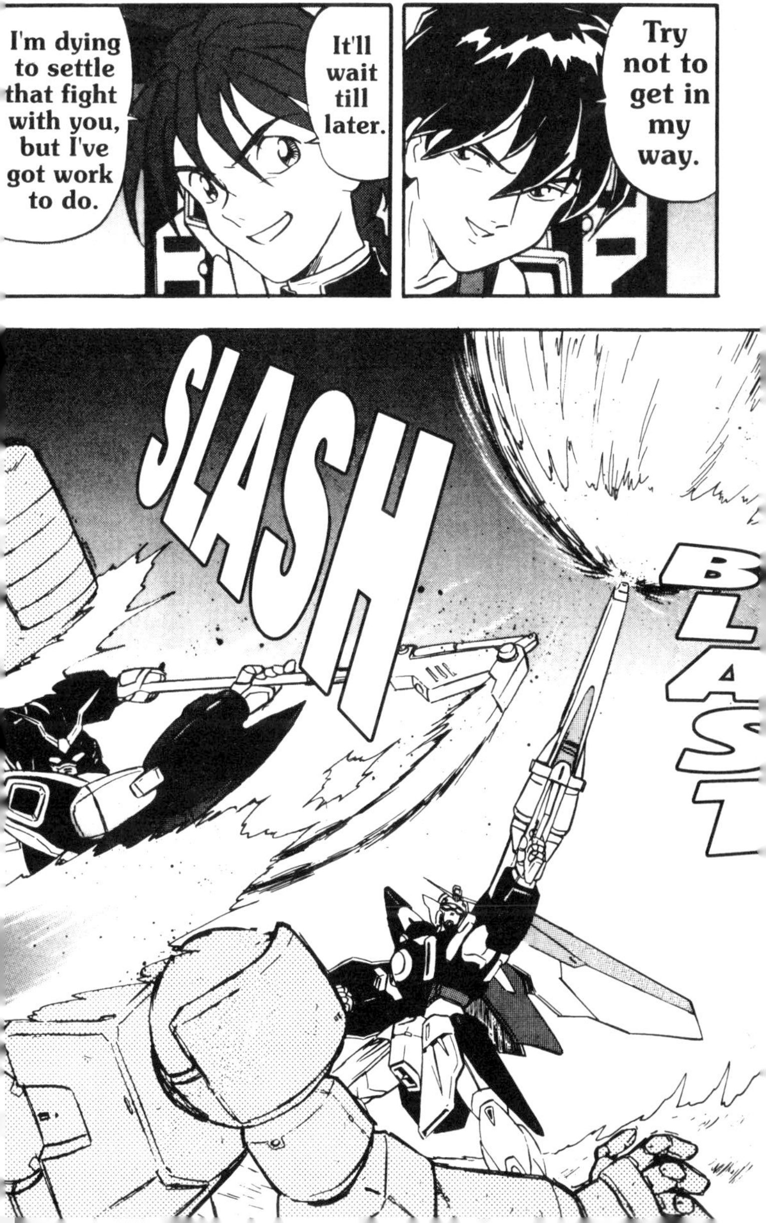

I'm dying to settle that fight with you, but I've got work to do.
It'll wait till later.
Try not to get in my way.
SLASH
BLAST

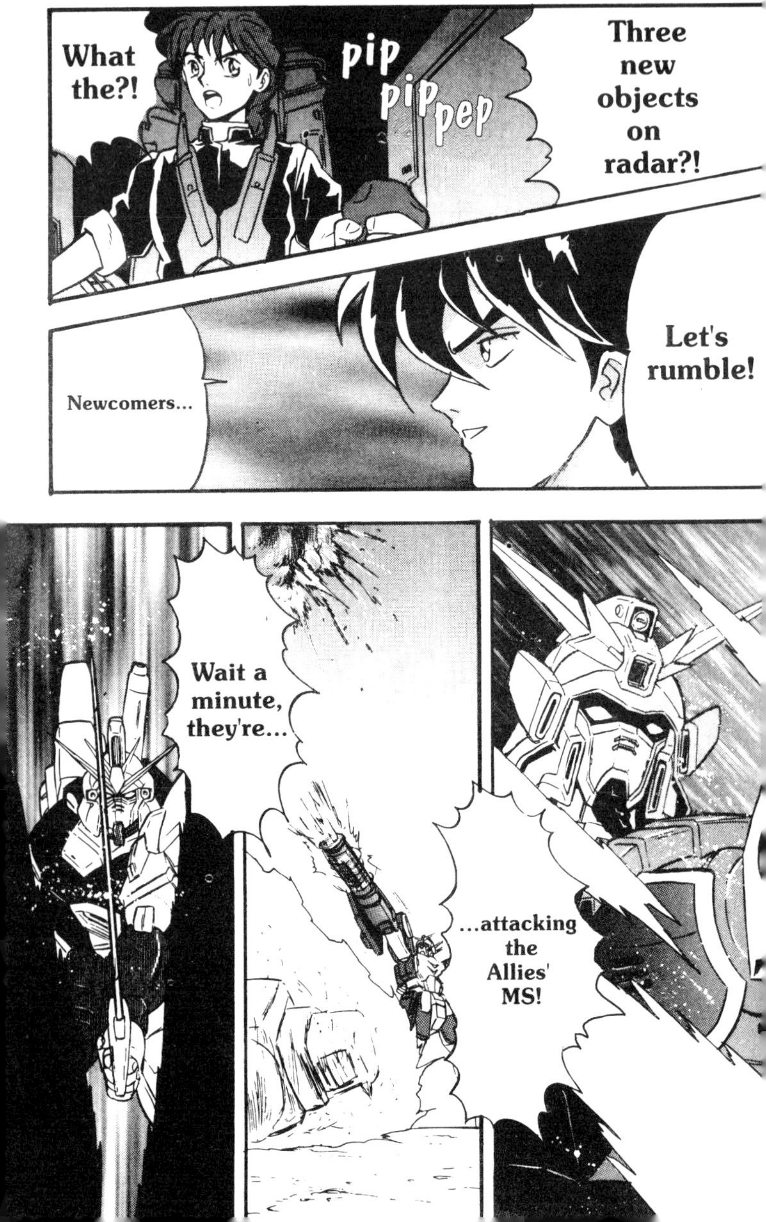

What the?!
pip pip pep
Three new objects on radar?!
Newcomers...
Let's rumble!
Wait a minute, they're...
...attacking the Allies' MS!

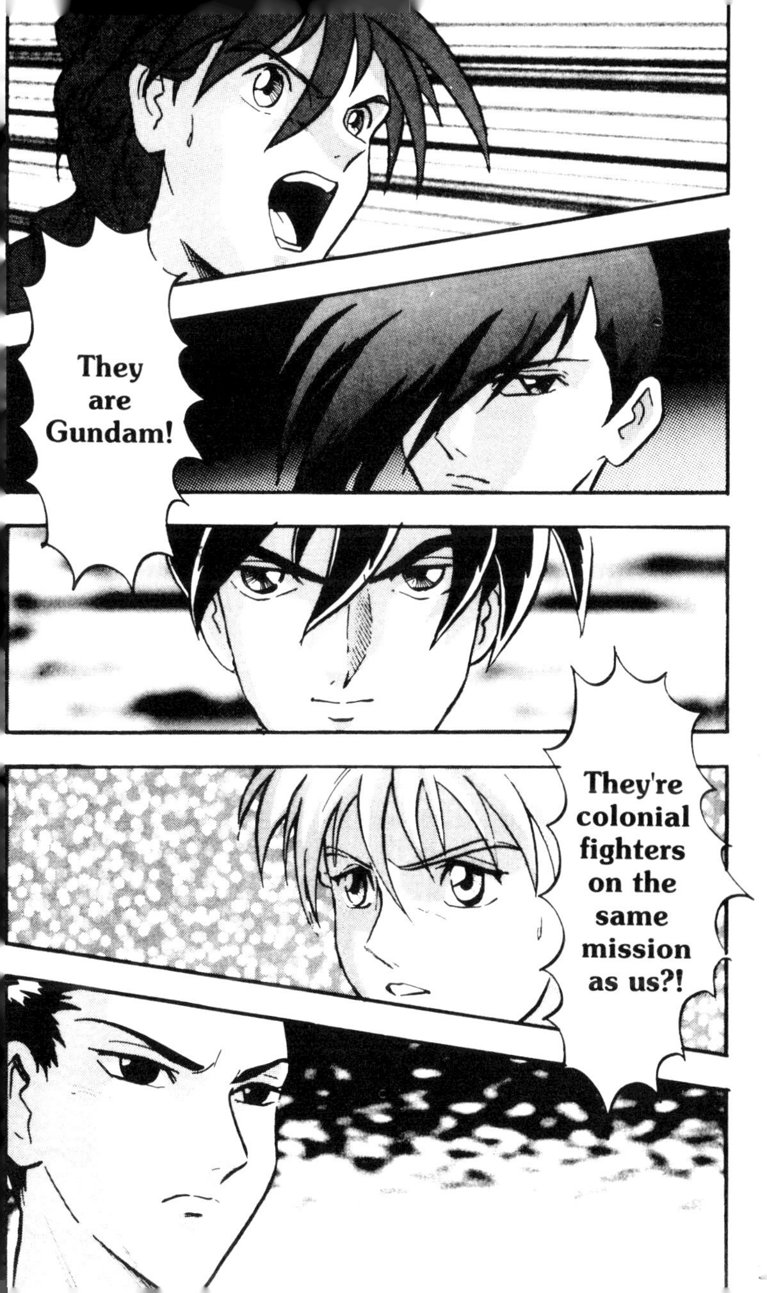
They are Gundam!
They're colonial fighters on the same mission as us?!

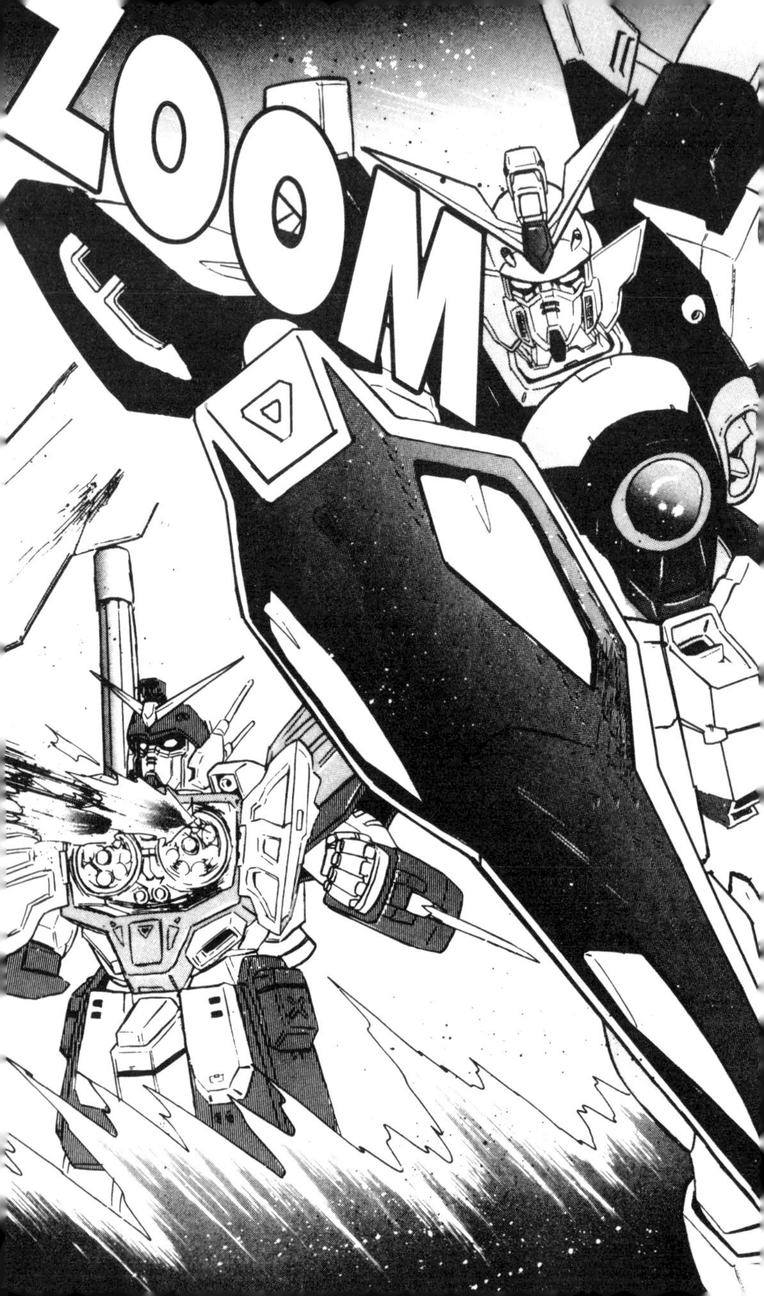
ZOOM

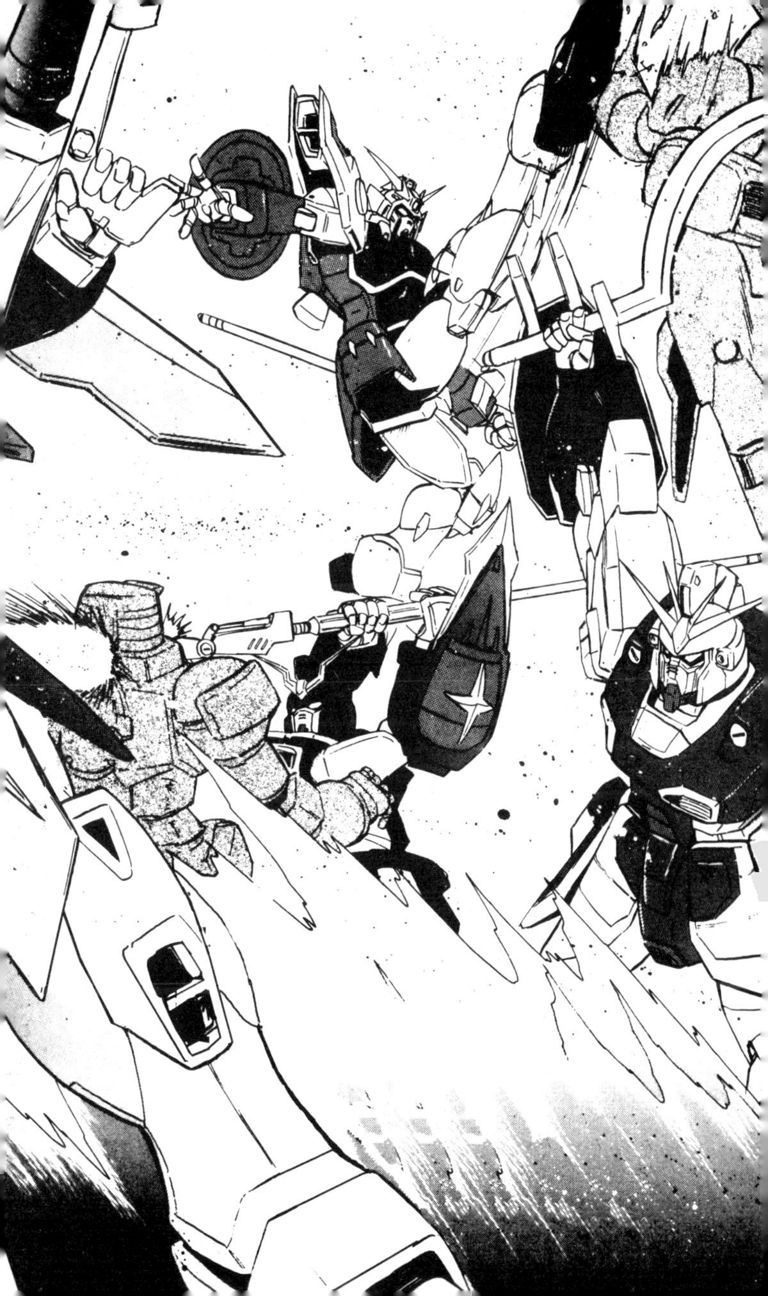

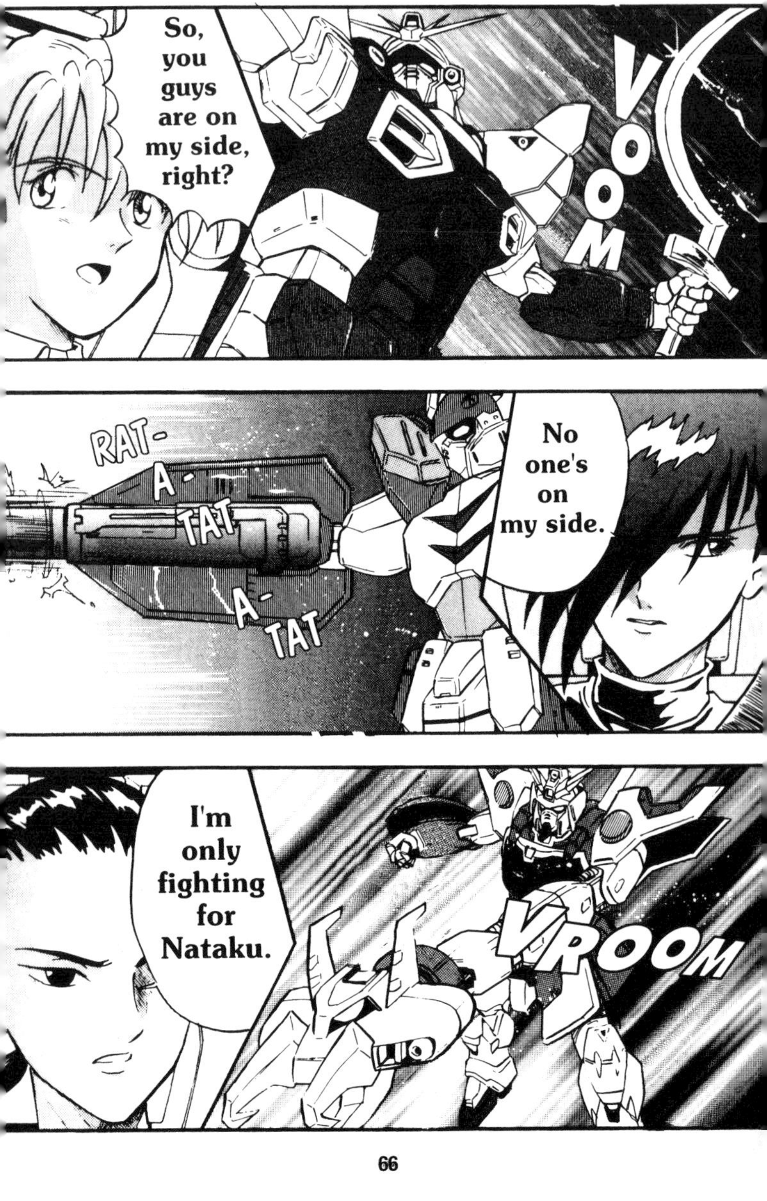

So, you guys are on my side, right?
VOOM
RAT-A-TAT-A-TAT
No one's on my side.
I'm only fighting for Nataku.
VROOM

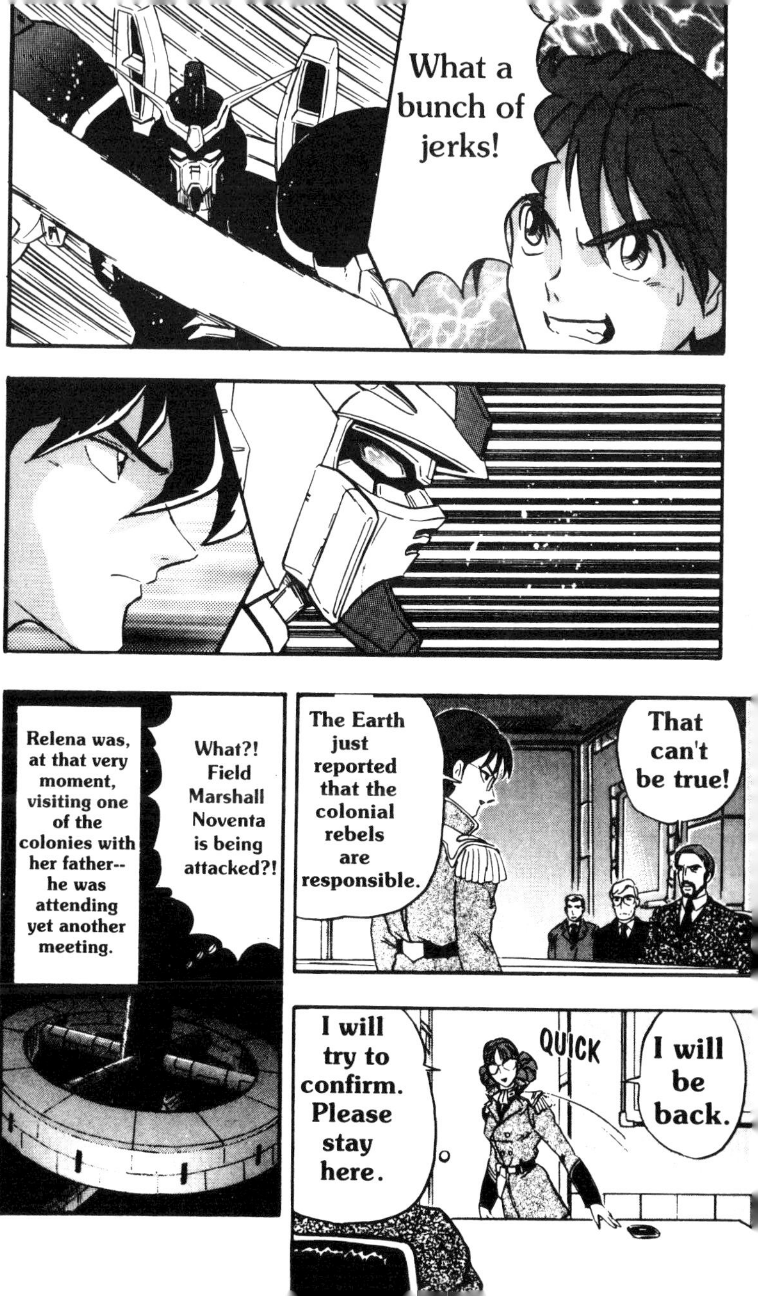

What a bunch of jerks!
Relena was, at that very moment, visiting one of the colonies with her father-- he was attending yet another meeting.
What?! Field Marshall Noventa is being attacked?!
The Earth just reported that the colonial rebels are responsible.
That can't be true!
I will try to confirm. Please stay here.
QUICK
I will be back.

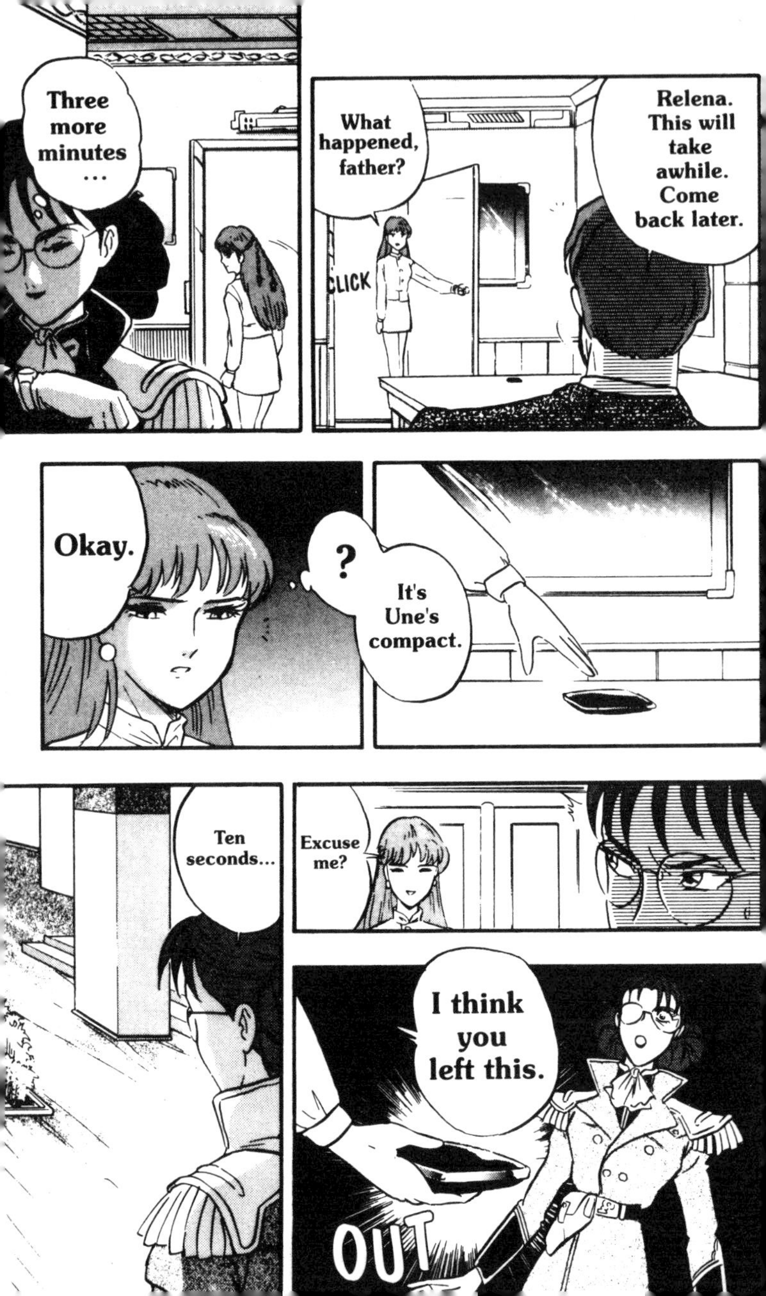
Three more minutes …
What happened, father?
CLICK
Relena. This will take awhile. Come back later.
Okay.
?
It's Une's compact.
Ten seconds…
Excuse me?
I think you left this.
OUT

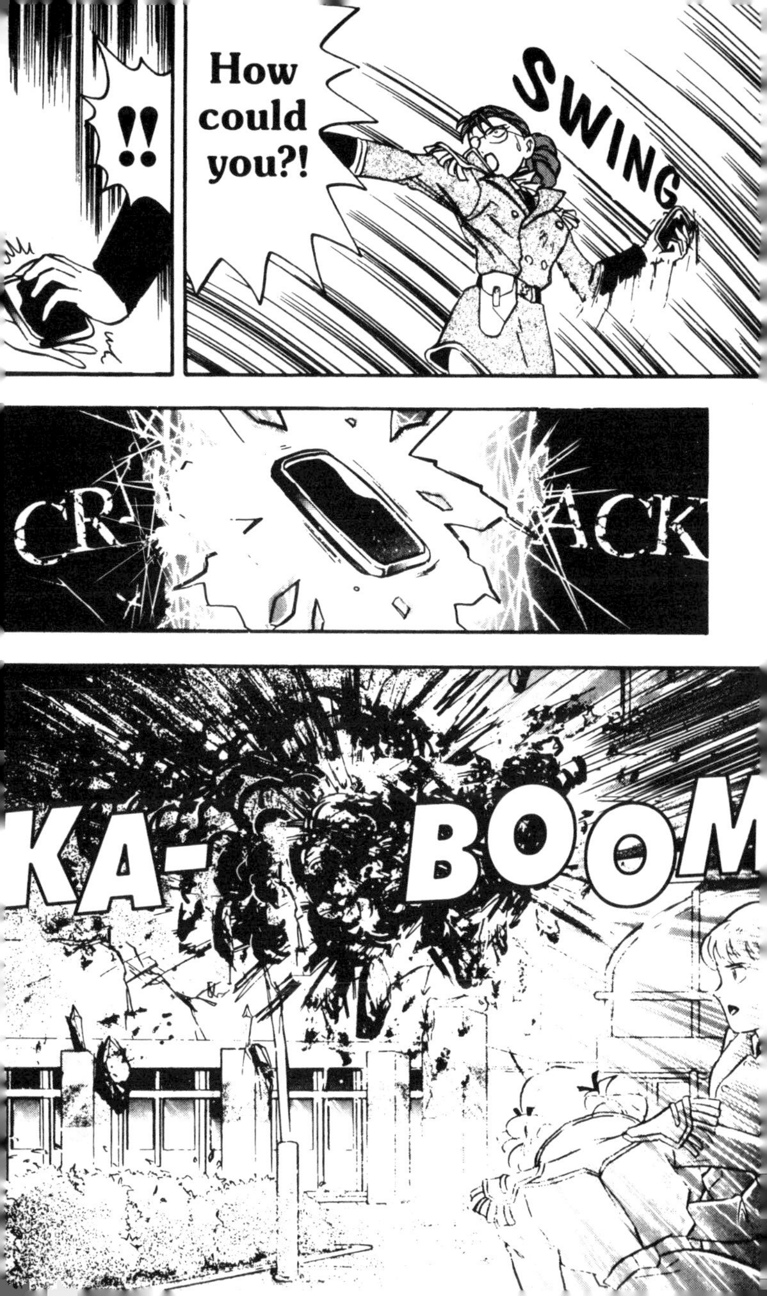

!!
How could you?!
SWING
CRACK
KA-BOOM

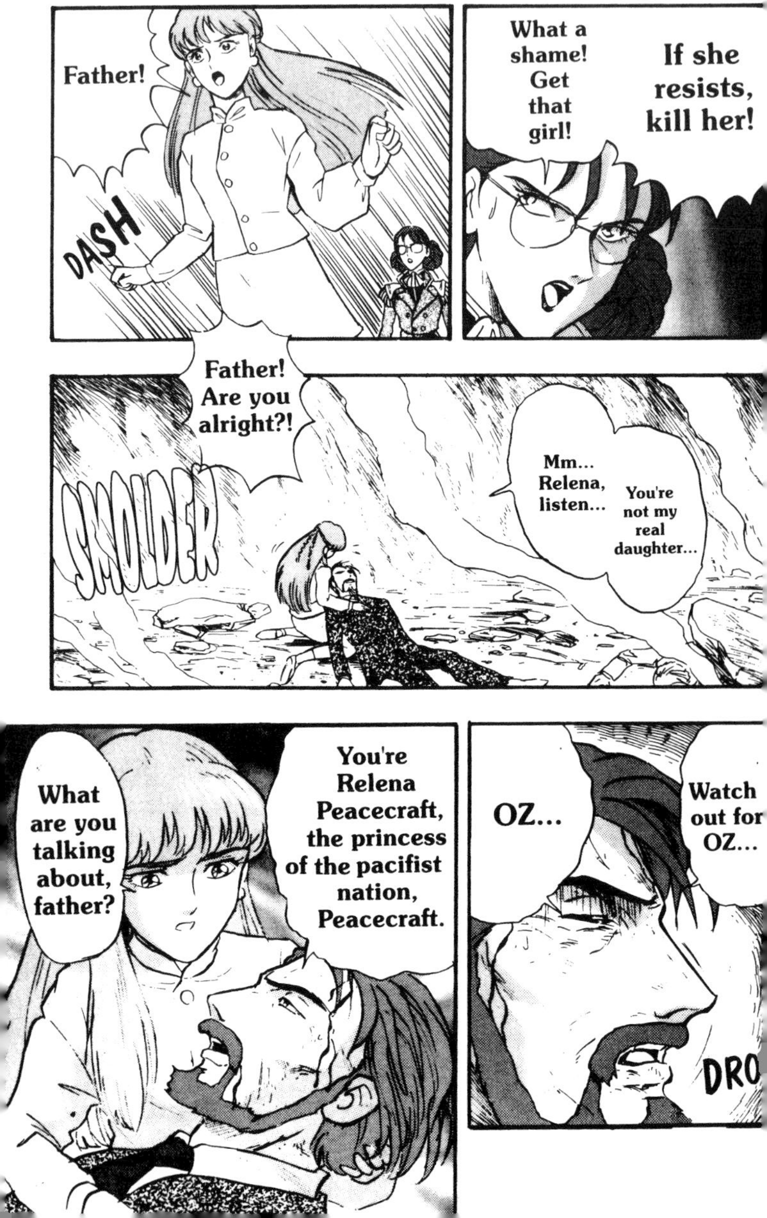
Father!
DASH
What a shame! Get that girl!
If she resists, kill her!
Father! Are you alright?!
SMOLDER
Mm... Relena, listen...
You're not my real daughter...
What are you talking about, father?
You're Relena Peacecraft, the princess of the pacifist nation, Peacecraft.
OZ...
Watch out for OZ...
DRO

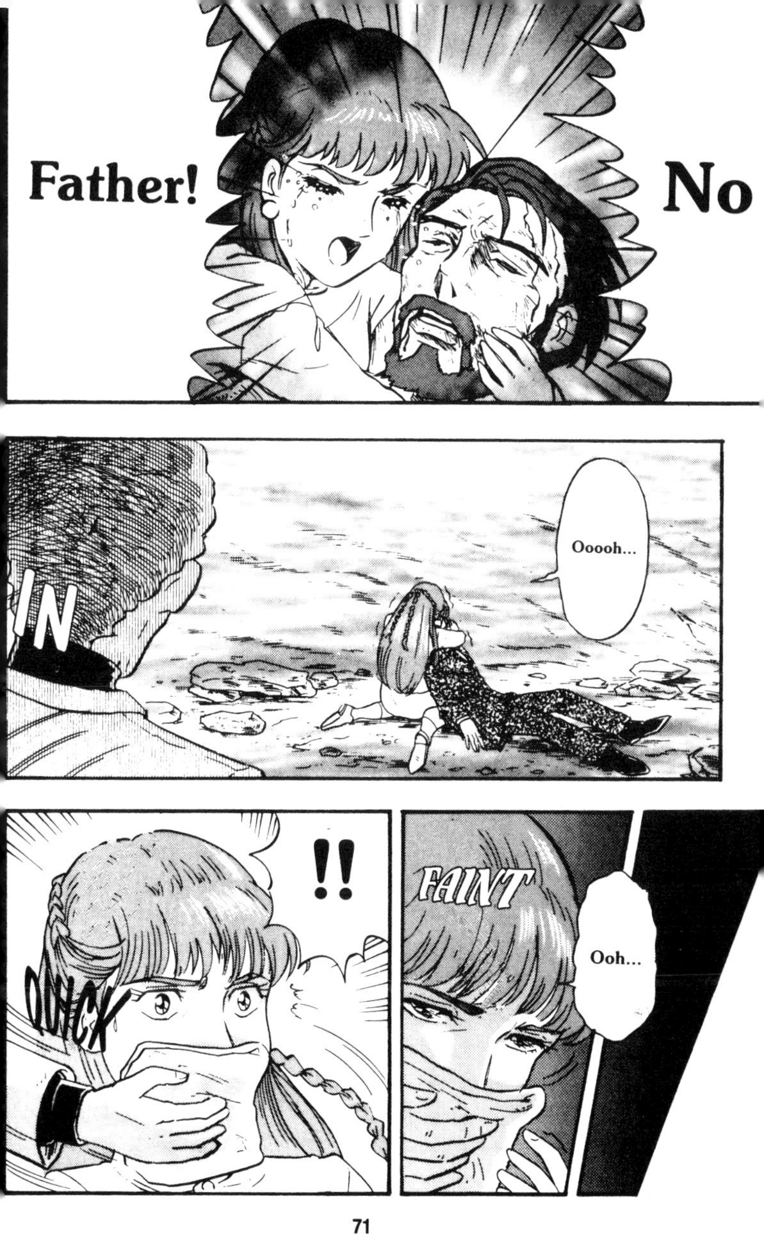
Father!
No
IN
Ooooh...
QUICK
!!
FAINT
Ooh...

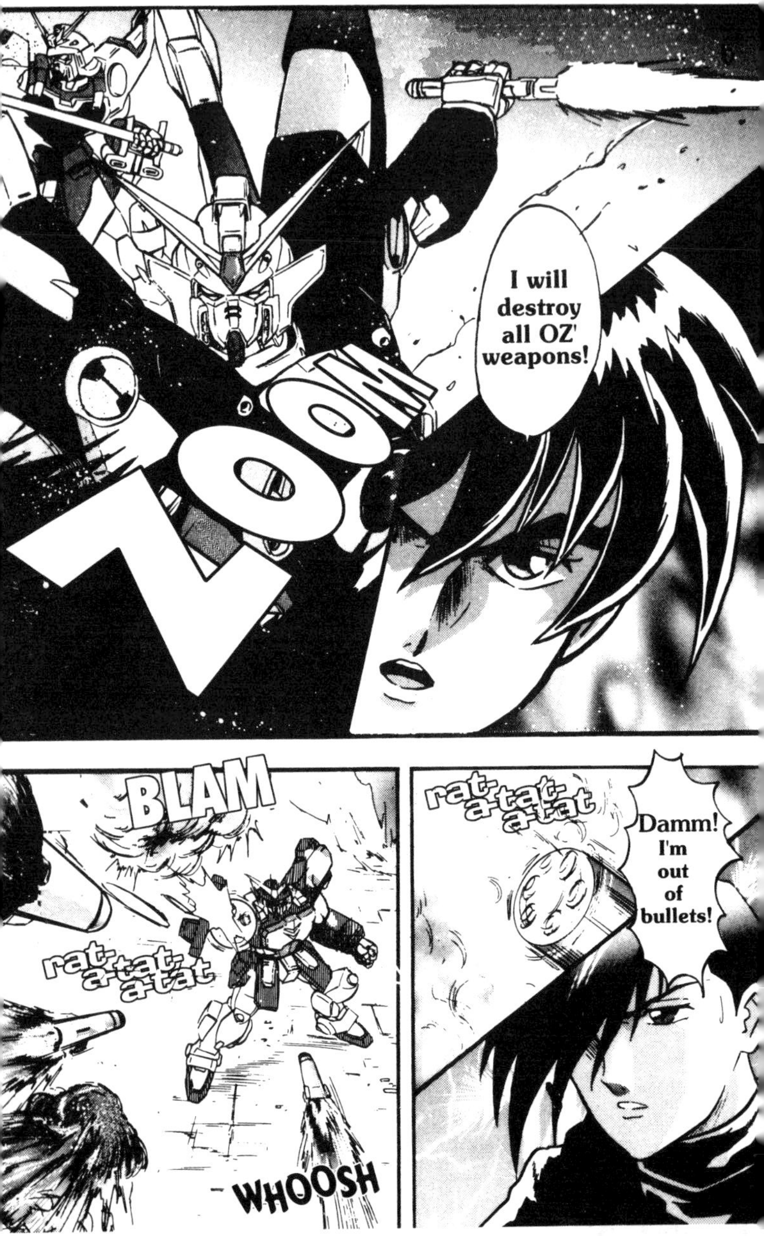
ZOOM
I will destroy all OZ' weapons!
BLAM
rat-a-tat-a-tat
WHOOSH
rat-a-tat-a-tat
Damm! I'm out of bullets!

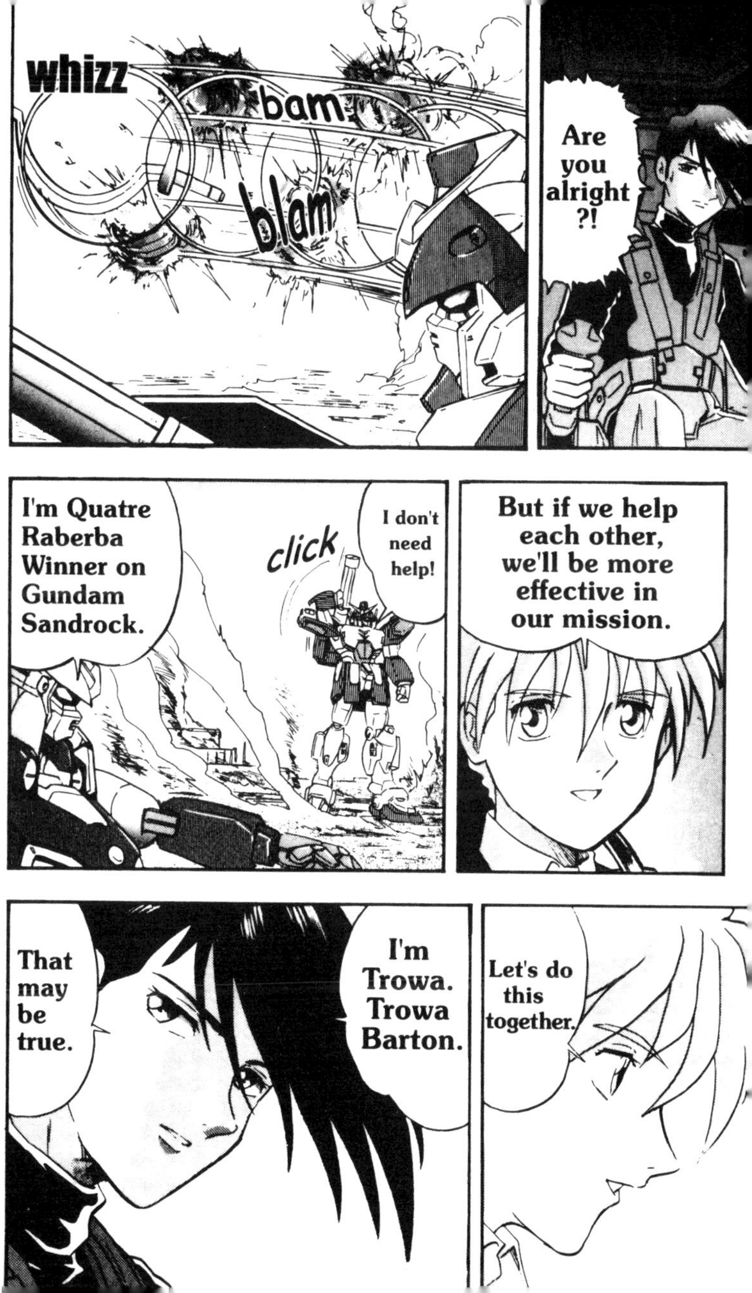
whizz
bam
blam
Are you alright ?!
I'm Quatre Raberba Winner on Gundam Sandrock.
click
I don't need help!
But if we help each other, we'll be more effective in our mission.
That may be true.
I'm Trowa. Trowa Barton.
Let's do this together.

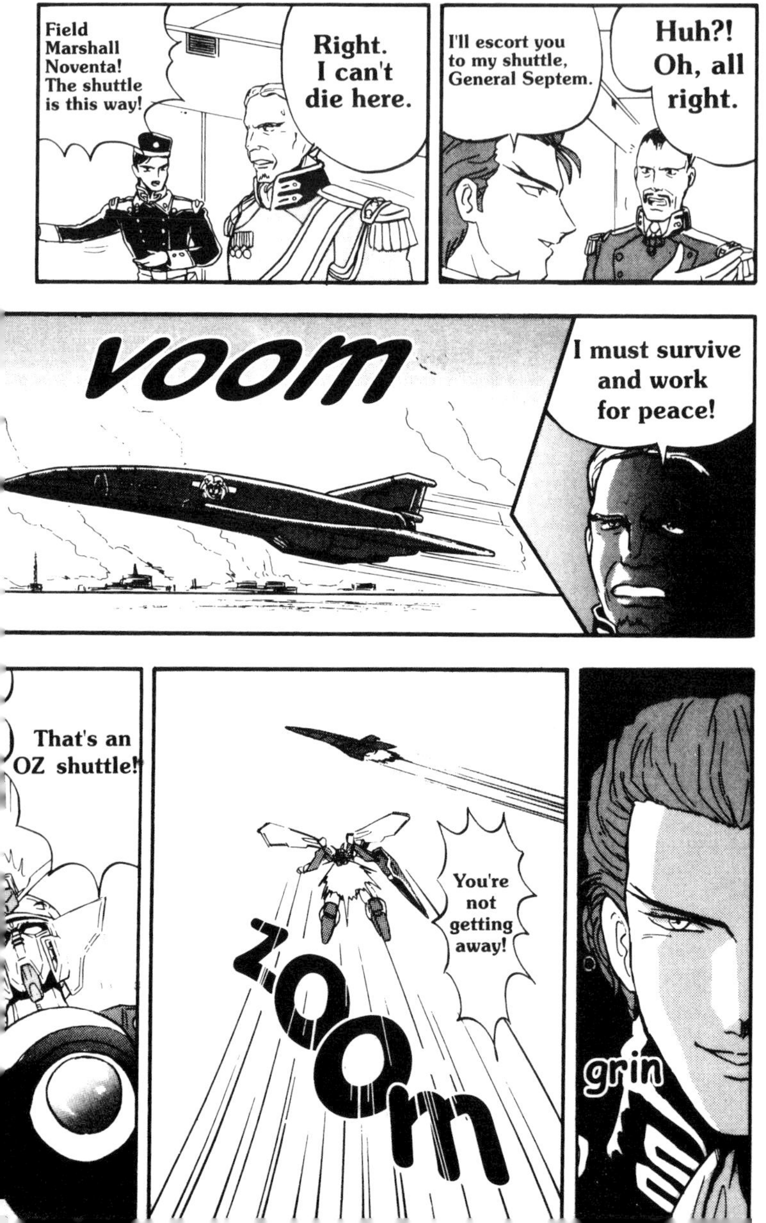
Field Marshall Noventa! The shuttle is this way!
Right. I can't die here.
I'll escort you to my shuttle, General Septem.
Huh?! Oh, all right.
voom
I must survive and work for peace!
That's an OZ shuttle!
You're not getting away!
zoom
grin

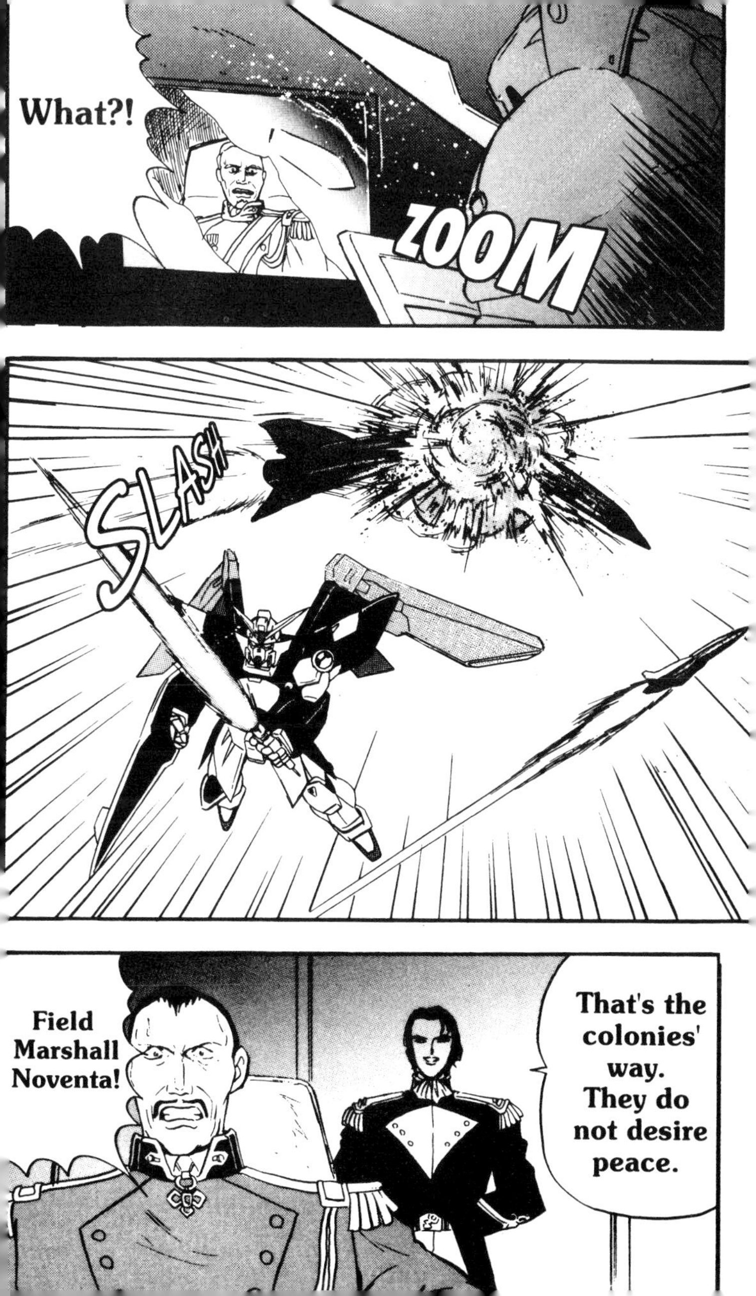
What?!
ZOOM
SLASH
Field Marshall Noventa!
That's the colonies' way. They do not desire peace.

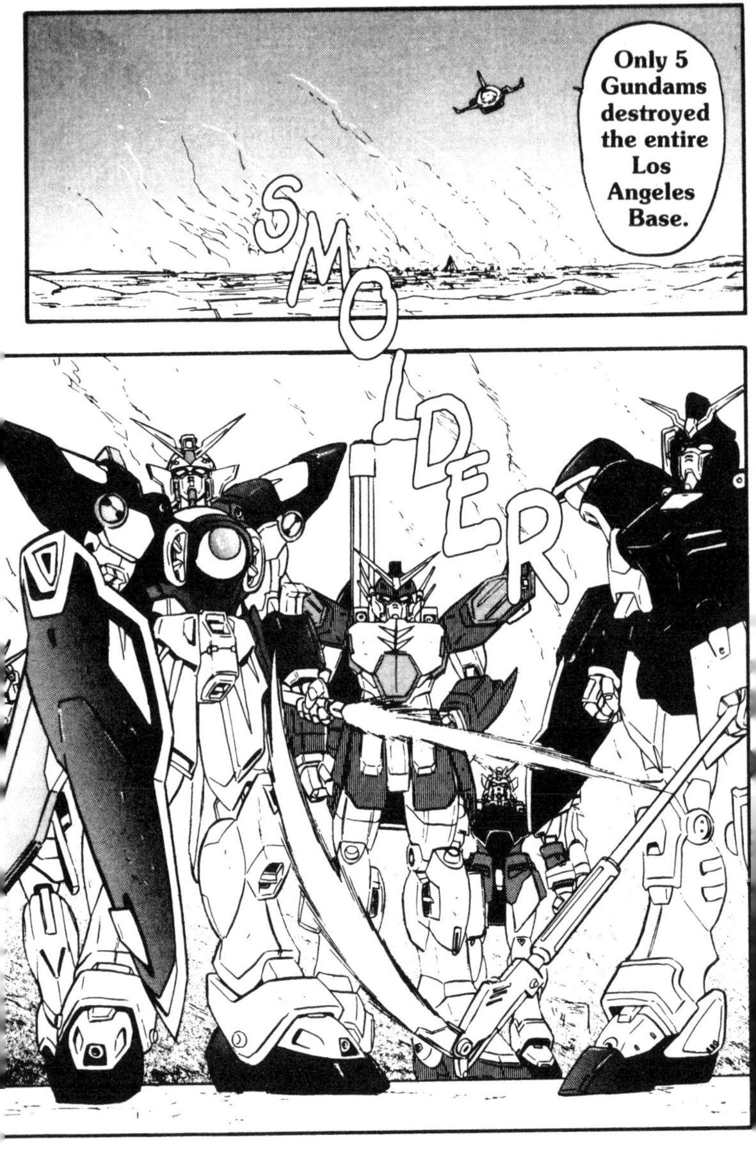
Only 5 Gundams destroyed the entire Los Angeles Base.
SMOLDER

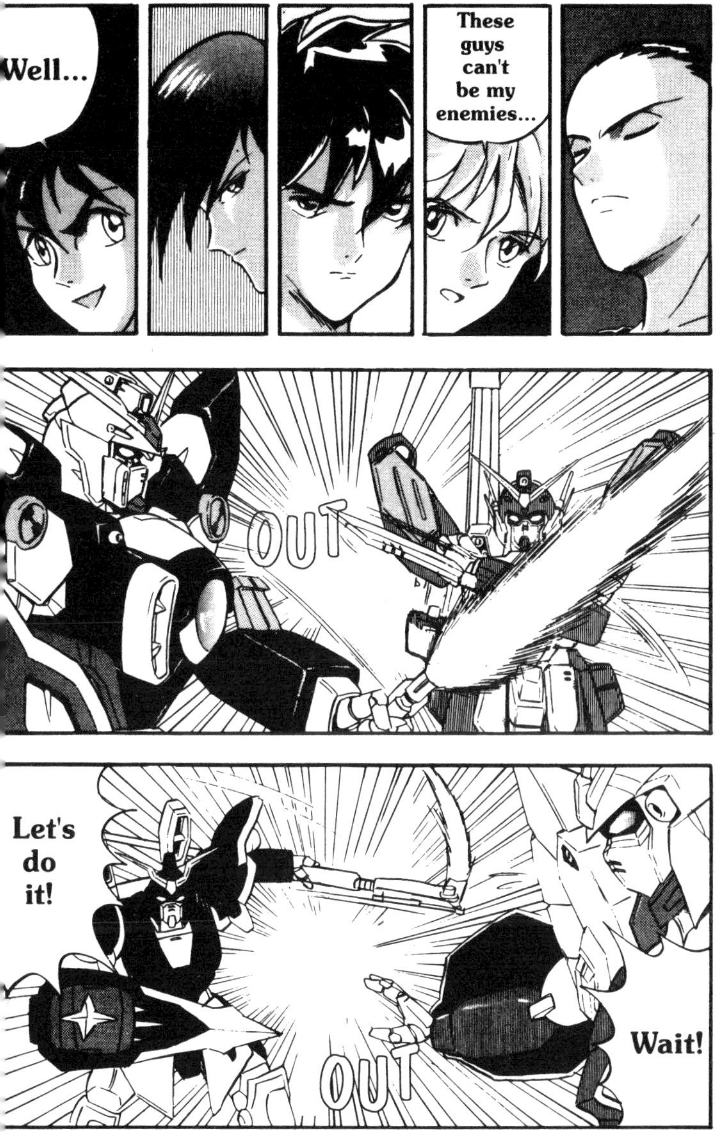
Well...
These guys can't be my enemies...
OUT
Let's do it!
OUT
Wait!

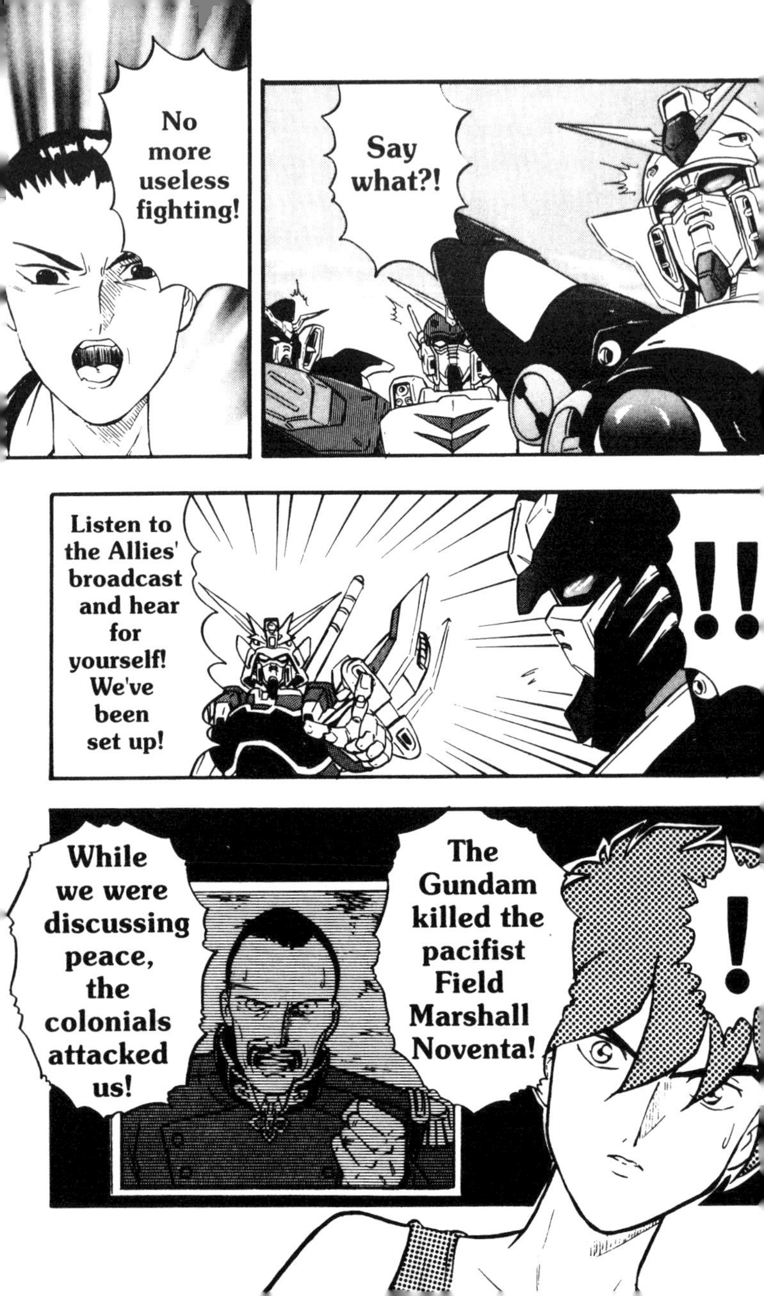
No more useless fighting!
Say what?!
Listen to the Allies' broadcast and hear for yourself! We've been set up!
!!
While we were discussing peace, the colonials attacked us!
The Gundam killed the pacifist Field Marshall Noventa!
!

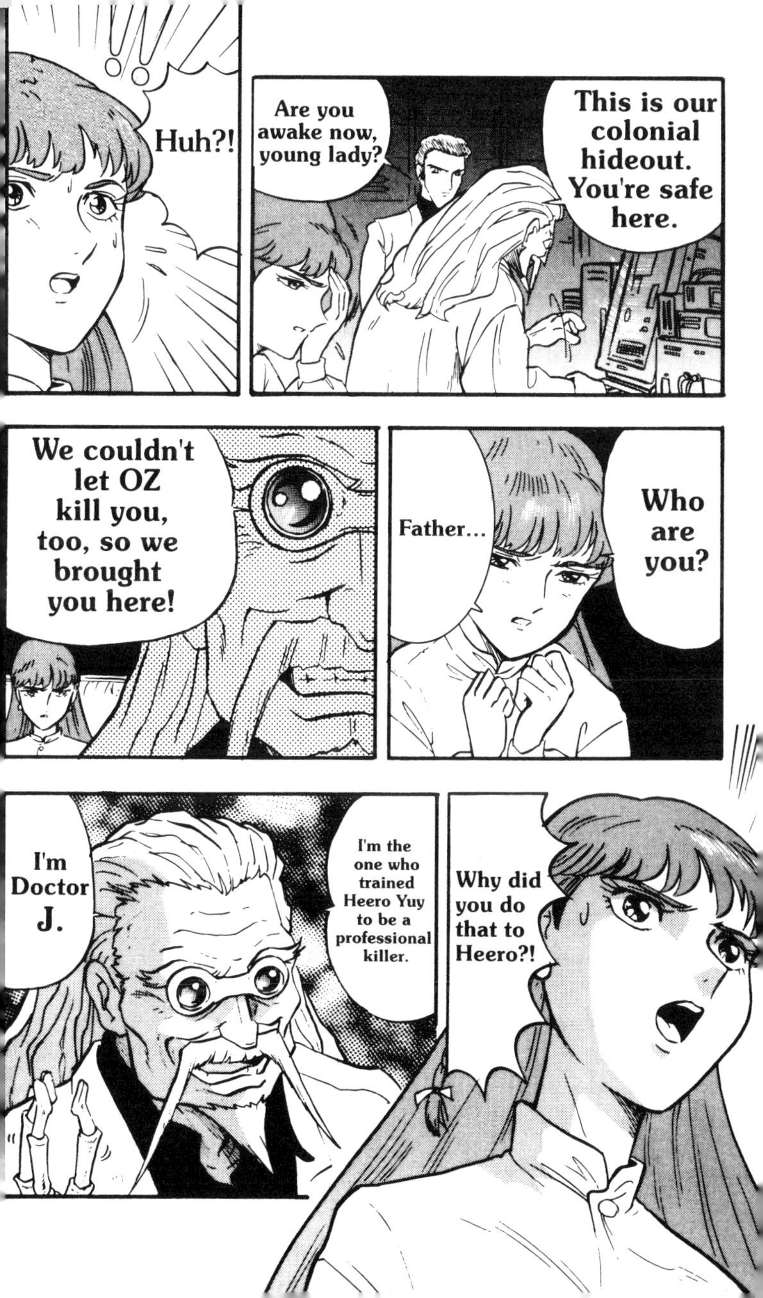
Huh?!
Are you awake now, young lady?
This is our colonial hideout. You're safe here.
We couldn't let OZ kill you, too, so we brought you here!
Father...
Who are you?
I'm Doctor J.
I'm the one who trained Heero Yuy to be a professional killer.
Why did you do that to Heero?!

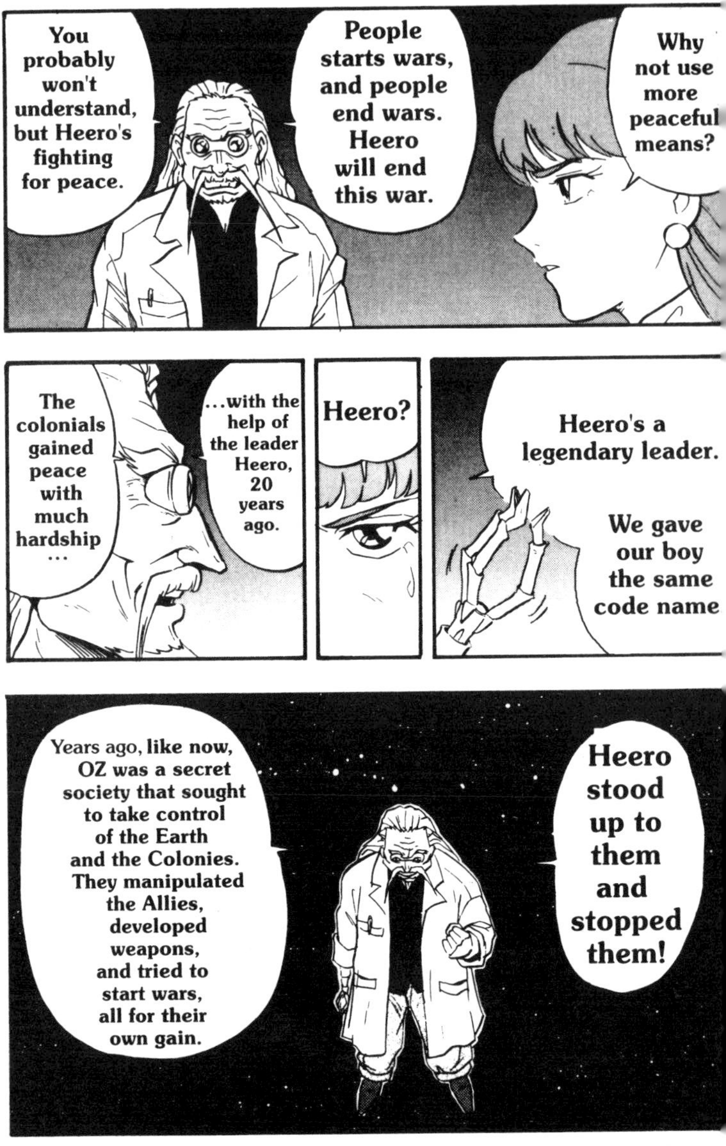
You probably won't understand, but Heero's fighting for peace.
People starts wars, and people end wars. Heero will end this war.
Why not use more peaceful means?
The colonials gained peace with much hardship...
...with the help of the leader Heero, 20 years ago.
Heero?
Heero's a legendary leader.
We gave our boy the same code name
Years ago, like now, OZ was a secret society that sought to take control of the Earth and the Colonies. They manipulated the Allies, developed weapons, and tried to start wars, all for their own gain.
Heero stood up to them and stopped them!

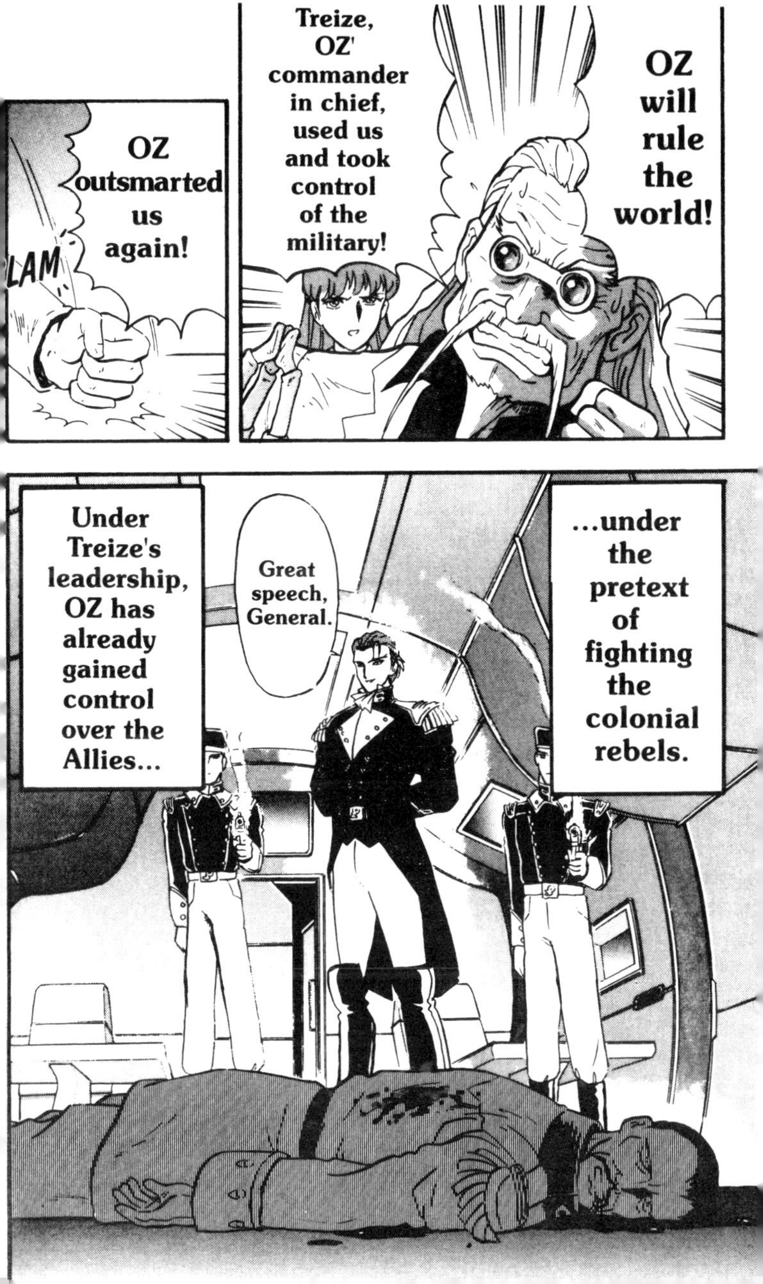
LAM
OZ outsmarted us again!
Treize, OZ' commander in chief, used us and took control of the military!
OZ will rule the world!
Under Treize's leadership, OZ has already gained control over the Allies...
Great speech, General.
...under the pretext of fighting the colonial rebels.

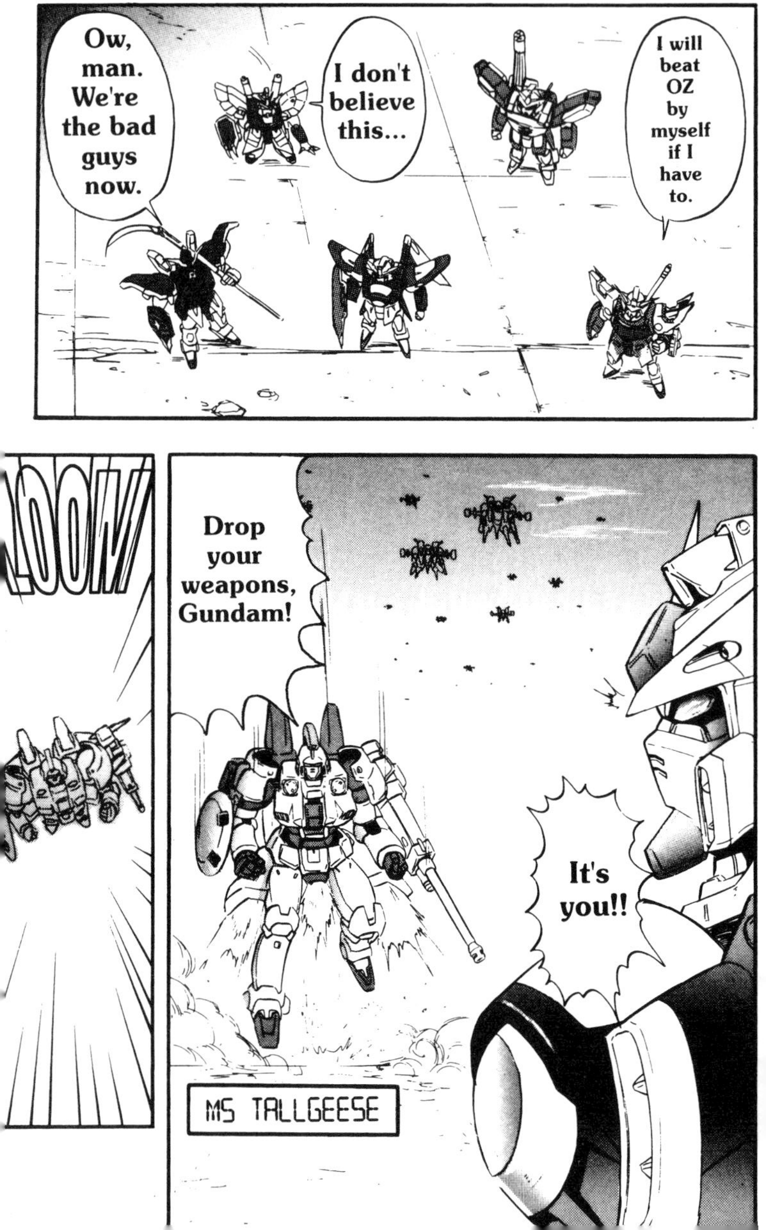
Ow, man. We're the bad guys now.
I don't believe this...
I will beat OZ by myself if I have to.
Drop your weapons, Gundam!
MS TALLGEESE
It's you!!

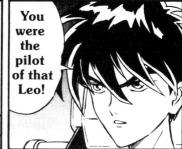

We meet again, bird Gundam. I'm Zechs of OZ.

You were the pilot of that Leo!

I've come for a rematch.

This Tallgeese should have the same output as your Gundam!

Fight me!

I don't think so, Zechs!

KABOOM

What?! Lady Une! What did you do?!

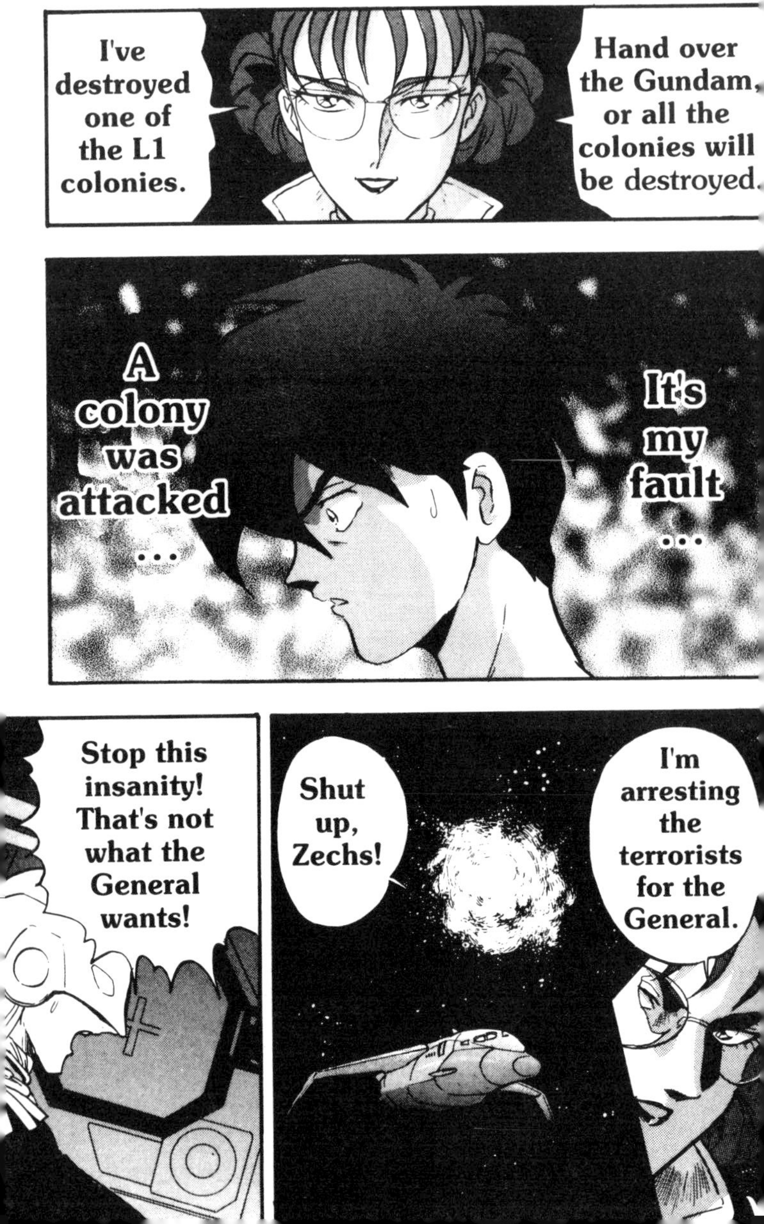
I've destroyed one of the L1 colonies.
Hand over the Gundam, or all the colonies will be destroyed.
A colony was attacked ...
It's my fault ...
Stop this insanity! That's not what the General wants!
Shut up, Zechs!
I'm arresting the terrorists for the General.

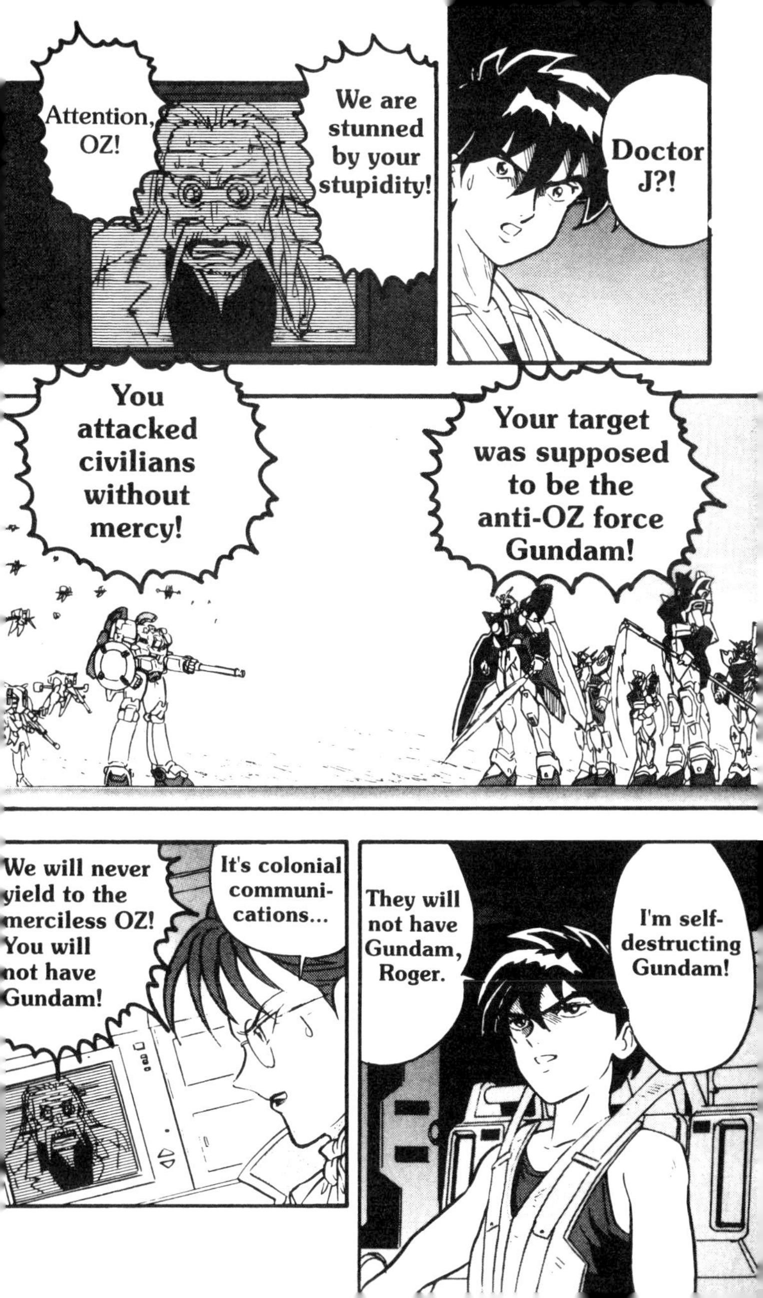
Attention, OZ!
We are stunned by your stupidity!
Doctor J?!
You attacked civilians without mercy!
Your target was supposed to be the anti-OZ force Gundam!
We will never yield to the merciless OZ! You will not have Gundam!
It's colonial communi-cations...
They will not have Gundam, Roger.
I'm self-destructing Gundam!

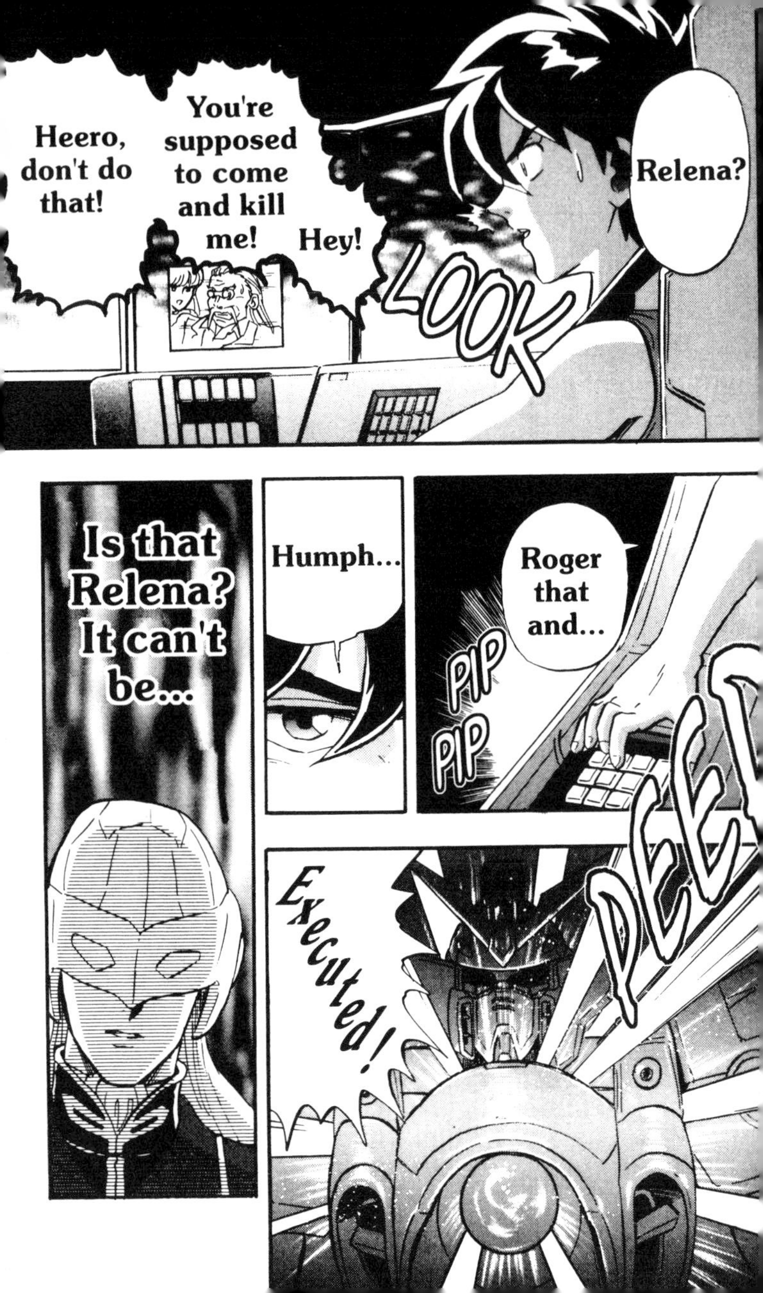
Heero, don't do that!
You're supposed to come and kill me!
Hey!
LOOK
Relena?
Is that Relena? It can't be...
Humph...
Roger that and...
PIP PIP
PEEP
Executed!

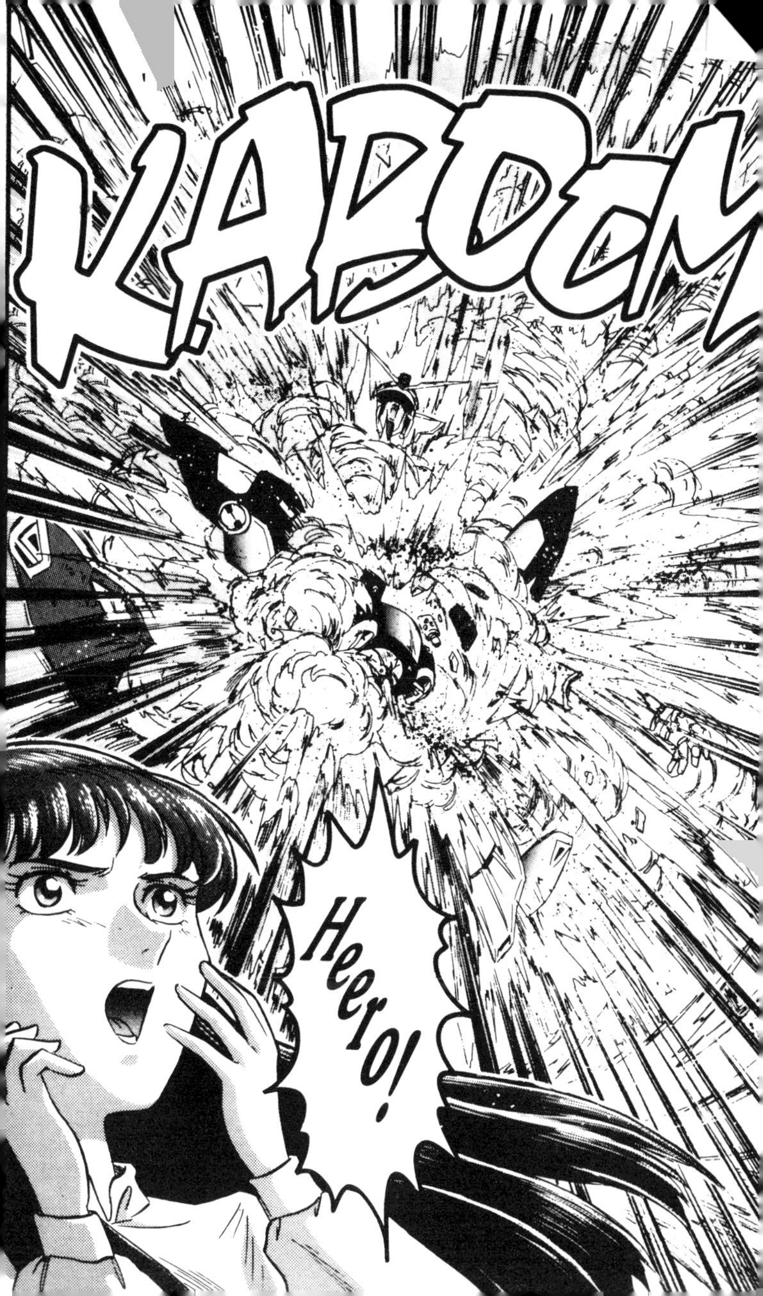
KABOOM
Heero!

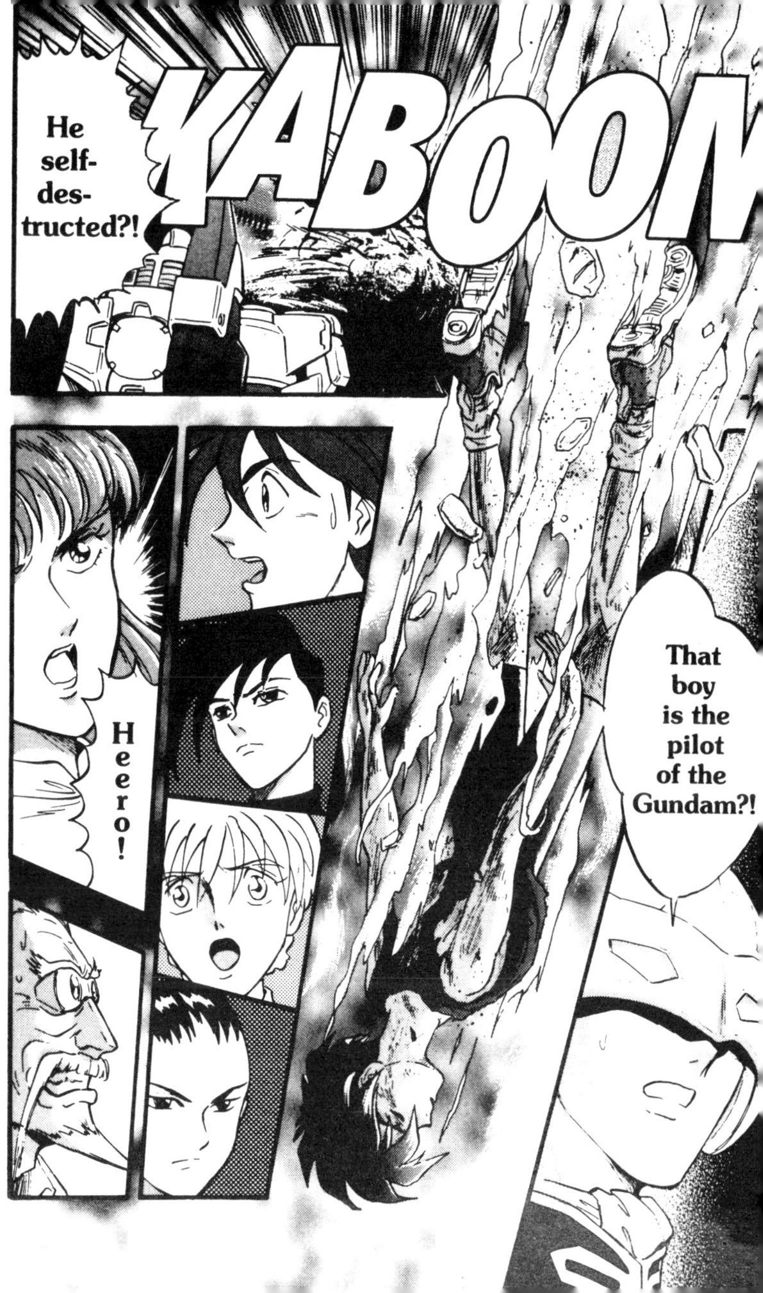
He self-des-tructed?!
KABOOM
Heero!
That boy is the pilot of the Gundam?!

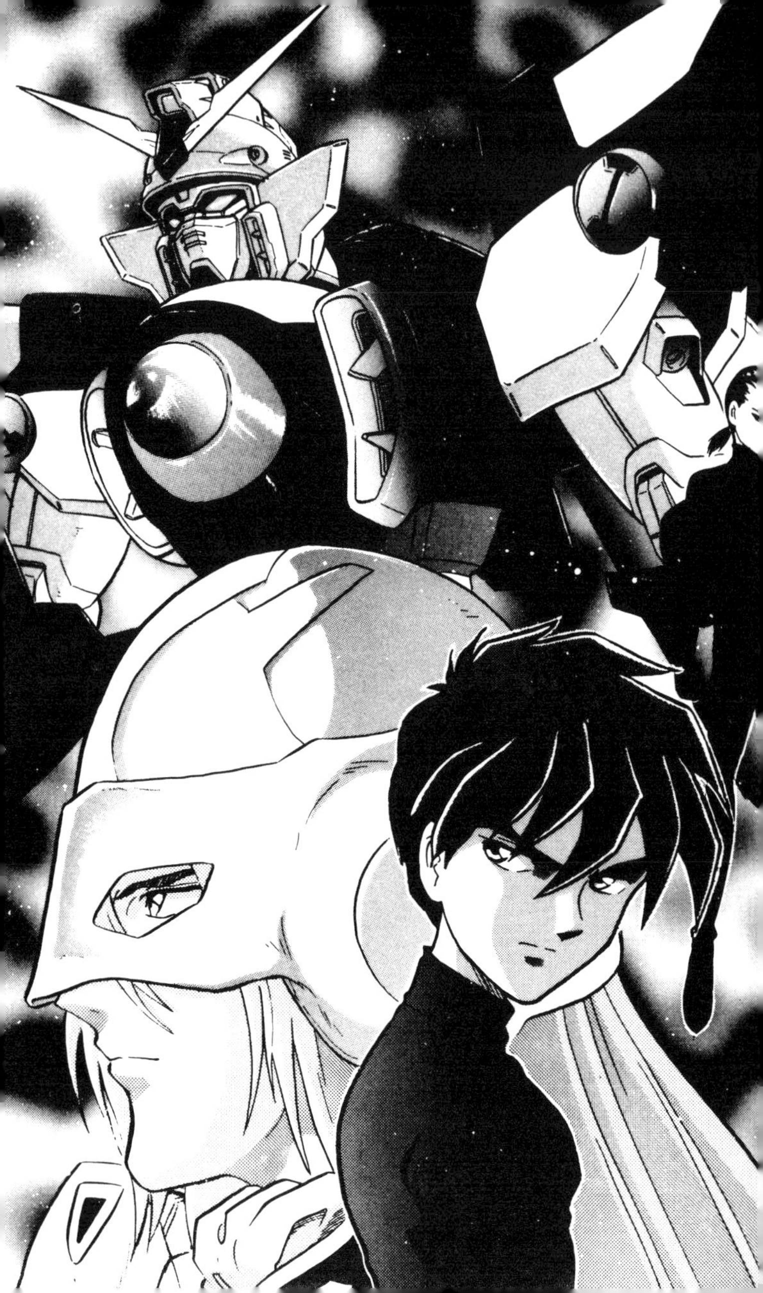

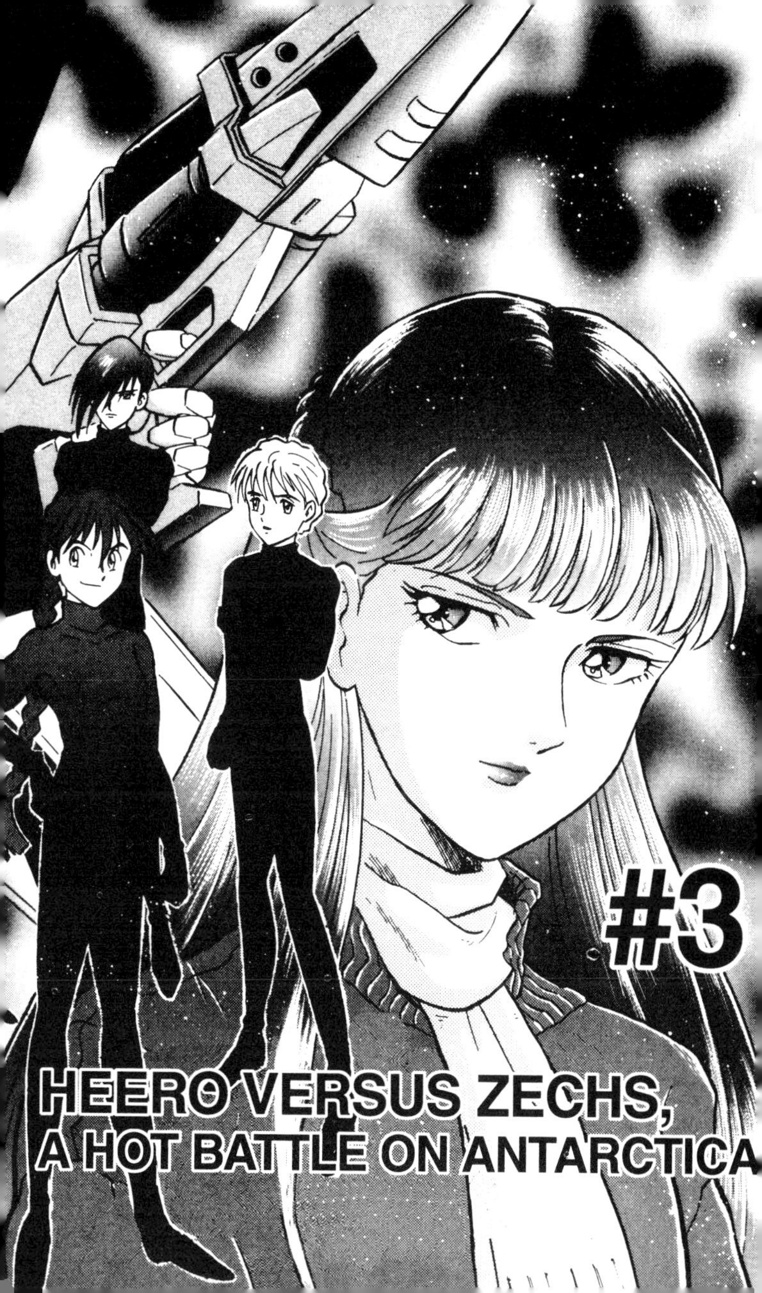
#3
HEERO VERSUS ZECHS,
A HOT BATTLE ON ANTARCTICA

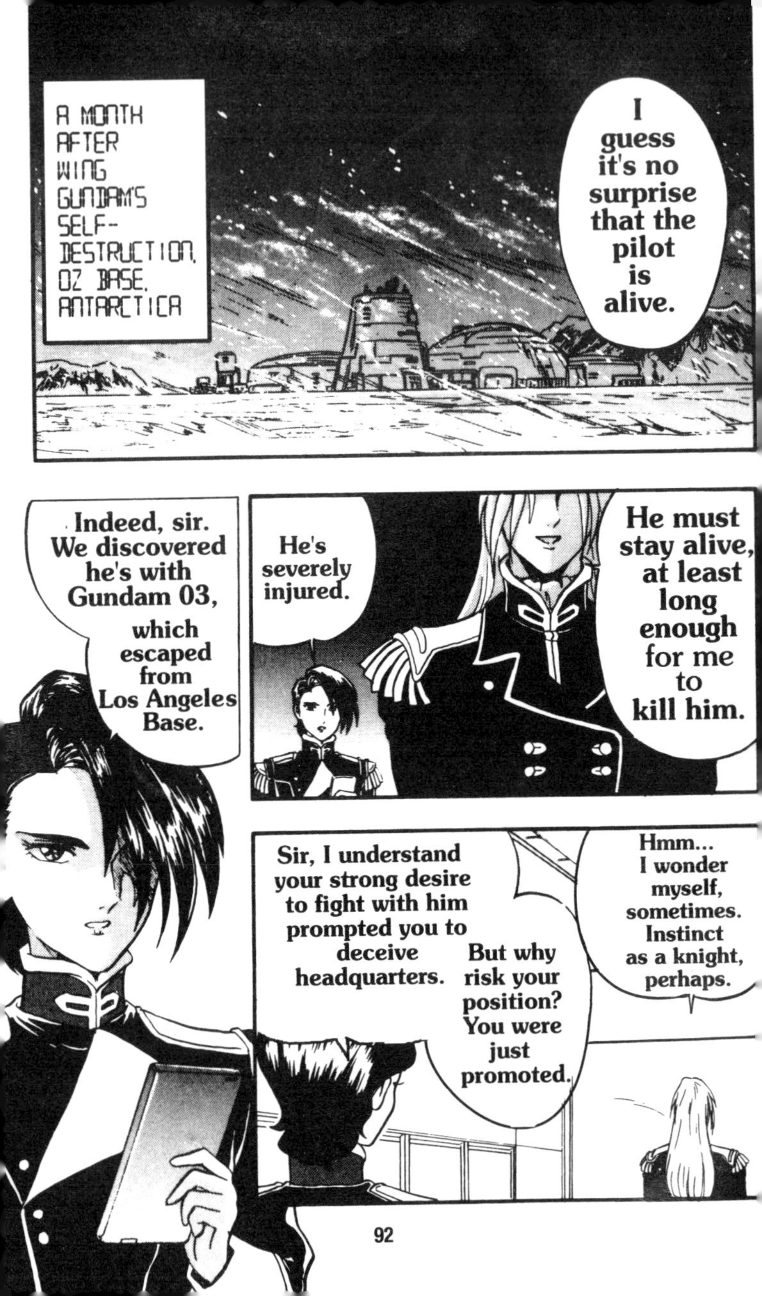
A MONTH AFTER WING GUNDAM'S SELF-DESTRUCTION. OZ BASE. ANTARCTICA
I guess it's no surprise that the pilot is alive.
Indeed, sir. We discovered he's with Gundam 03, which escaped from Los Angeles Base.
He's severely injured.
He must stay alive, at least long enough for me to kill him.
Sir, I understand your strong desire to fight with him prompted you to deceive headquarters.
But why risk your position? You were just promoted.
Hmm... I wonder myself, sometimes. Instinct as a knight, perhaps.

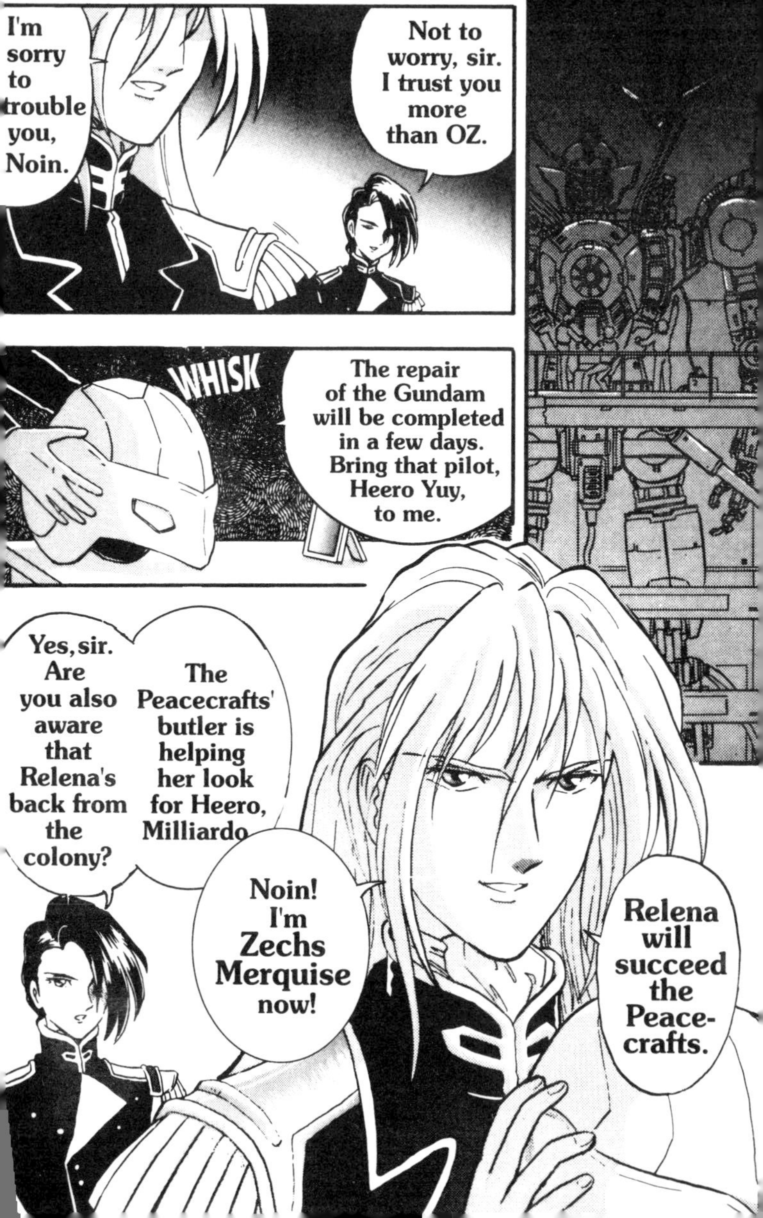
I'm sorry to trouble you, Noin.
Not to worry, sir. I trust you more than OZ.
WHISK
The repair of the Gundam will be completed in a few days. Bring that pilot, Heero Yuy, to me.
Yes, sir. Are you also aware that Relena's back from the colony?
The Peacecrafts' butler is helping her look for Heero, Milliardo
Noin! I'm Zechs Merquise now!
Relena will succeed the Peace-crafts.

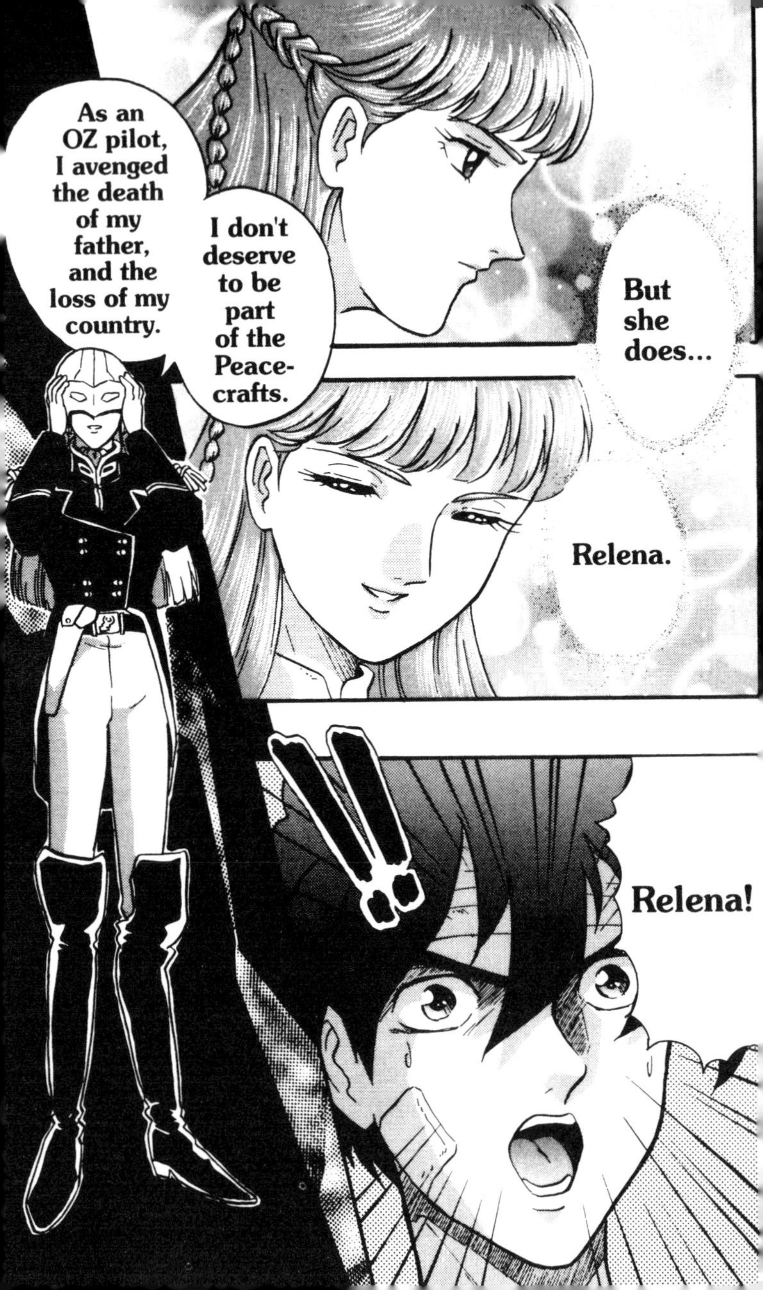
As an OZ pilot, I avenged the death of my father, and the loss of my country.
I don't deserve to be part of the Peace-crafts.
But she does...
Relena.
Relena!

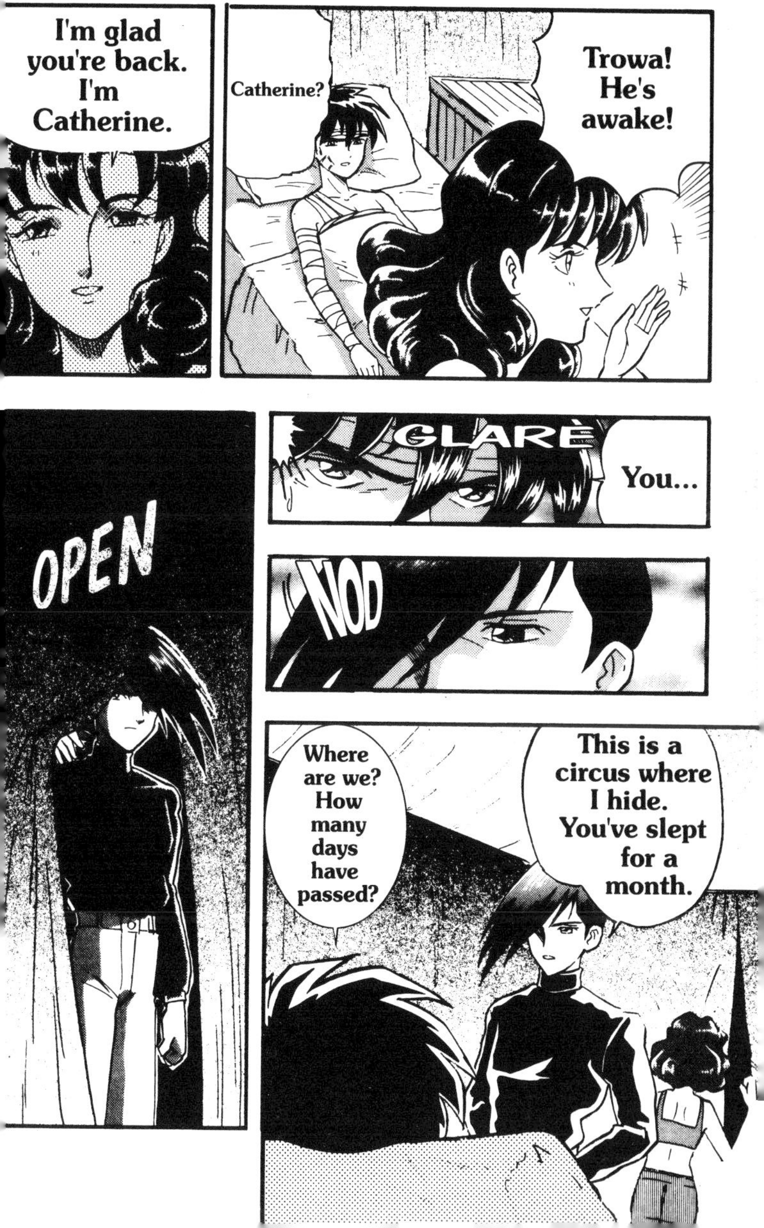
I'm glad you're back. I'm Catherine.
Catherine?
Trowa! He's awake!
OPEN
GLARE
You...
NOD
Where are we? How many days have passed?
This is a circus where I hide. You've slept for a month.

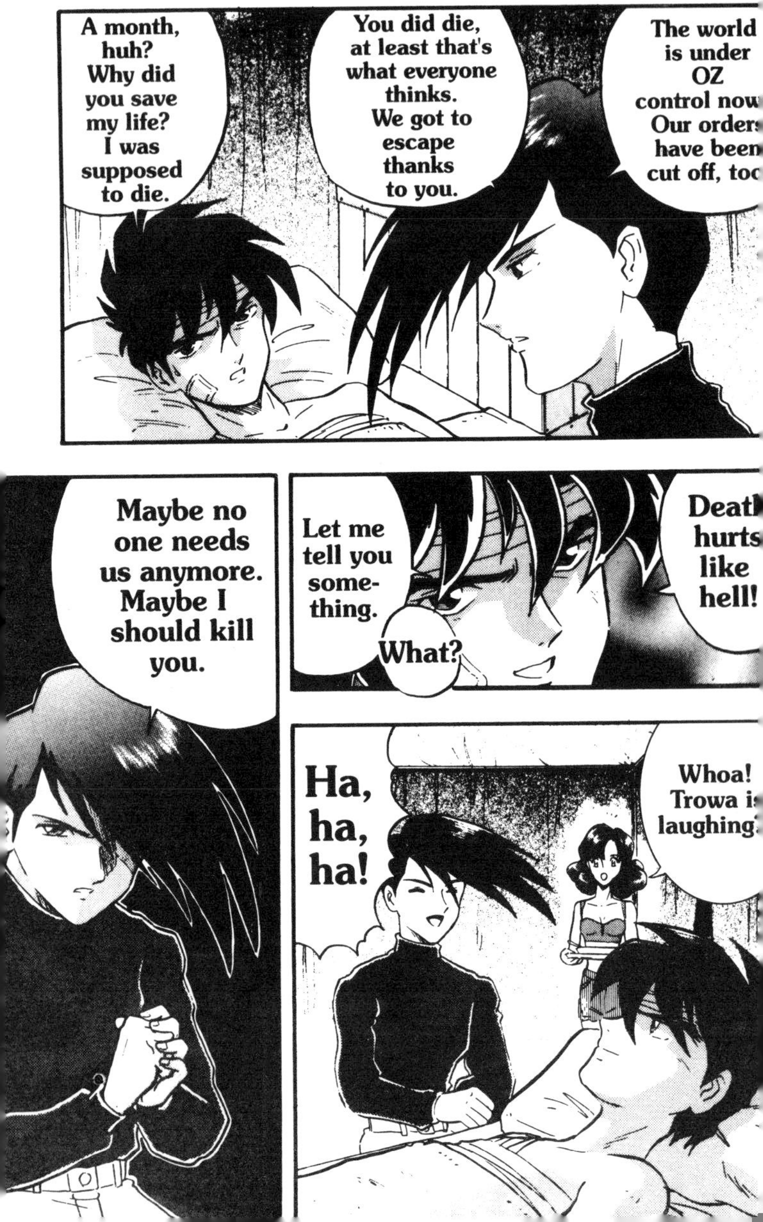
A month, huh? Why did you save my life? I was supposed to die.
You did die, at least that's what everyone thinks. We got to escape thanks to you.
The world is under OZ control now Our orders have been cut off, too
Maybe no one needs us anymore. Maybe I should kill you.
Let me tell you some-thing.
What?
Death hurts like hell!
Ha, ha, ha!
Whoa! Trowa is laughing

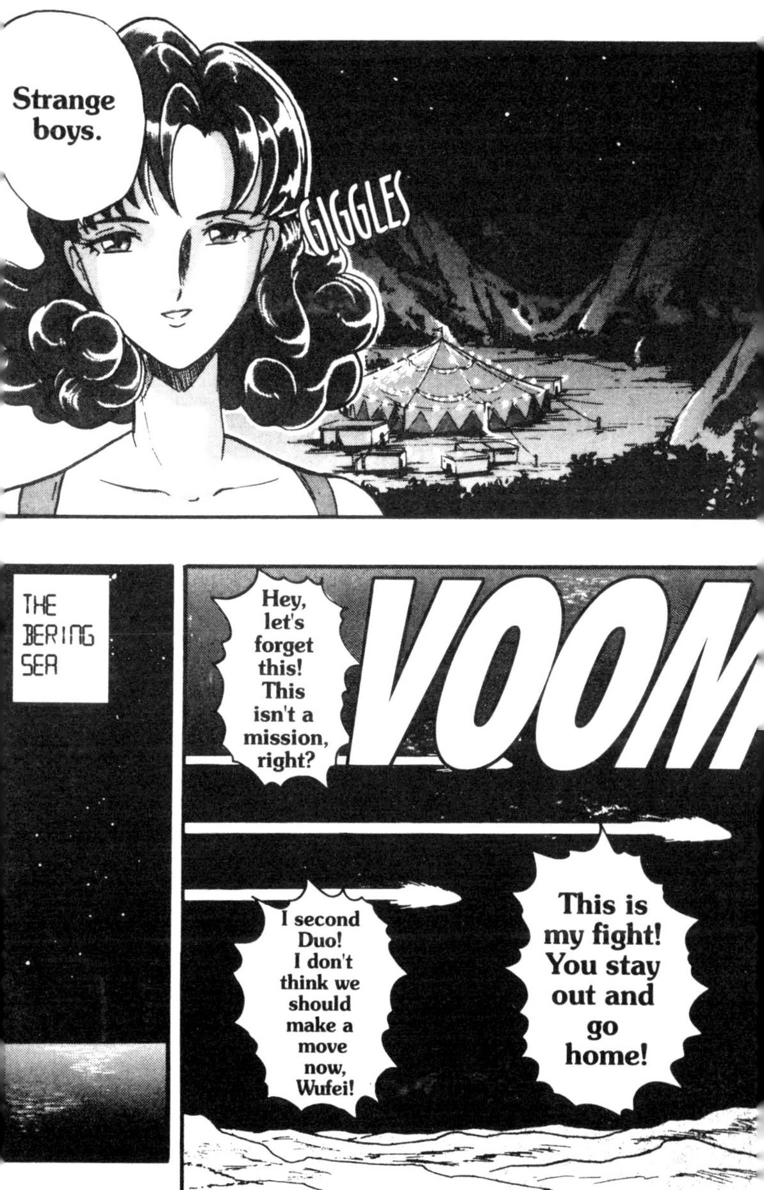
Strange boys.
GIGGLES
THE BERING SEA
Hey, let's forget this! This isn't a mission, right?
VOOM
I second Duo! I don't think we should make a move now, Wufei!
This is my fight! You stay out and go home!

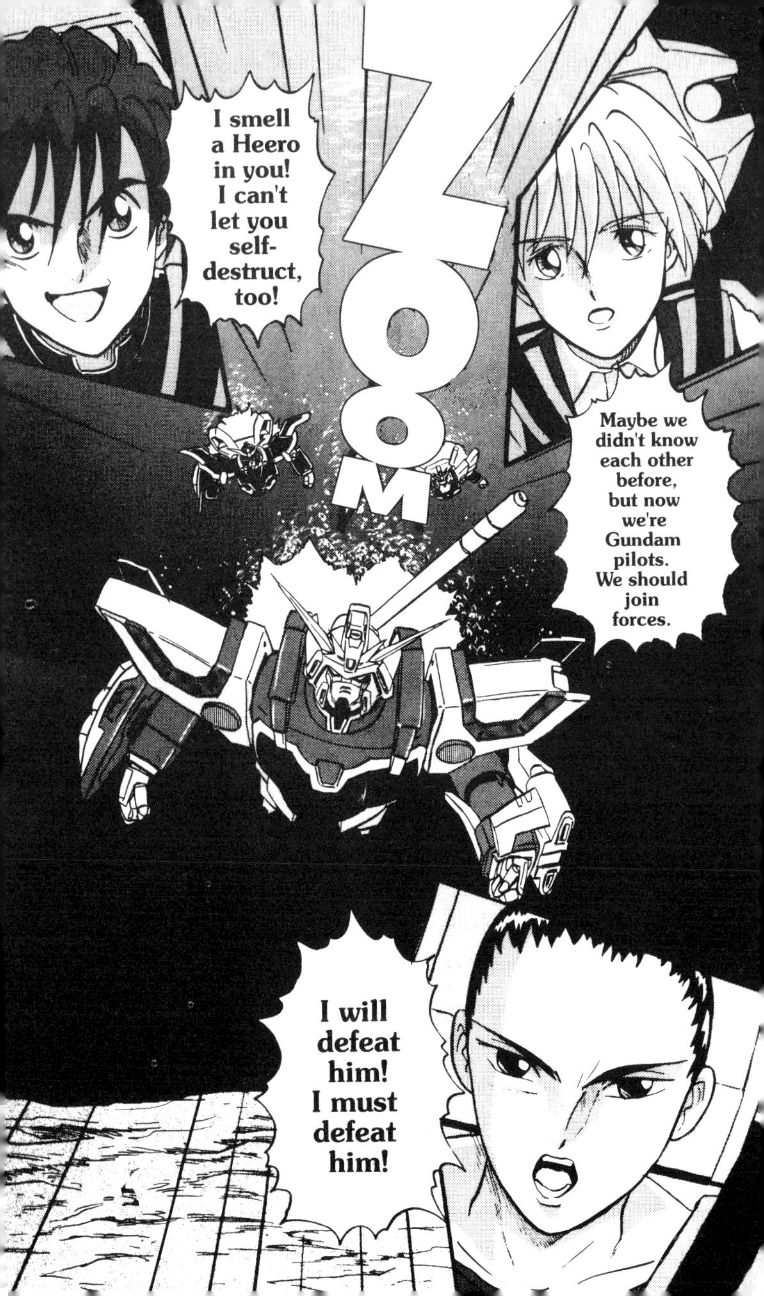
I smell a Heero in you! I can't let you self-destruct, too!
Maybe we didn't know each other before, but now we're Gundam pilots. We should join forces.
I will defeat him! I must defeat him!

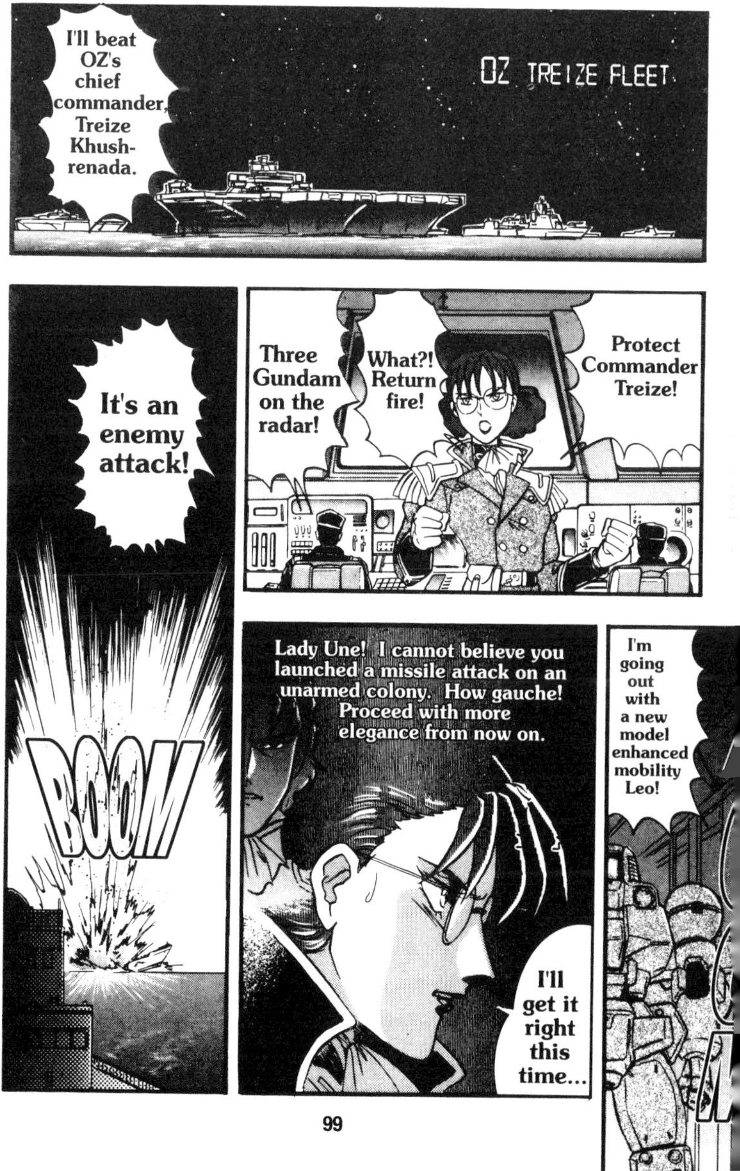
I'll beat OZ's chief commander, Treize Khush-renada.
OZ TREIZE FLEET
It's an enemy attack!
BOOM
Three Gundam on the radar!
What?! Return fire!
Protect Commander Treize!
Lady Une! I cannot believe you launched a missile attack on an unarmed colony. How gauche! Proceed with more elegance from now on.
I'll get it right this time...
I'm going out with a new model enhanced mobility Leo!

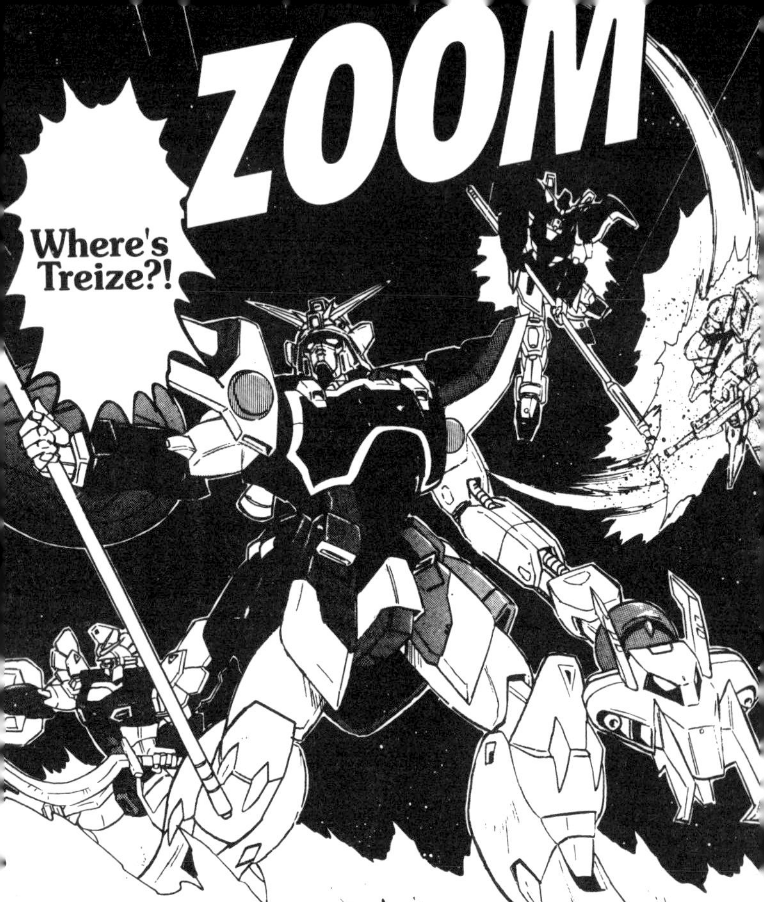
ZOOM
Where's Treize?!
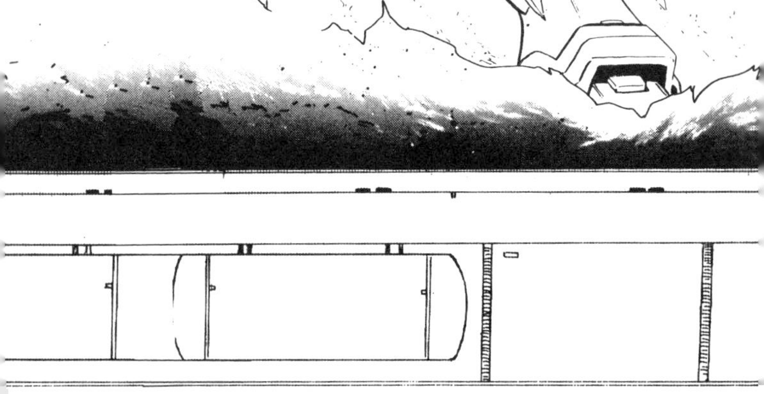

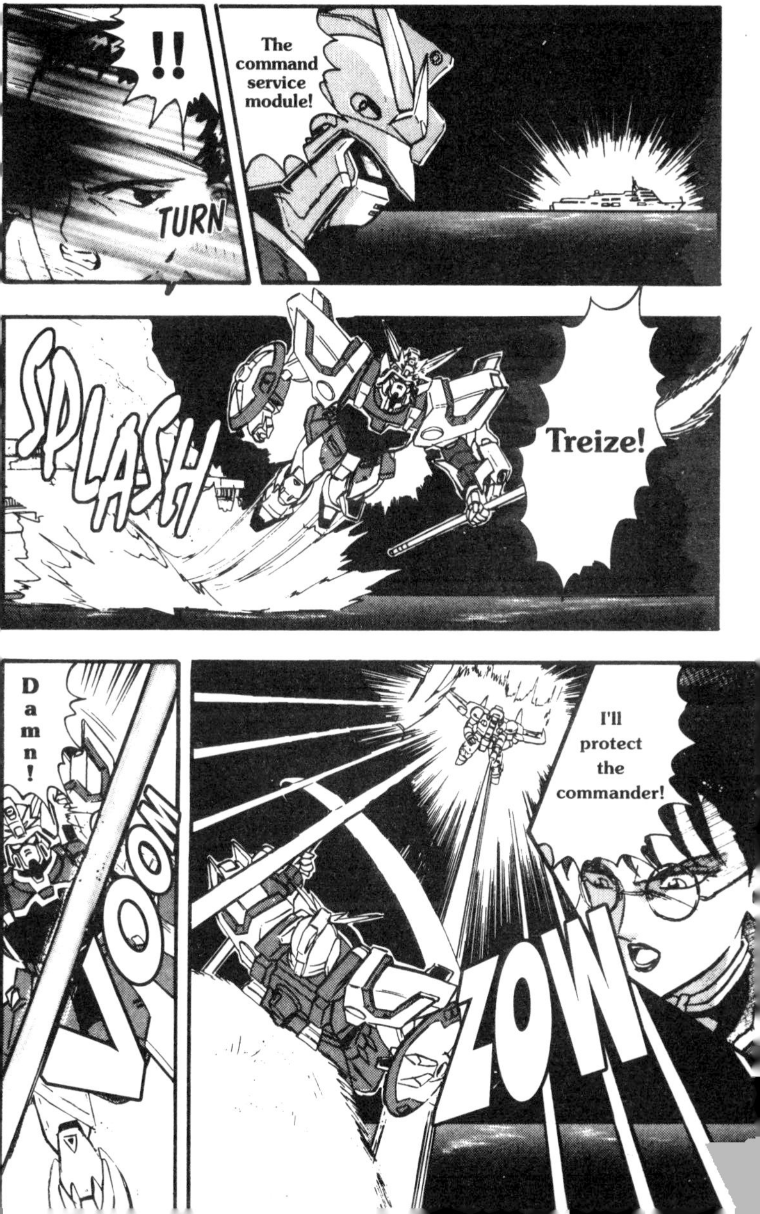
!!
TURN
The command service module!
SPLASH
Treize!
Damn!
VOOM
I'll protect the commander!
ZOM

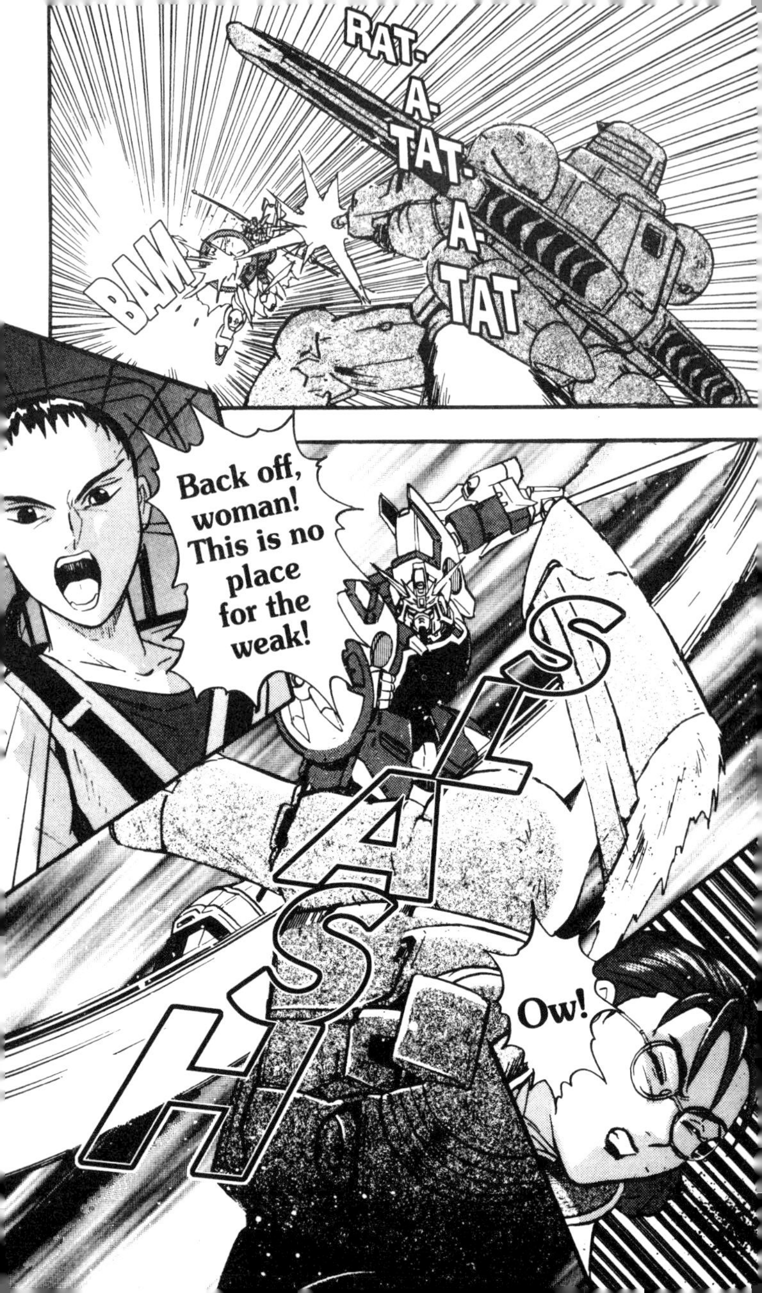

RAT-A-TAT-A-TAT
BAM
Back off, woman! This is no place for the weak!
SLASH
Ow!

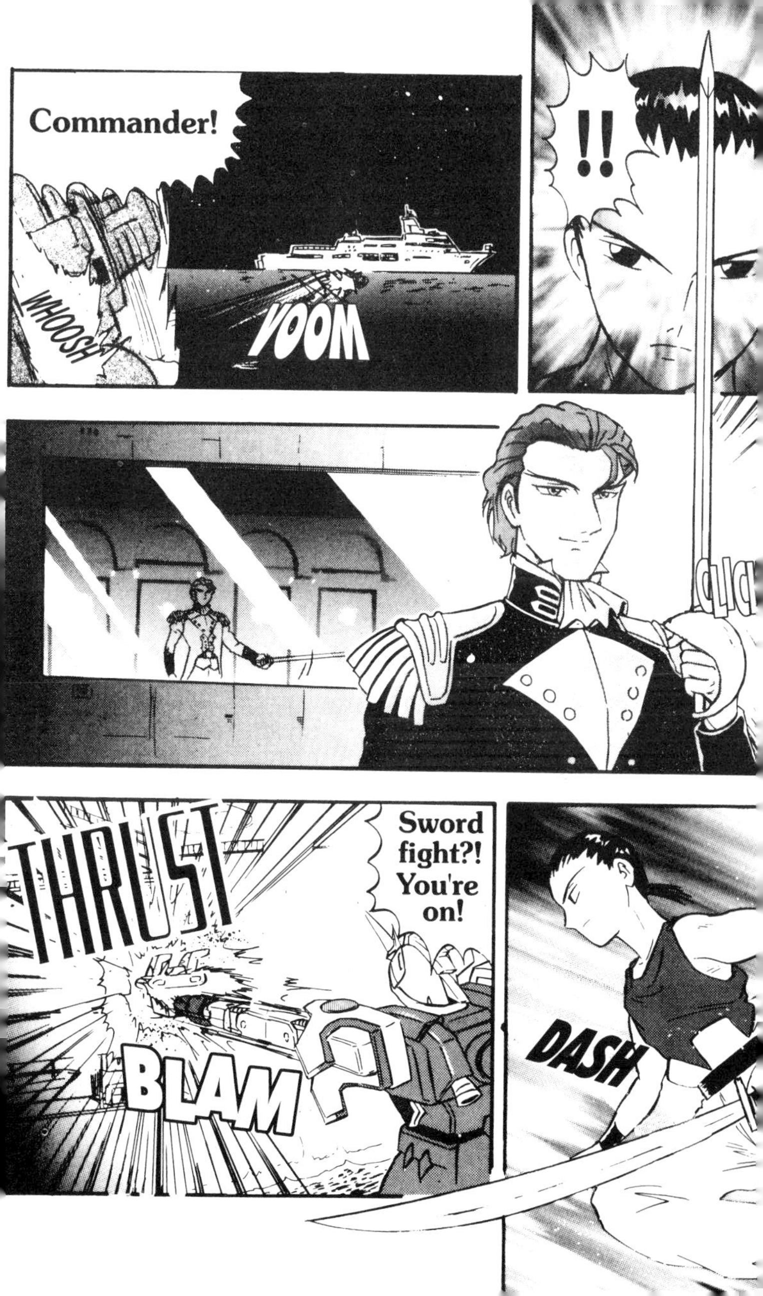
Commander!
WHOOSH
VOOM
!!
CLICK
THRUST
Sword fight?! You're on!
BLAM
DASH

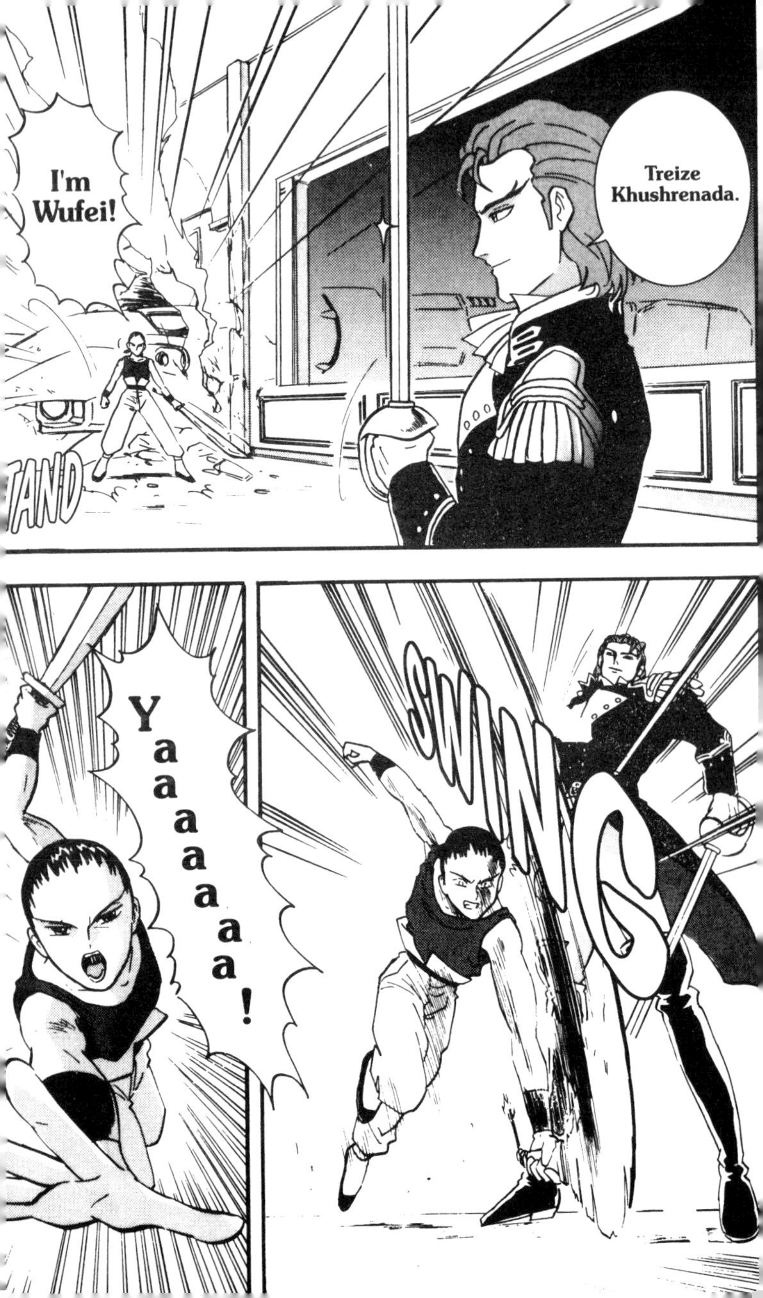
I'm Wufei!
TAND
Treize Khushrenada.
Yaaaaaaaa!
SWING

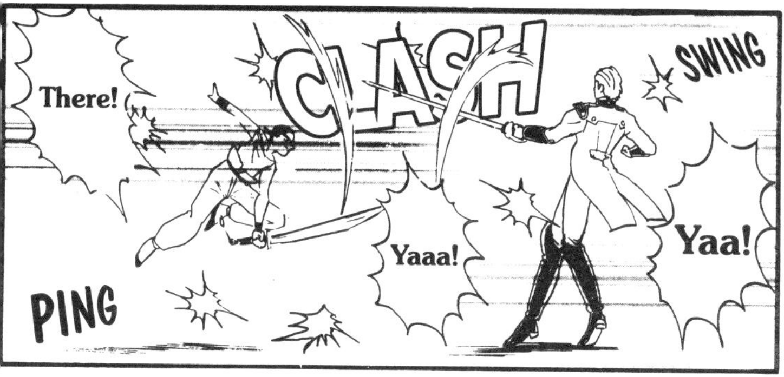
There!
CLASH
SWING
Yaaa!
Yaa!
PING

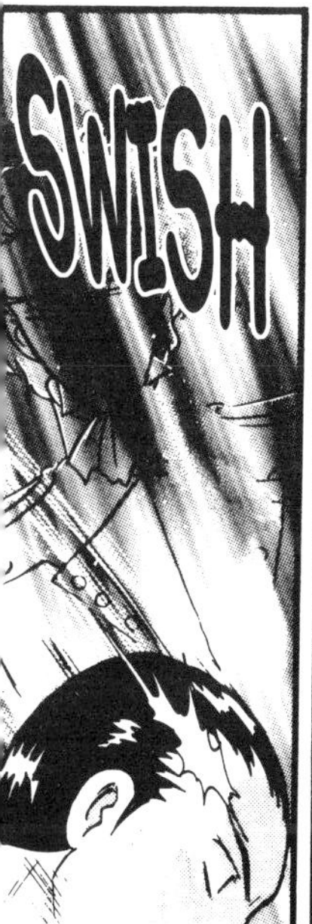
SWISH

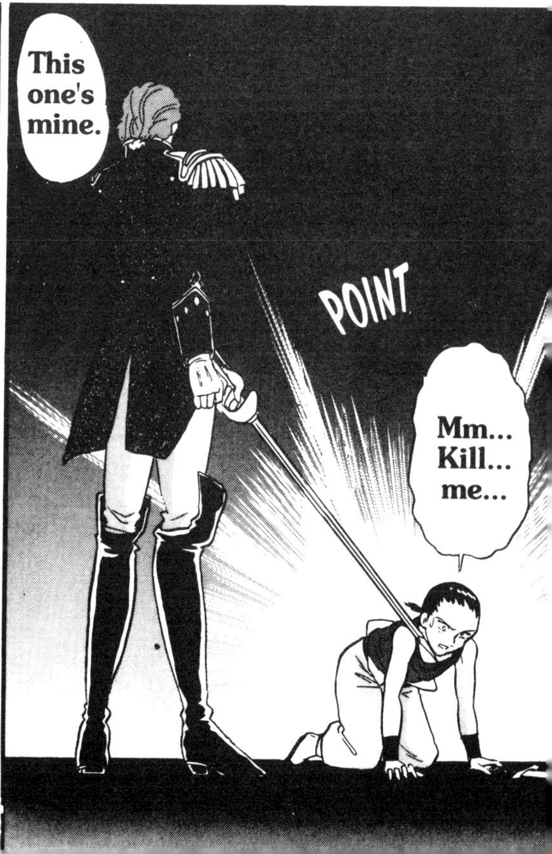
This one's mine.
POINT
Mm... Kill... me...

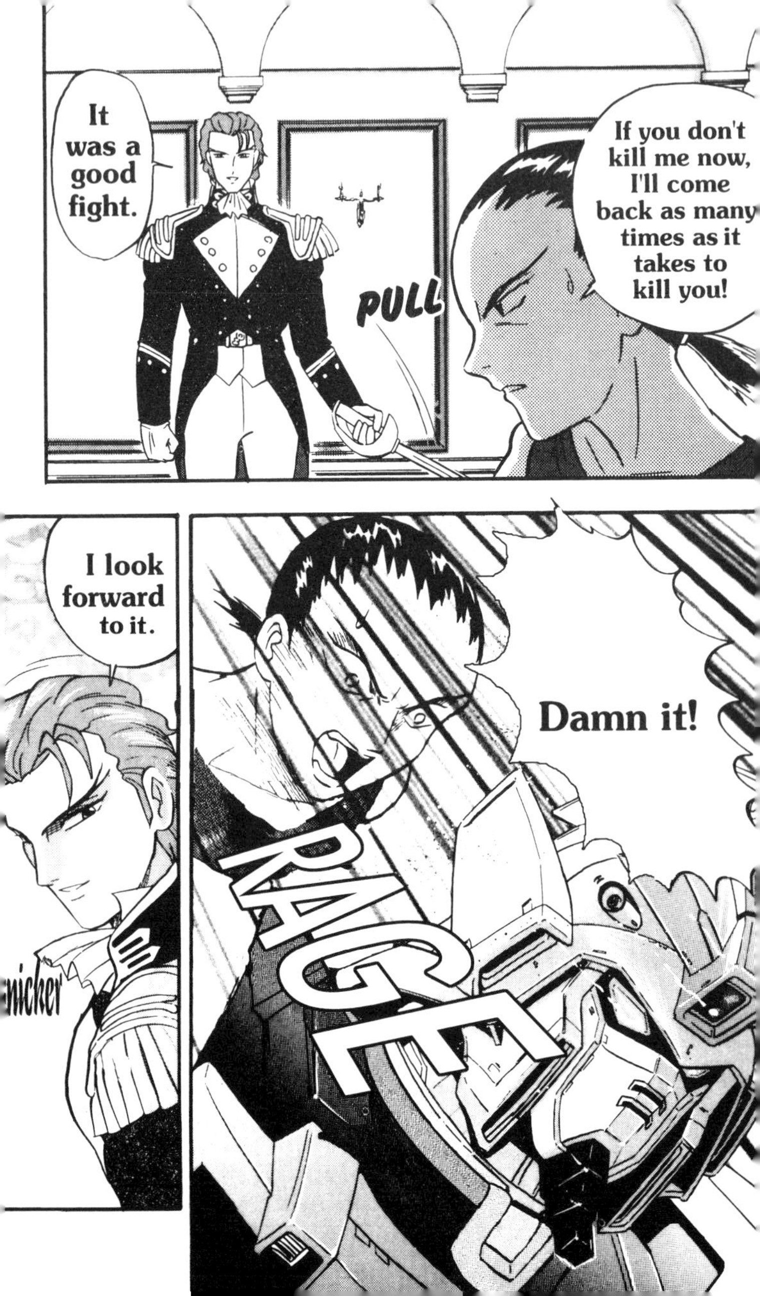
It was a good fight.
PULL
If you don't kill me now, I'll come back as many times as it takes to kill you!
I look forward to it.
nicker
Damn it!
RAGE

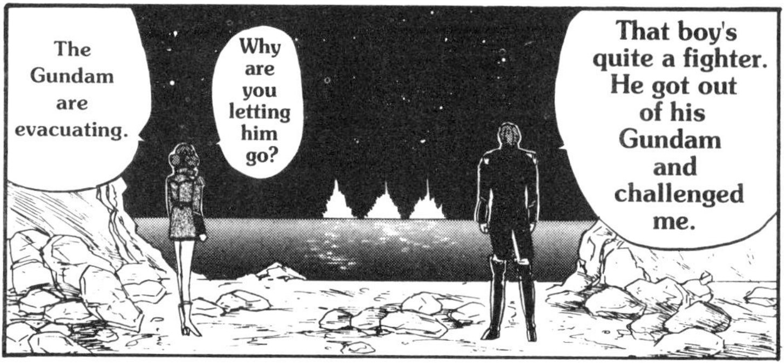
The Gundam are evacuating.
Why are you letting him go?
That boy's quite a fighter. He got out of his Gundam and challenged me.
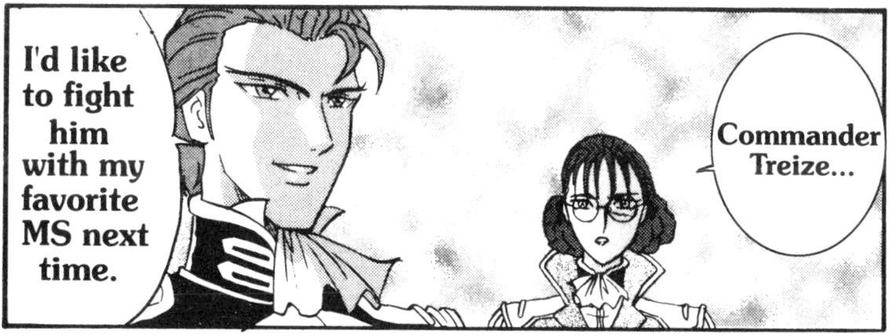
I'd like to fight him with my favorite MS next time.
Commander Treize...
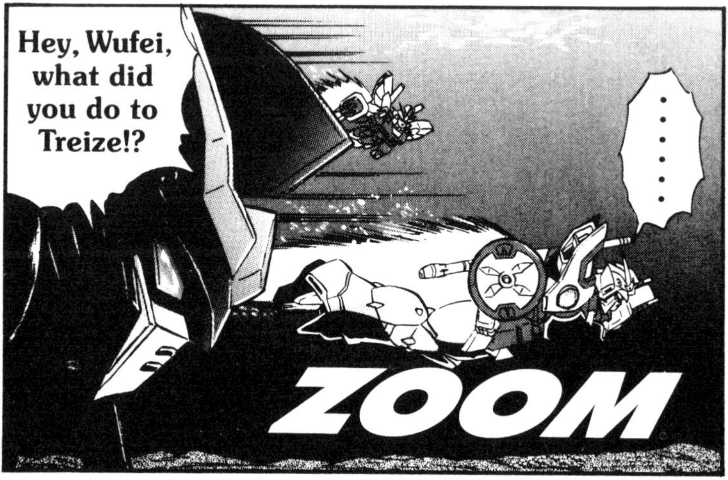
Hey, Wufei, what did you do to Treize!?
....
ZOOM

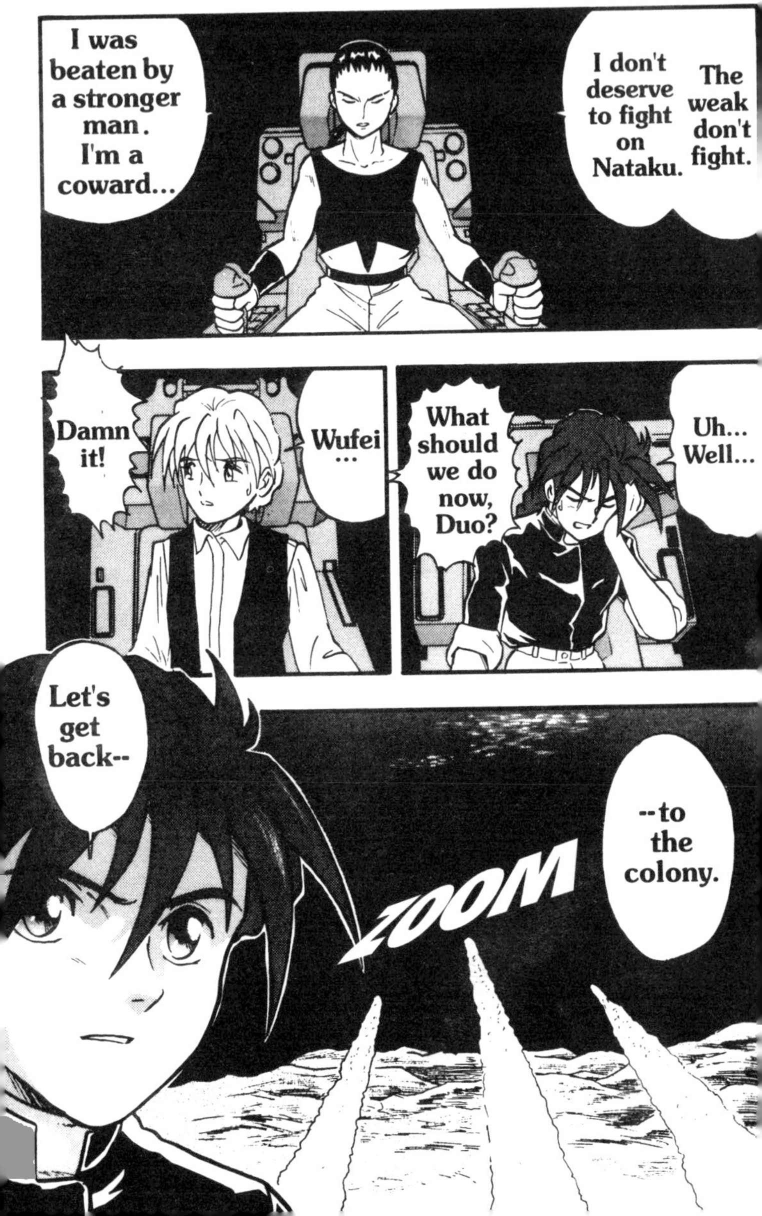
I was beaten by a stronger man. I'm a coward...
I don't deserve to fight on Nataku.
The weak don't fight.
Damn it!
Wufei...
What should we do now, Duo?
Uh... Well...
Let's get back--
ZOOM
--to the colony.

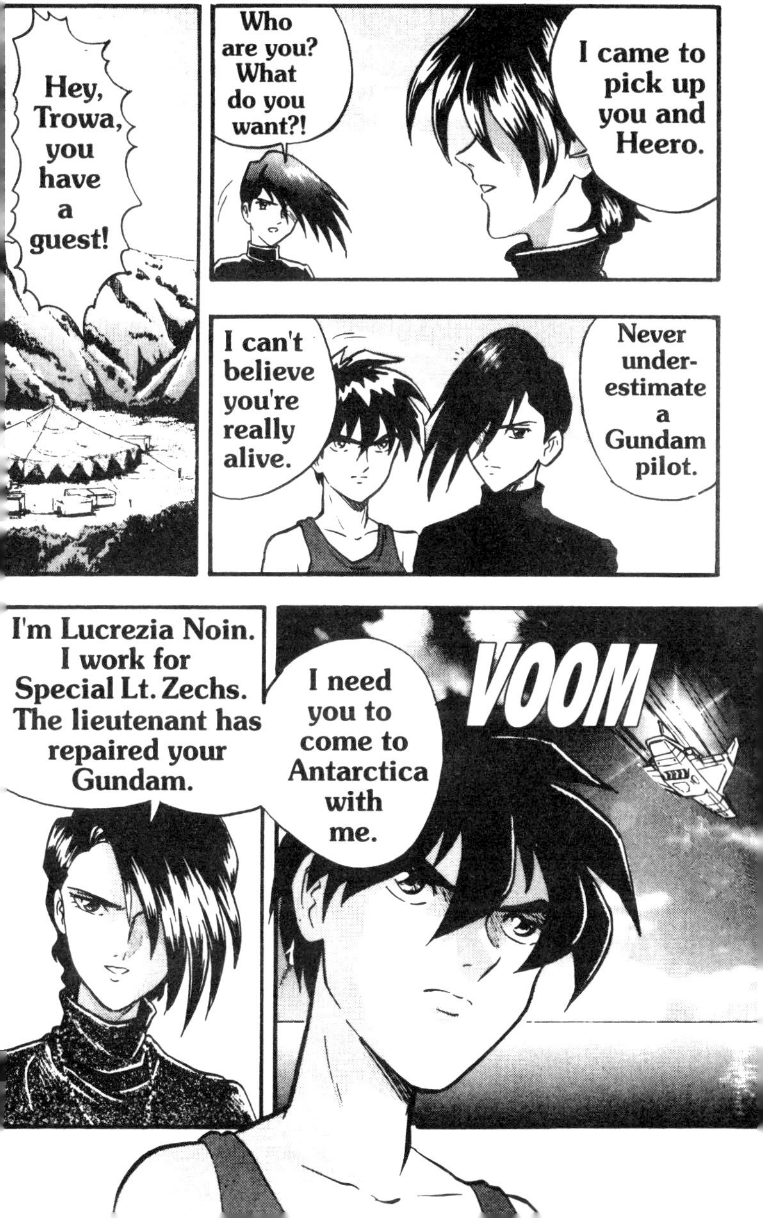
Hey, Trowa, you have a guest!
Who are you? What do you want?!
I came to pick up you and Heero.
I can't believe you're really alive.
Never under-estimate a Gundam pilot.
I'm Lucrezia Noin. I work for Special Lt. Zechs. The lieutenant has repaired your Gundam.
I need you to come to Antarctica with me.
VOOM

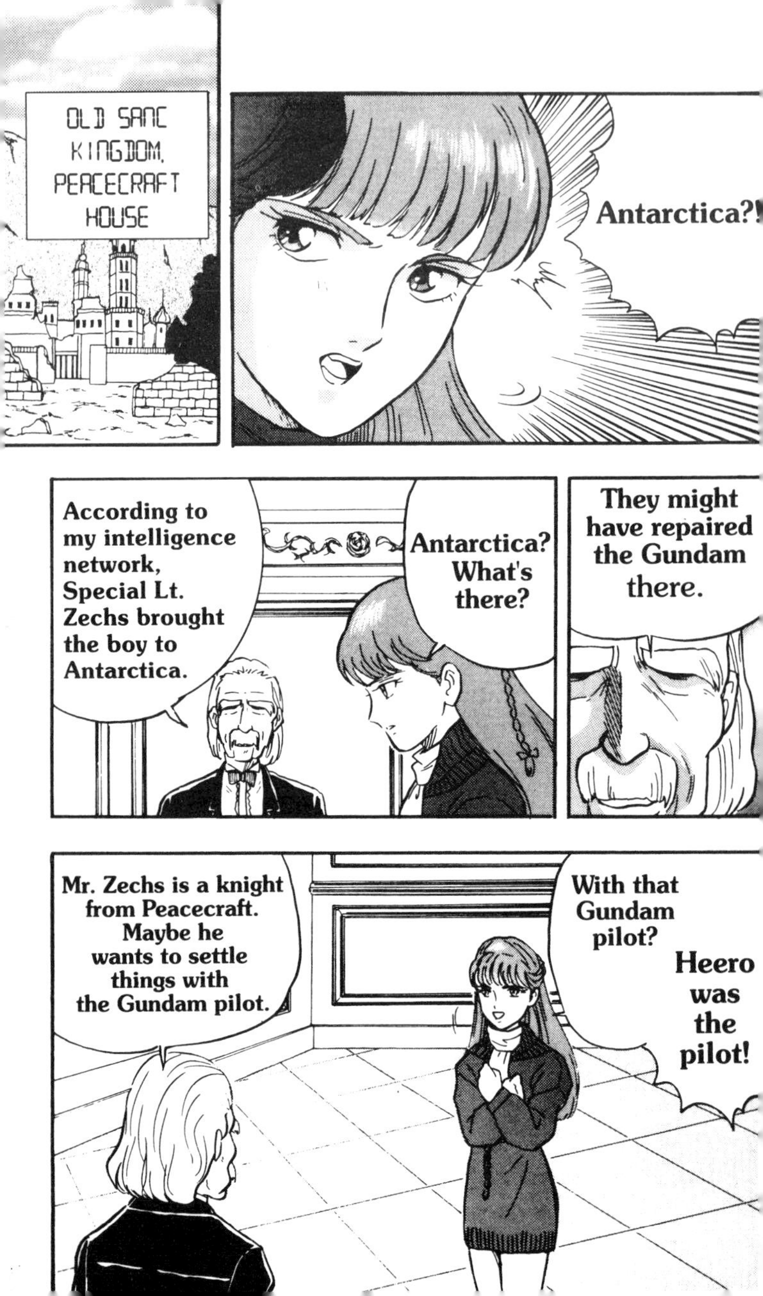
OLD SANC KINGDOM, PEACECRAFT HOUSE
Antarctica?!
According to my intelligence network, Special Lt. Zechs brought the boy to Antarctica.
Antarctica? What's there?
They might have repaired the Gundam there.
Mr. Zechs is a knight from Peacecraft. Maybe he wants to settle things with the Gundam pilot.
With that Gundam pilot?
Heero was the pilot!

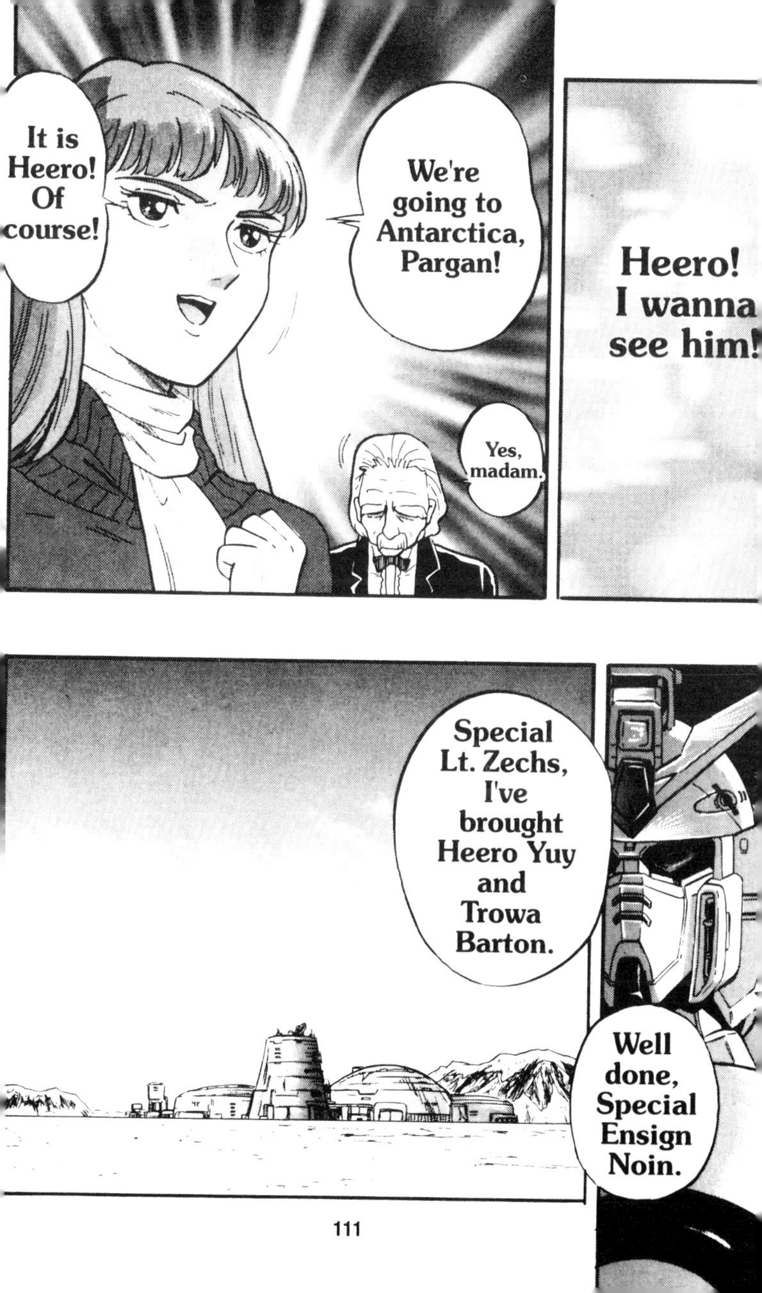
It is Heero! Of course!
We're going to Antarctica, Pargan!
Yes, madam.
Heero! I wanna see him!
Special Lt. Zechs, I've brought Heero Yuy and Trowa Barton.
Well done, Special Ensign Noin.

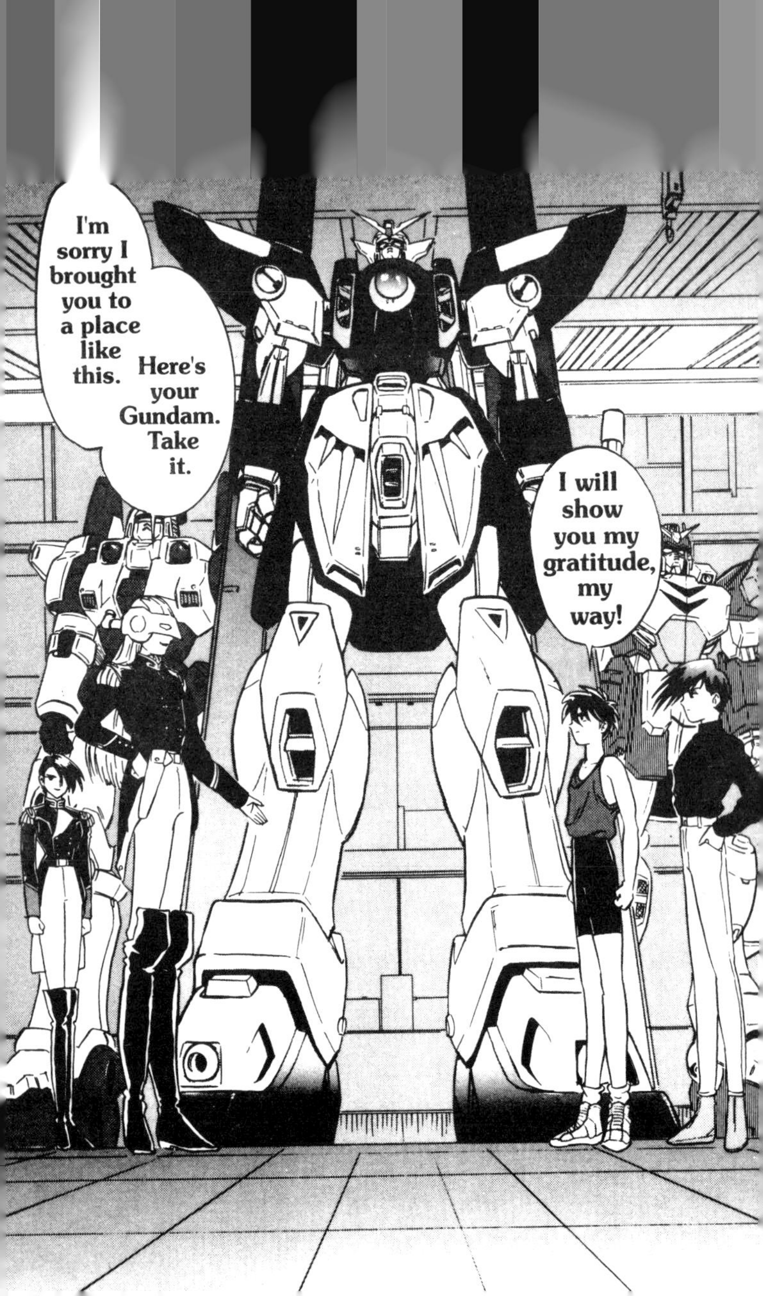
I'm sorry I brought you to a place like this.
Here's your Gundam. Take it.
I will show you my gratitude, my way!

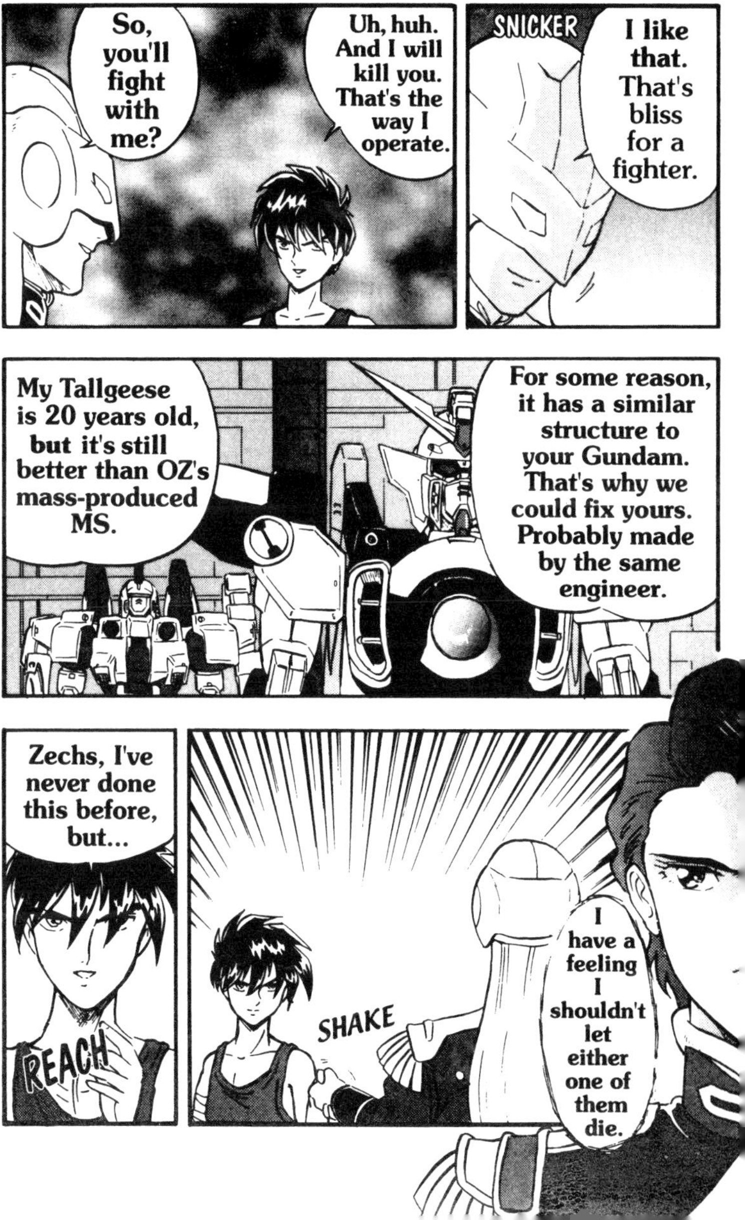
So, you'll fight with me?
Uh, huh. And I will kill you. That's the way I operate.
SNICKER
I like that. That's bliss for a fighter.
My Tallgeese is 20 years old, but it's still better than OZ's mass-produced MS.
For some reason, it has a similar structure to your Gundam. That's why we could fix yours. Probably made by the same engineer.
Zechs, I've never done this before, but...
REACH
SHAKE
I have a feeling I shouldn't let either one of them die.

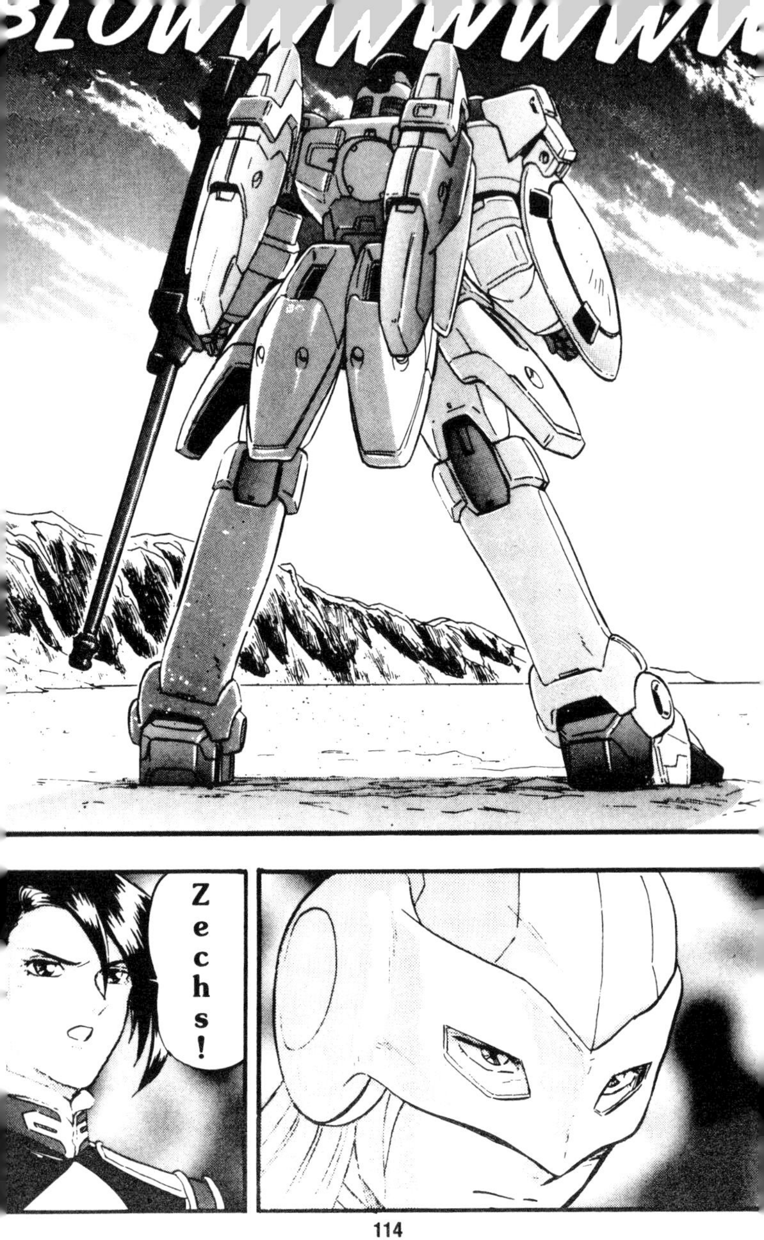
BLOWWWWWW
Zechs!

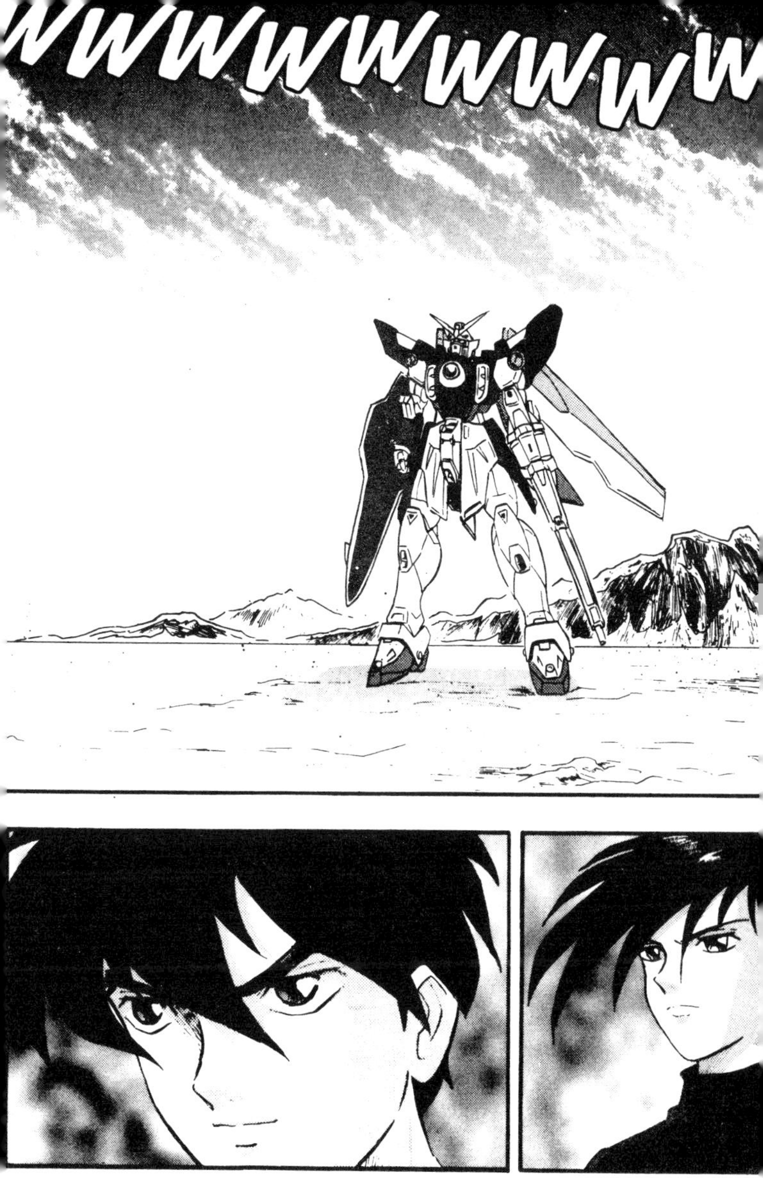
WWWWWWWWW

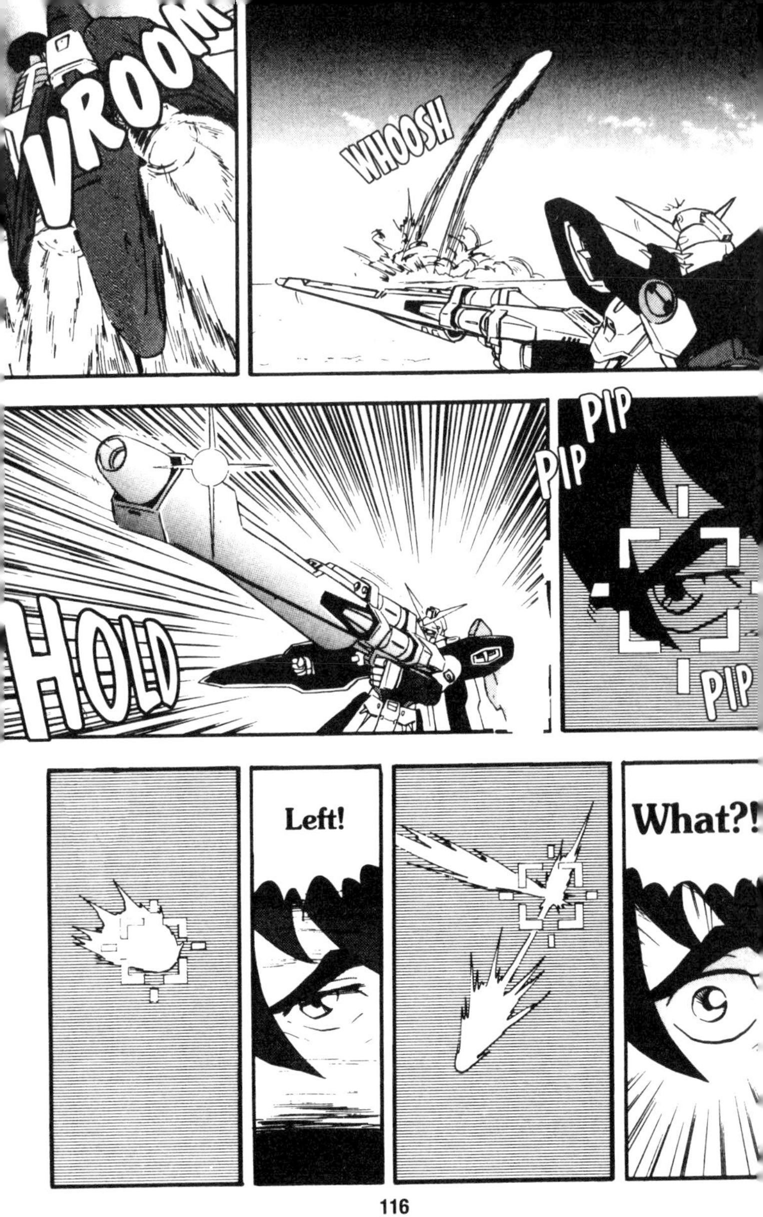
VROOM
WHOOSH
HOLD
PIP
PIP
PIP
Left!
What?!

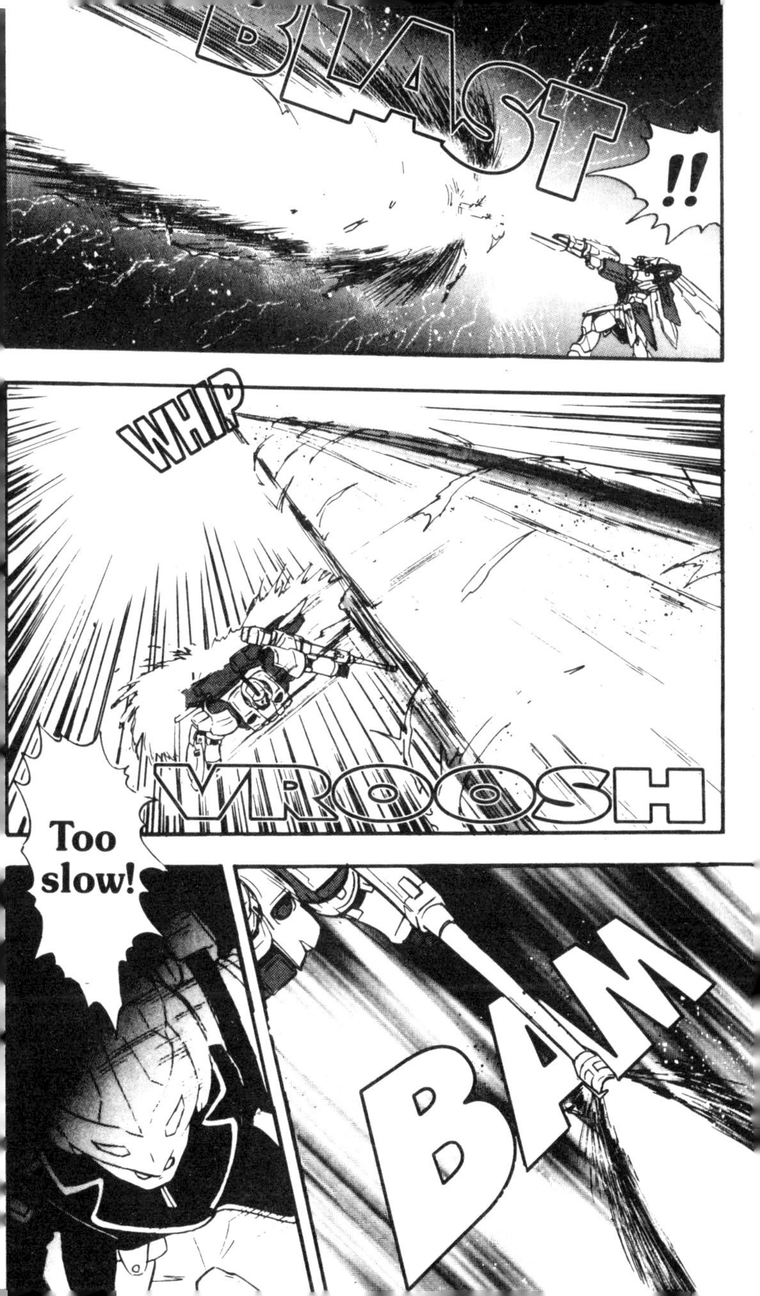

BLAST
!!
WHIP
VROOSH
Too slow!
BAM

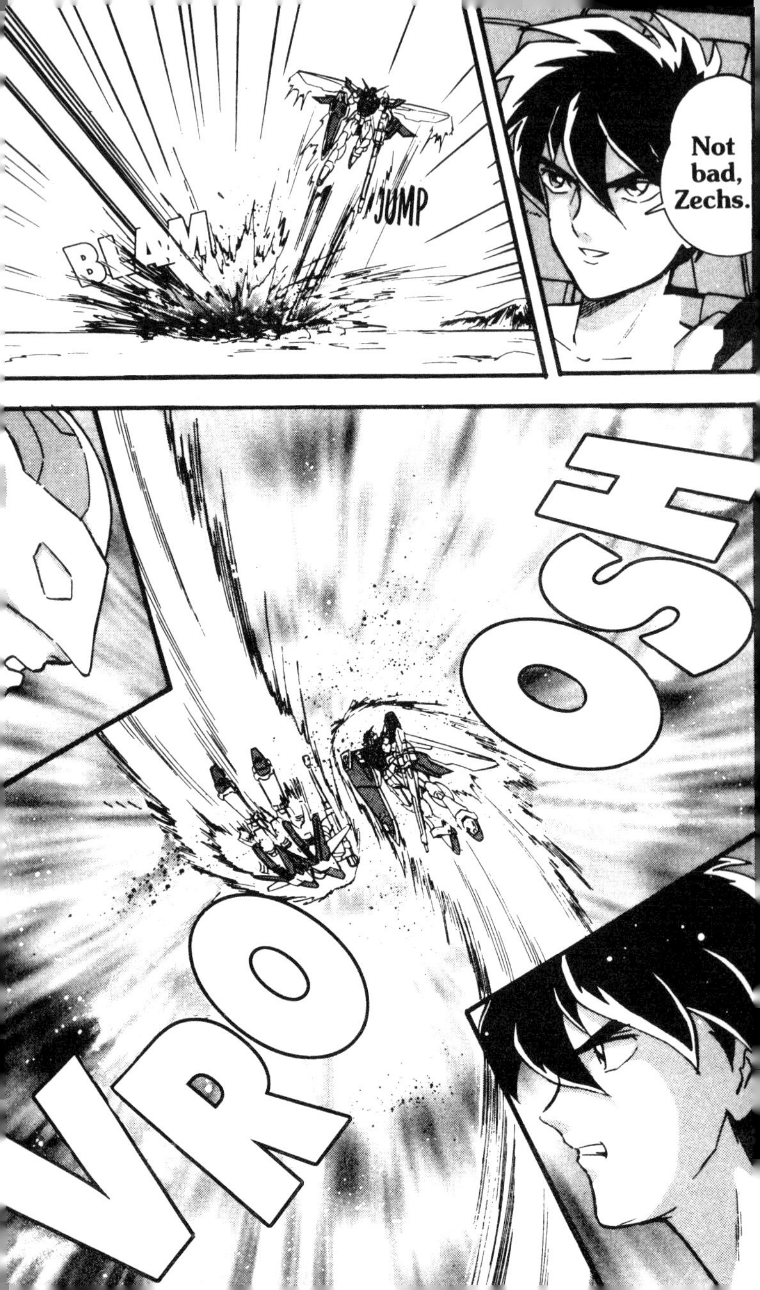
BLAM
JUMP
Not bad, Zechs.
VROOSH

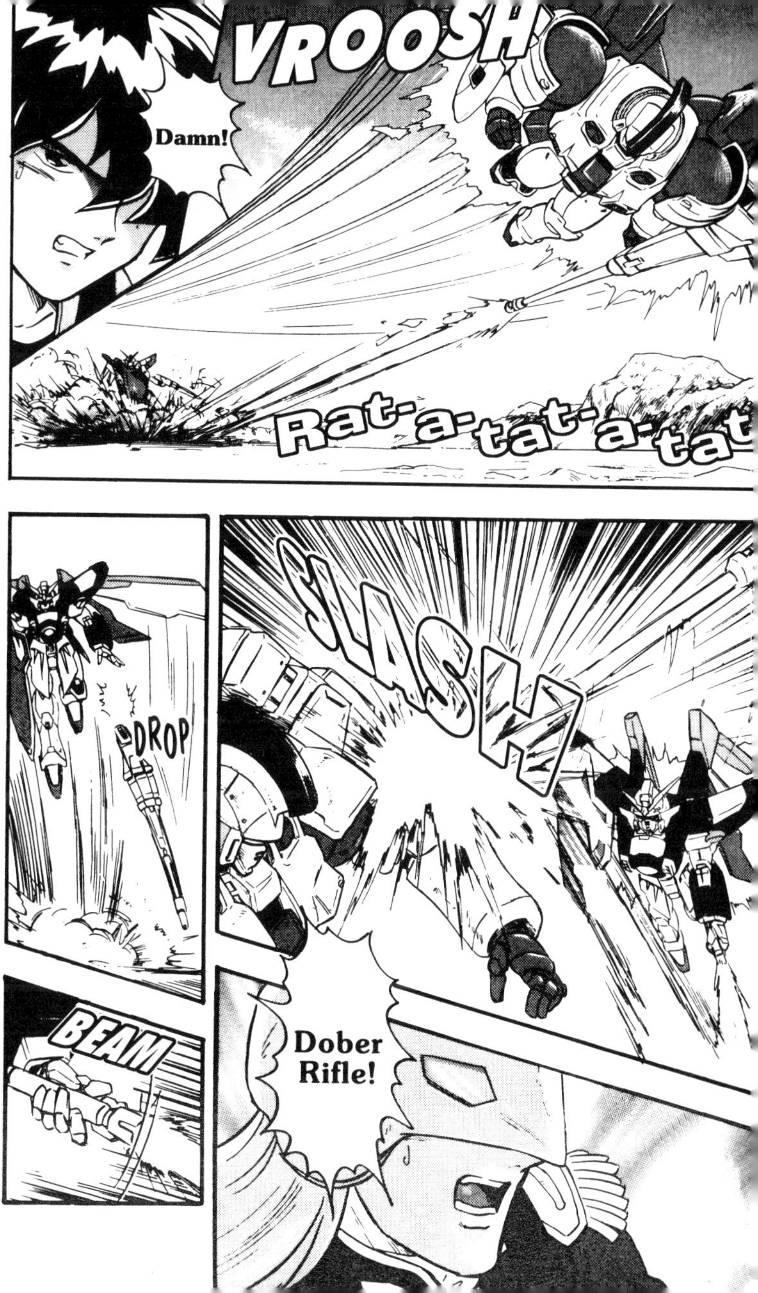
VROOSH
Damn!
Rat-a-tat-a-tat
DROP
SLASH
BEAM
Dober
Rifle!

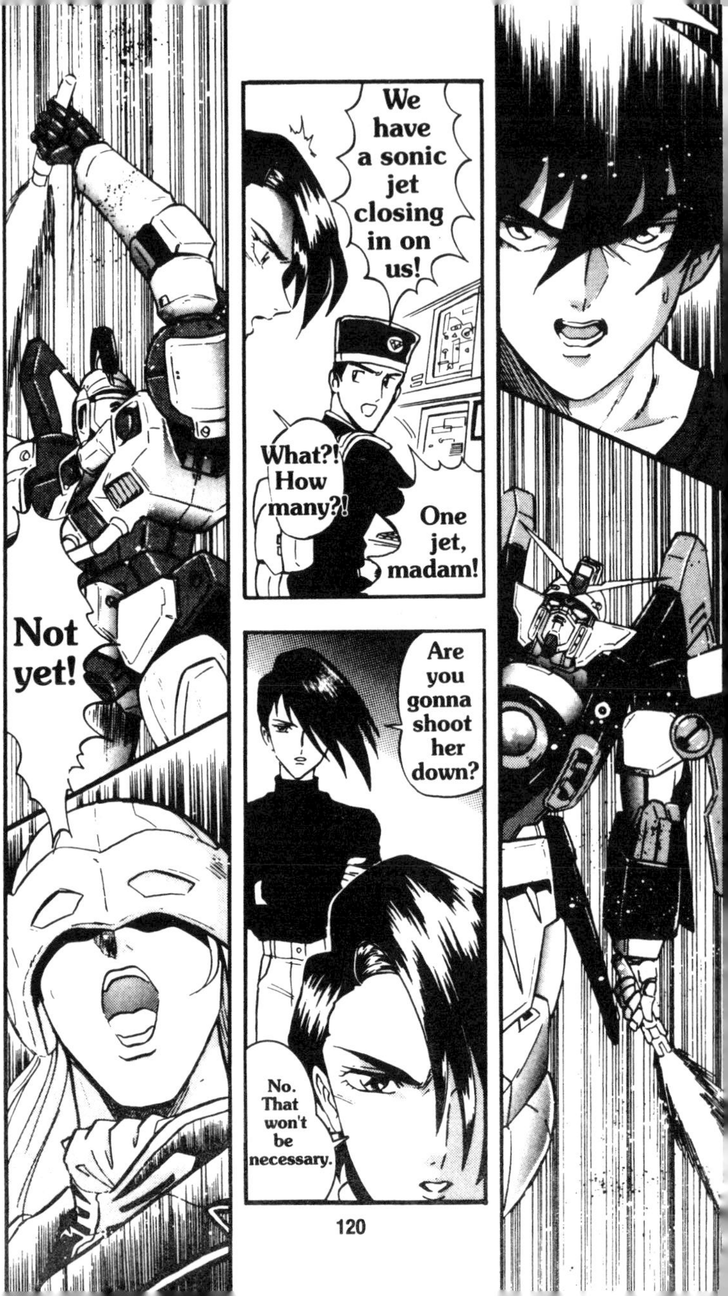
Not yet!
We have a sonic jet closing in on us!
What?! How many?!
One jet, madam!
Are you gonna shoot her down?
No. That won't be necessary.

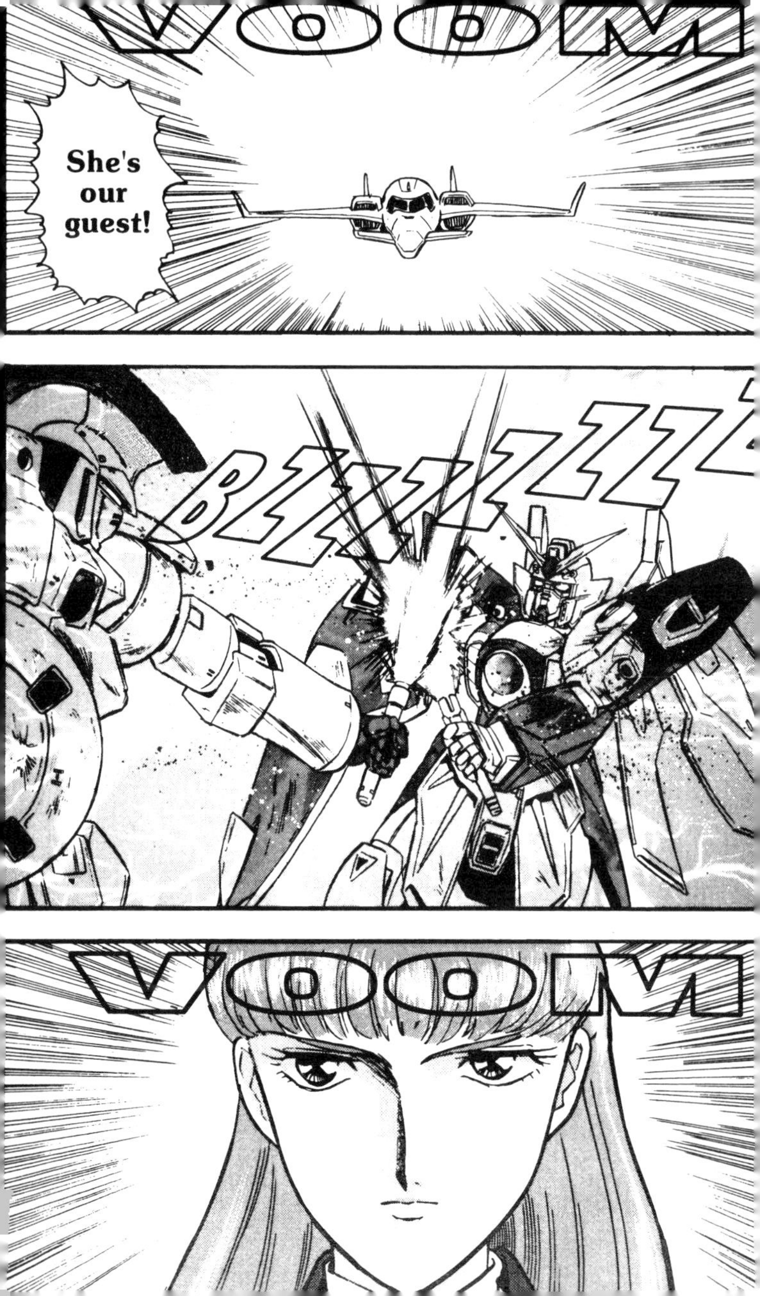
VOOM
She's our guest!
BZZZZZZZ
VOOM

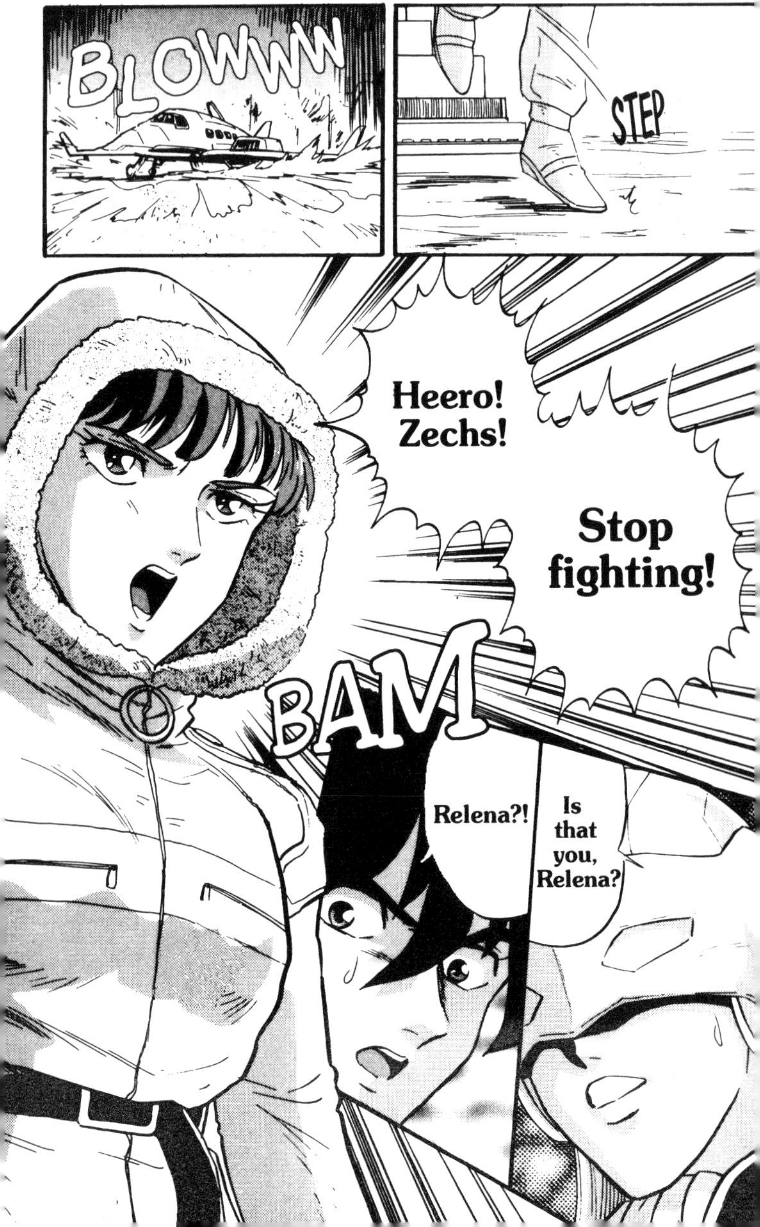
BLOWWW
STEP
Heero! Zechs!
Stop fighting!
BAM
Relena?!
Is that you, Relena?

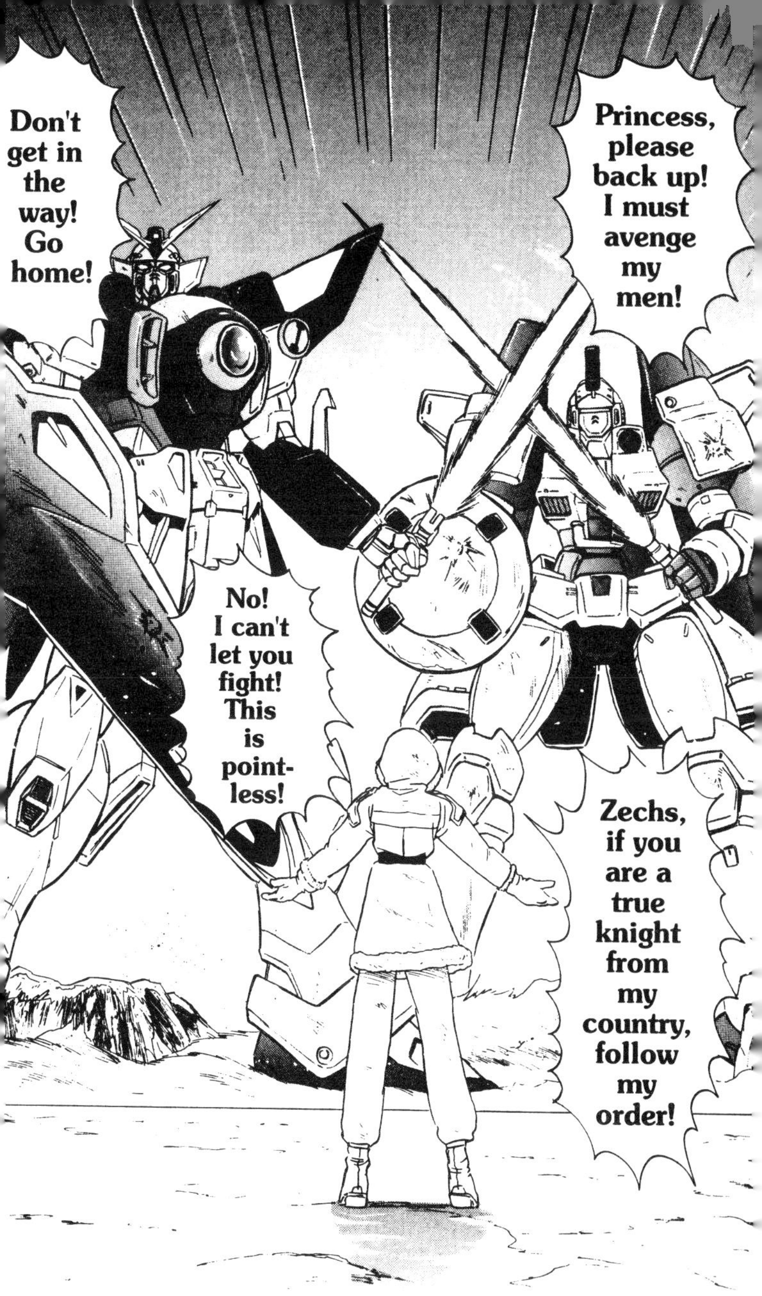
Don't get in the way! Go home!
Princess, please back up! I must avenge my men!
No! I can't let you fight! This is pointless!
Zechs, if you are a true knight from my country, follow my order!

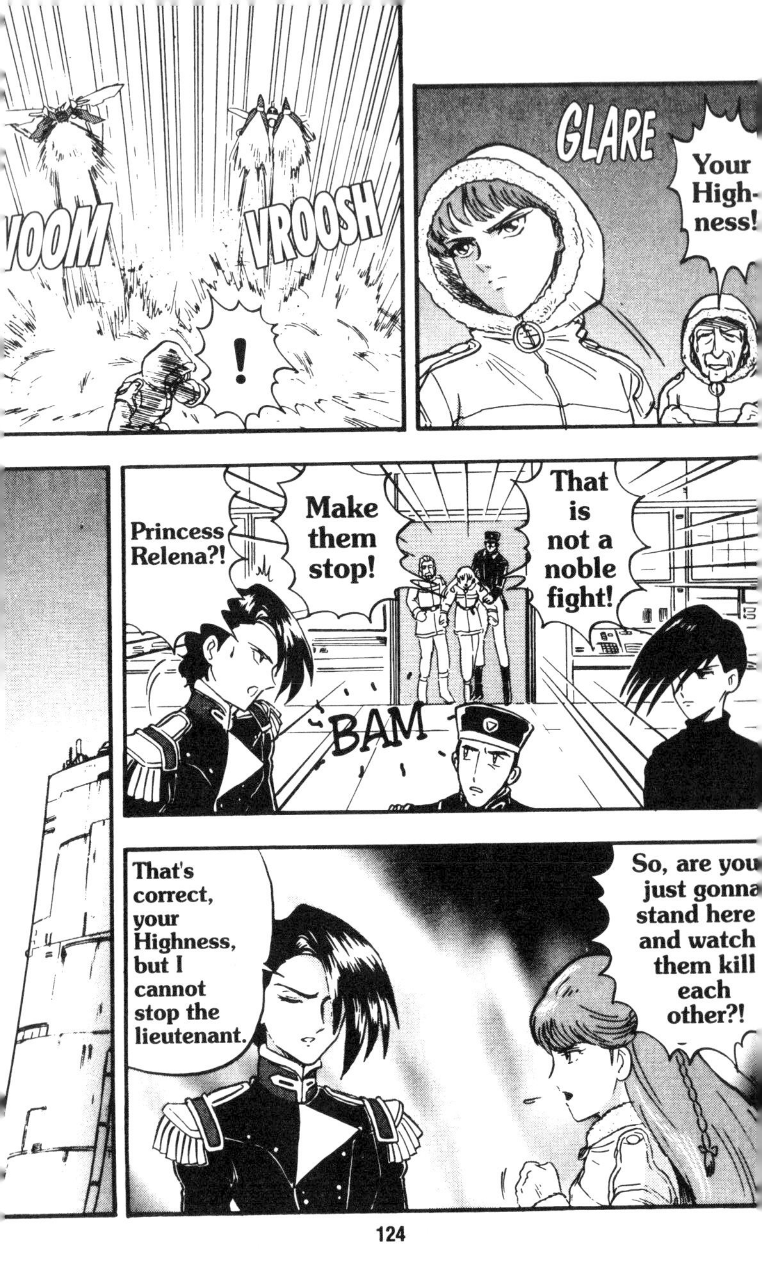
OOM
VROOSH
!
GLARE
Your High-ness!
Princess Relena?!
Make them stop!
That is not a noble fight!
BAM
That's correct, your Highness, but I cannot stop the lieutenant.
So, are you just gonna stand here and watch them kill each other?!

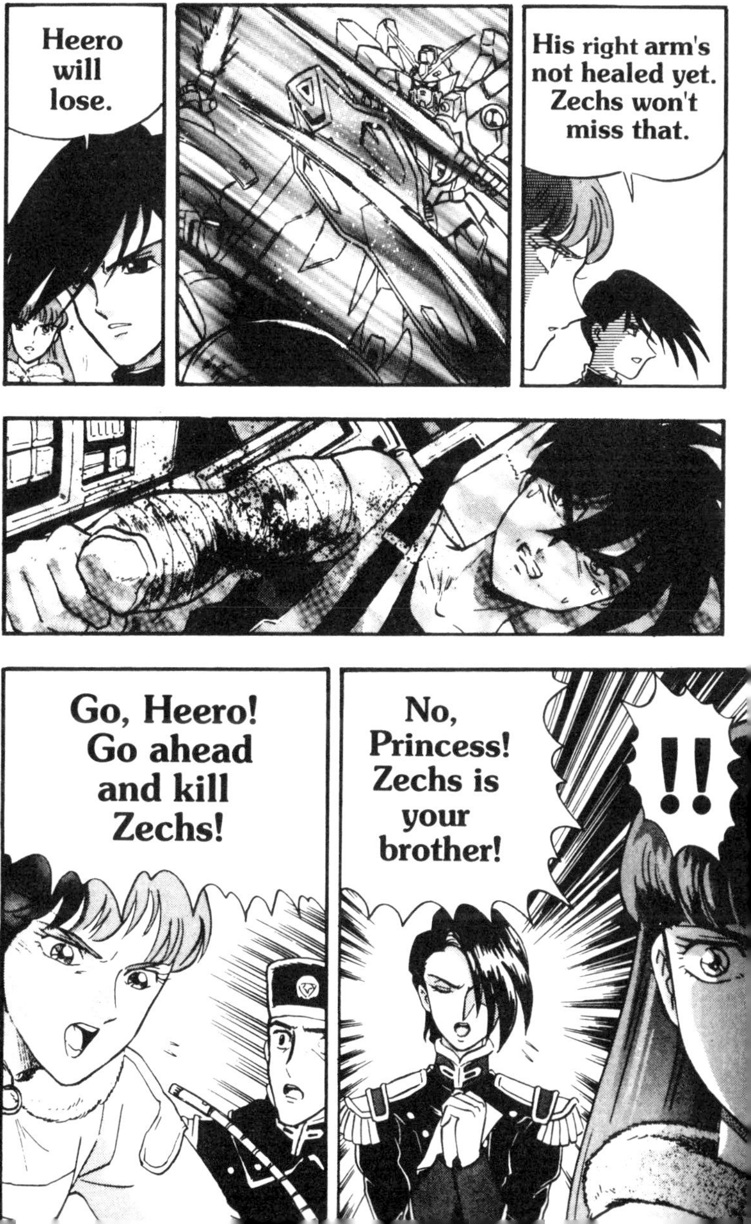
Heero will lose.
His right arm's not healed yet. Zechs won't miss that.
Go, Heero! Go ahead and kill Zechs!
No, Princess! Zechs is your brother!
!!

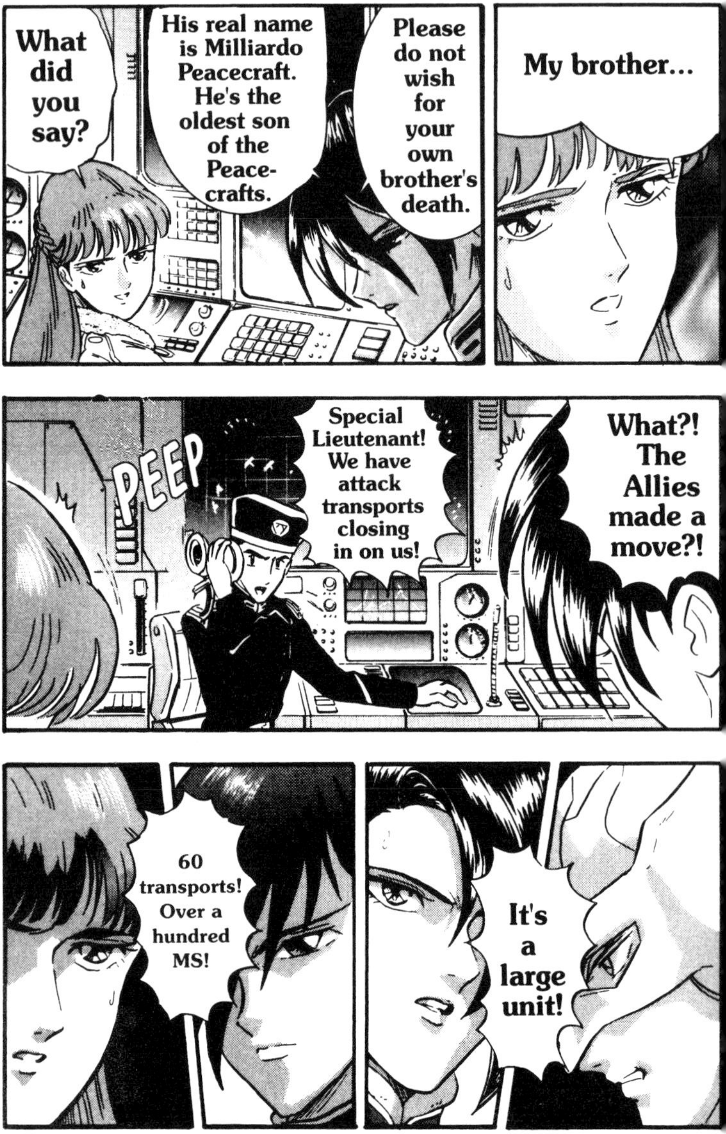

What did you say?
His real name is Milliardo Peacecraft. He's the oldest son of the Peace-crafts.
Please do not wish for your own brother's death.
My brother...
PEEP
Special Lieutenant! We have attack transports closing in on us!
What?! The Allies made a move?!
60 transports! Over a hundred MS!
It's a large unit!

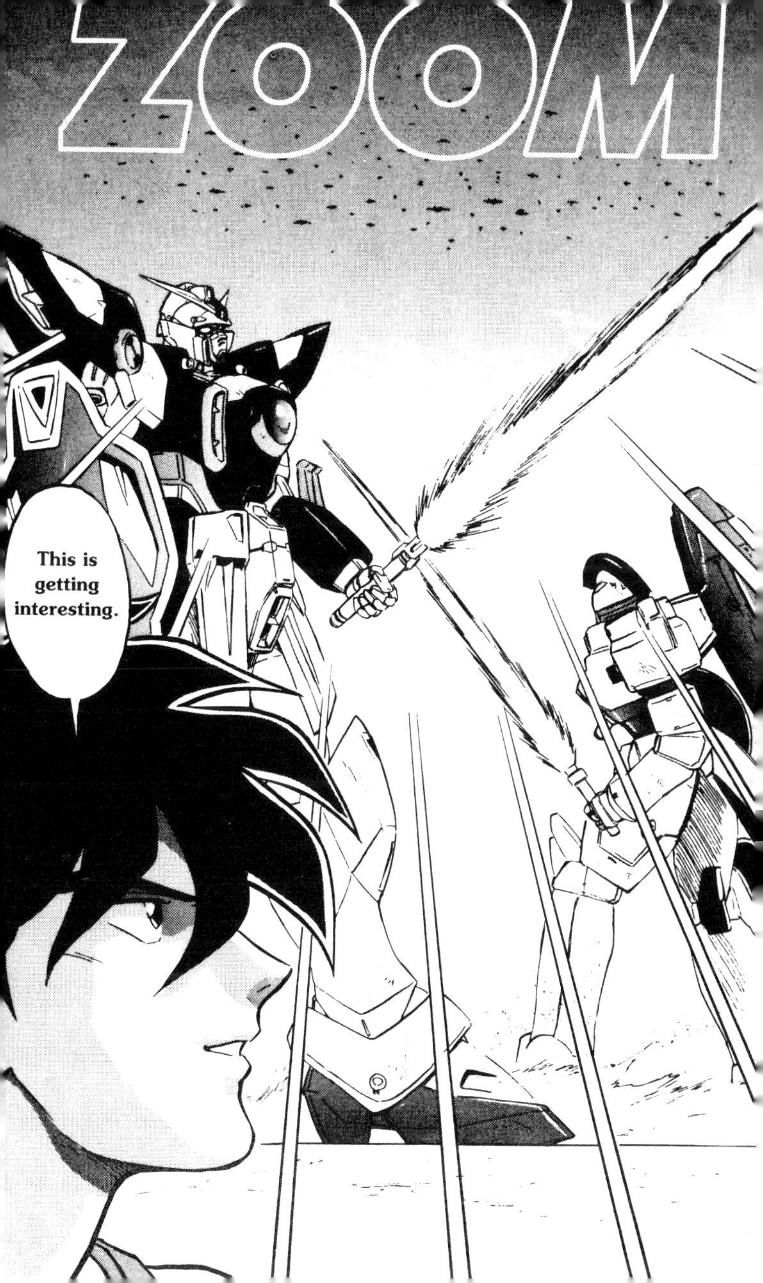
ZOOM
This is getting interesting.

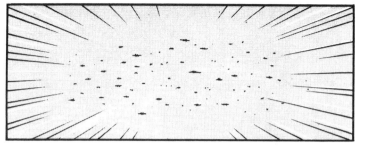

It just looks like the remaining Allies. But I have no more bullets!

Get ready!

Trowa.

My Heavy-arms is more effective for long distance shooting!

STOMP STOMP

We're still at a disadvantage, though.

#4 BOYS WANDER

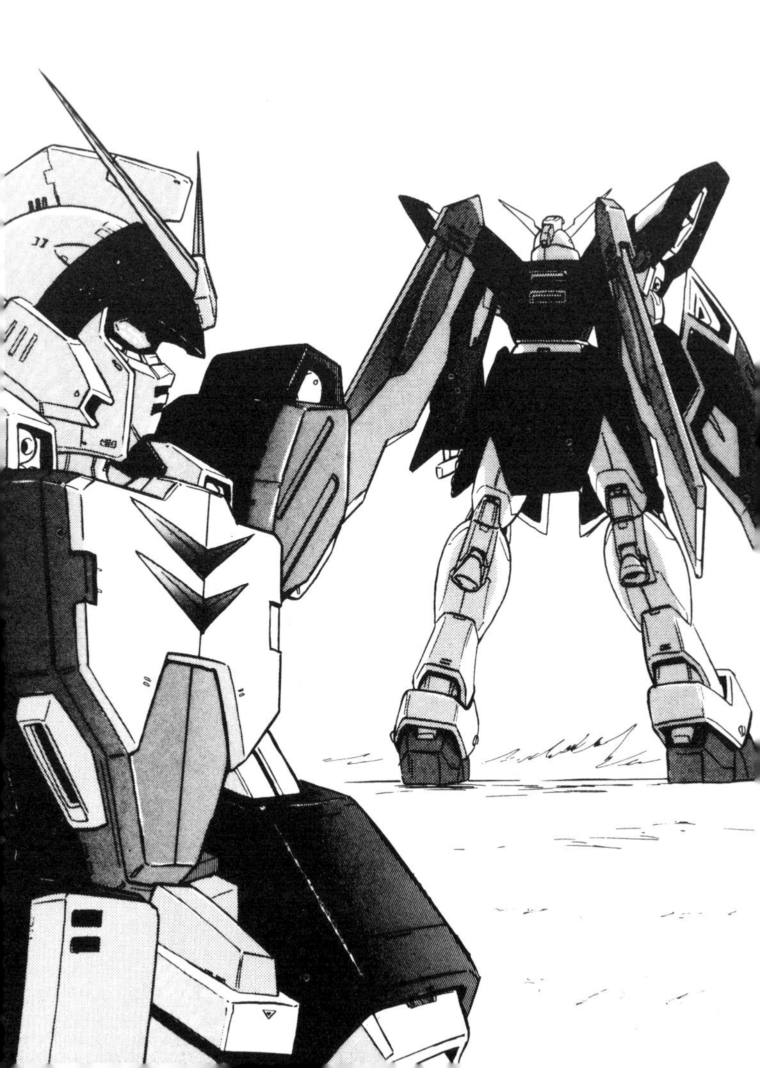

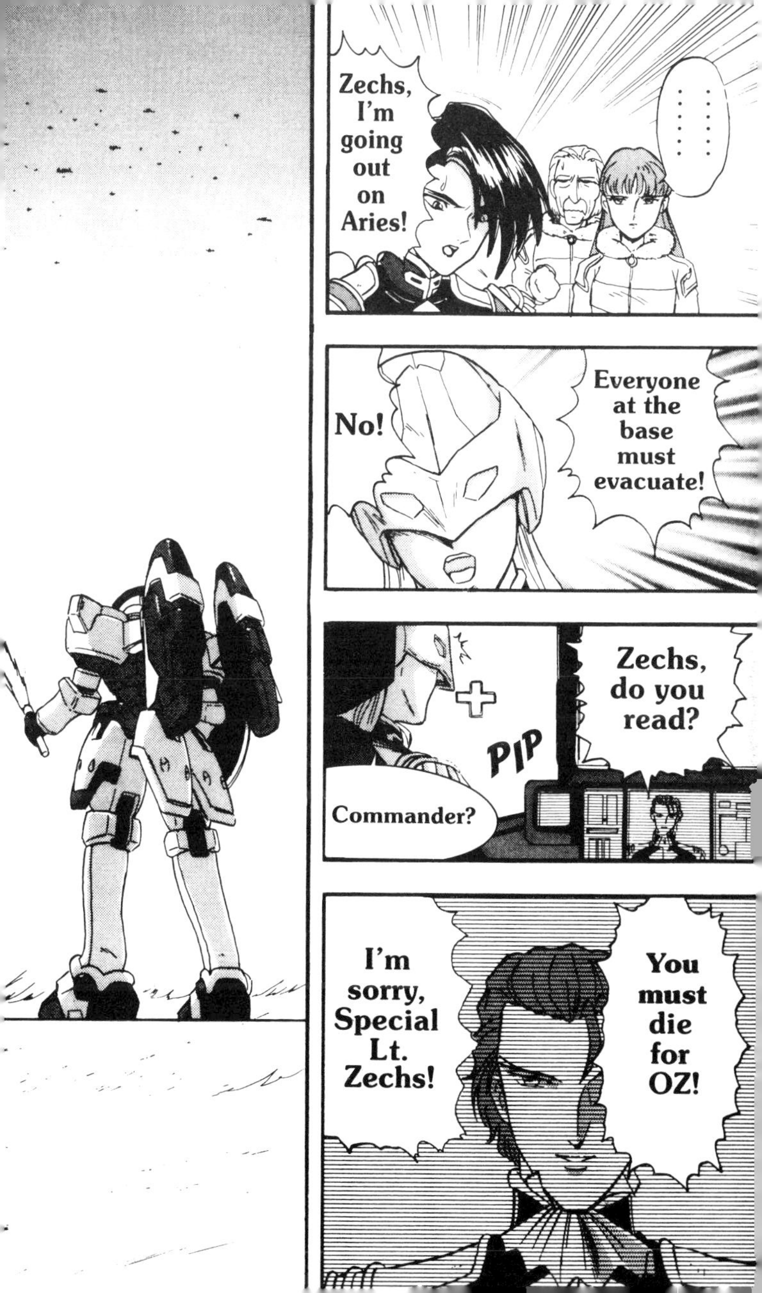

Zechs, I'm going out on Aries!
......
No!
Everyone at the base must evacuate!
Zechs, do you read?
PIP
Commander?
I'm sorry, Special Lt. Zechs!
You must die for OZ!

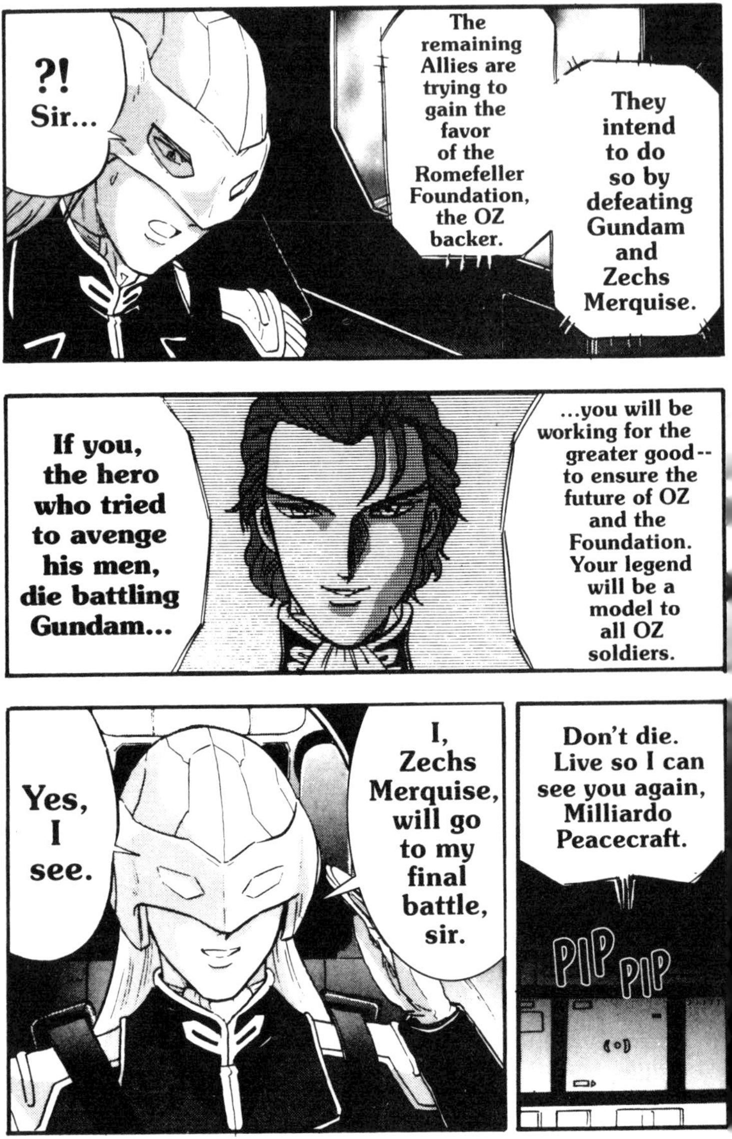
?! Sir...
The remaining Allies are trying to gain the favor of the Romefeller Foundation, the OZ backer.
They intend to do so by defeating Gundam and Zechs Merquise.
If you, the hero who tried to avenge his men, die battling Gundam...
...you will be working for the greater good-- to ensure the future of OZ and the Foundation. Your legend will be a model to all OZ soldiers.
Yes, I see.
I, Zechs Merquise, will go to my final battle, sir.
Don't die. Live so I can see you again, Milliardo Peacecraft.
PIP PIP

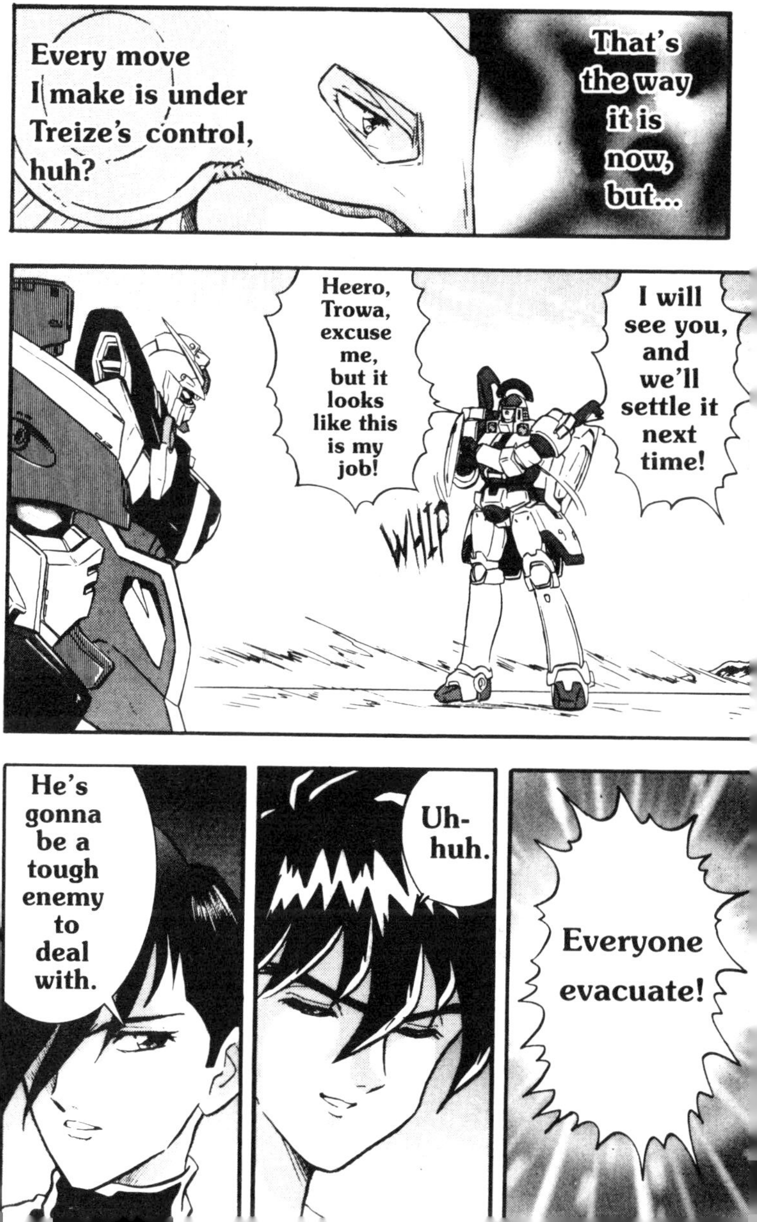

Every move I make is under Treize's control, huh?
That's the way it is now, but...
Heero, Trowa, excuse me, but it looks like this is my job!
I will see you, and we'll settle it next time!
WHIP
He's gonna be a tough enemy to deal with.
Uh-huh.
Everyone evacuate!

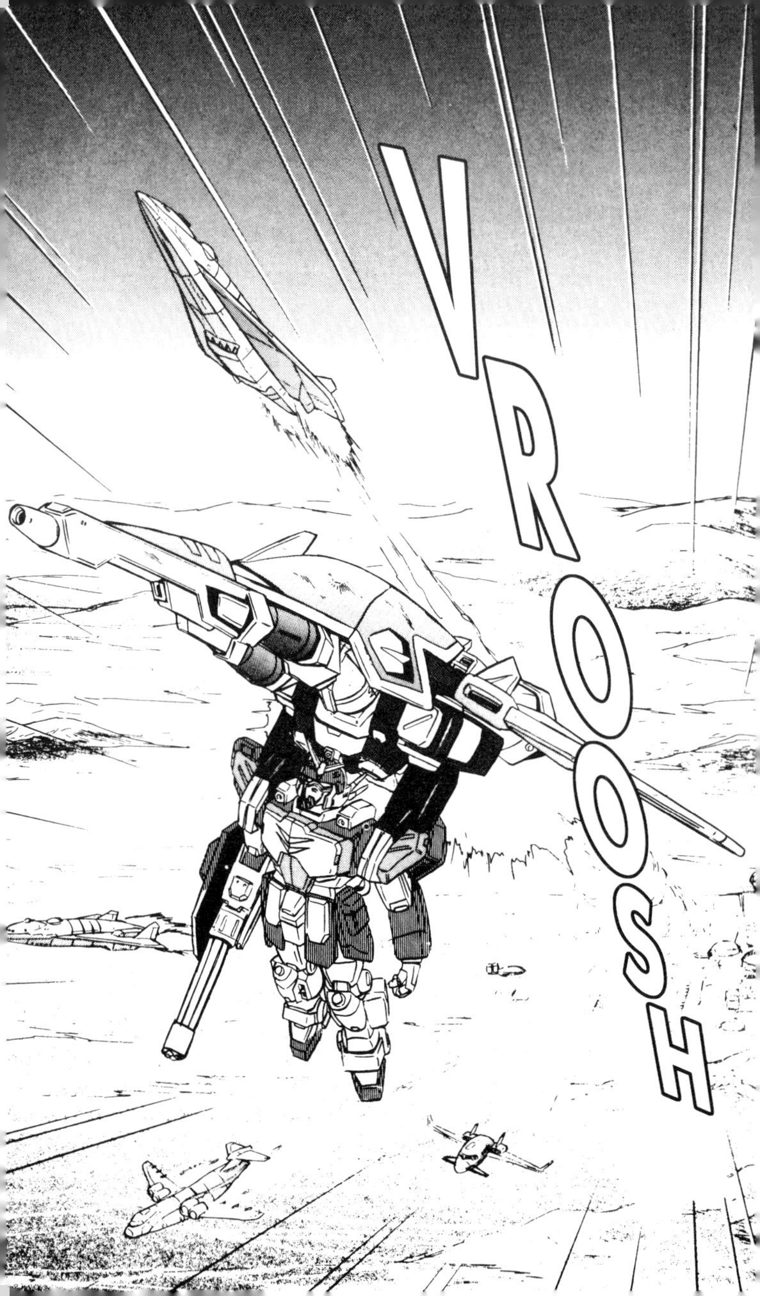
VROOOOSH

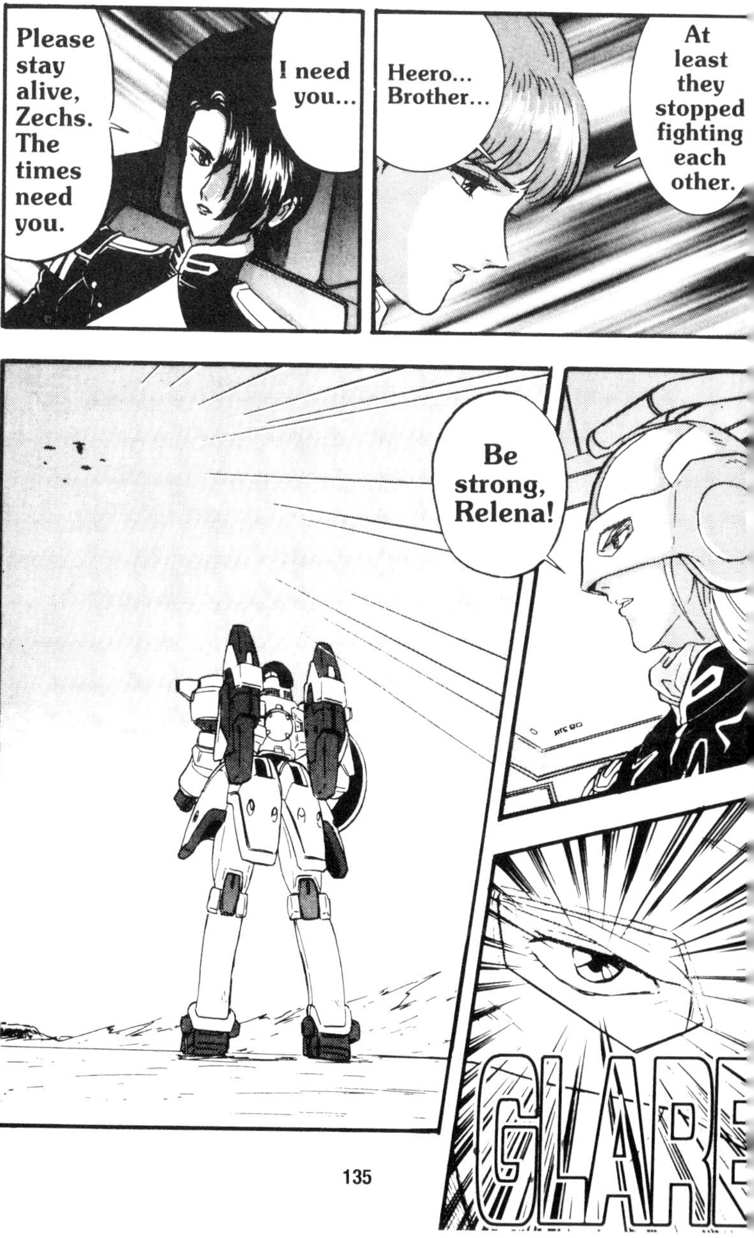
At least they stopped fighting each other.
Heero... Brother...
Please stay alive, Zechs. The times need you.
I need you...
Be strong, Relena!
GLARE

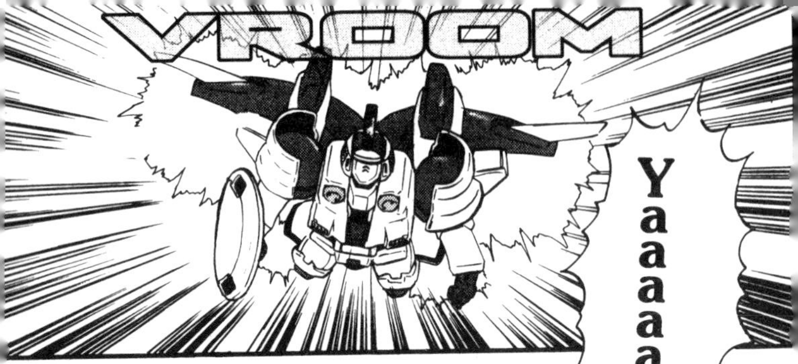
VROOM
Yaaaaaa!
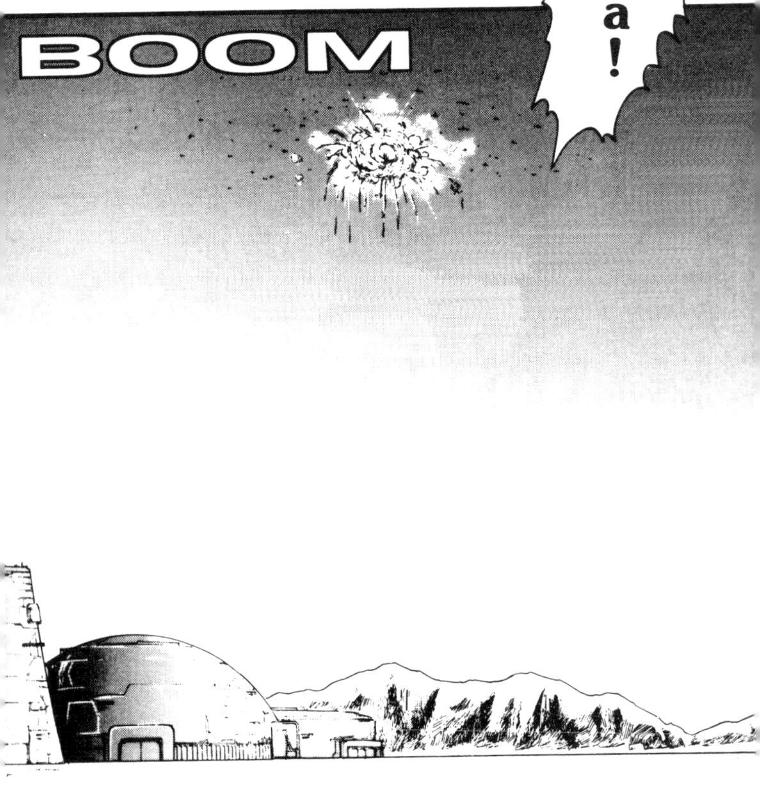
BOOM

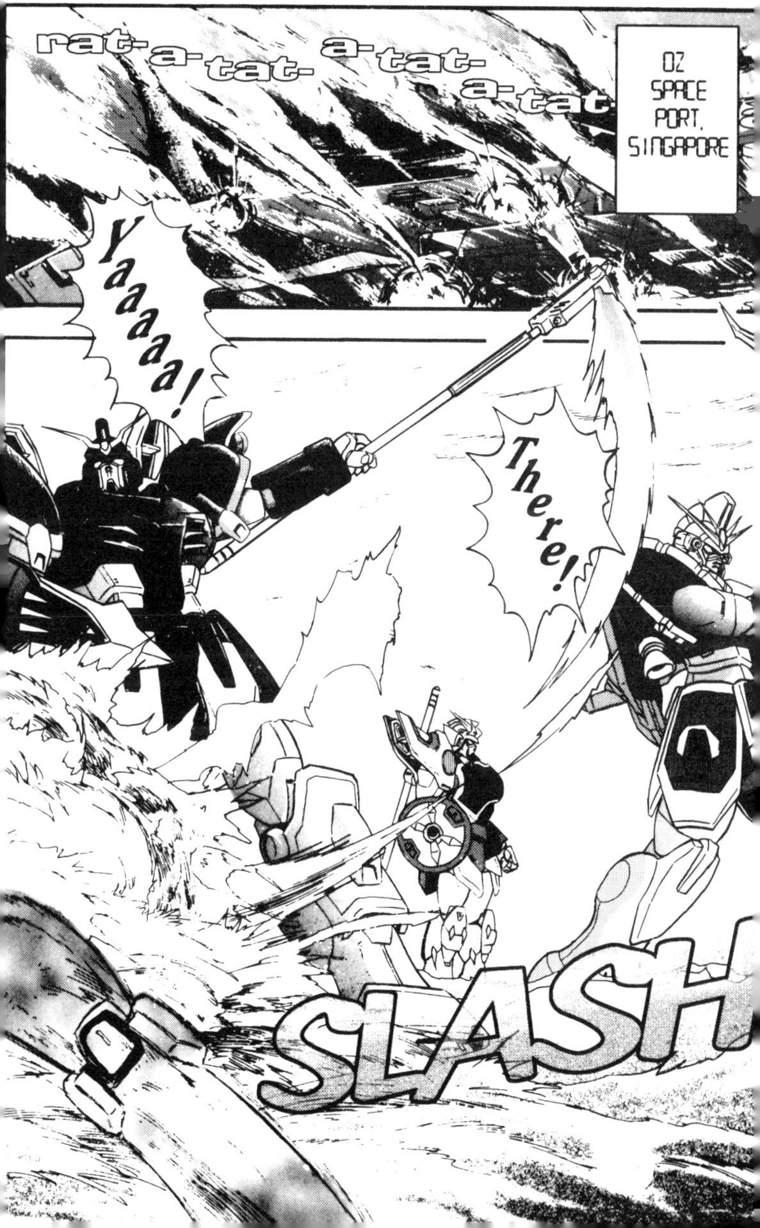
rat-a-tat- a-tat-a-tat-
OZ SPACE PORT, SINGAPORE
Yaaaaaa!
There!
SLASH

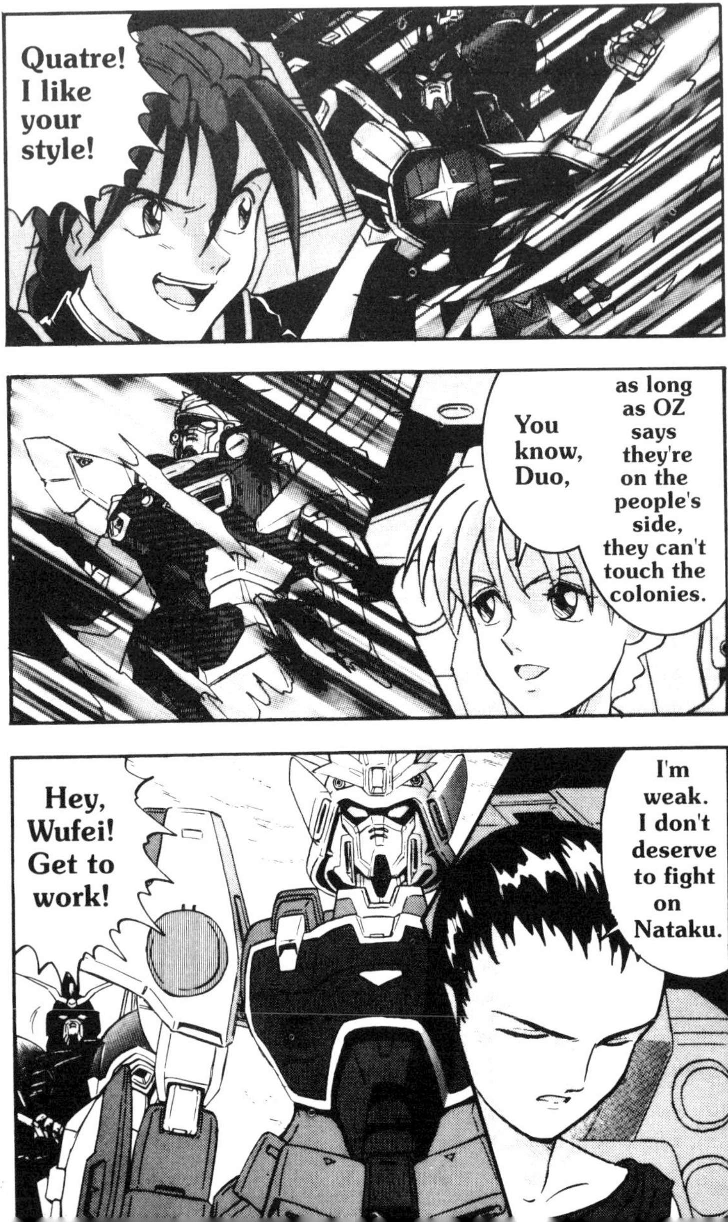
Quatre! I like your style!
You know, Duo,
as long as OZ says they're on the people's side, they can't touch the colonies.
Hey, Wufei! Get to work!
I'm weak. I don't deserve to fight on Nataku.

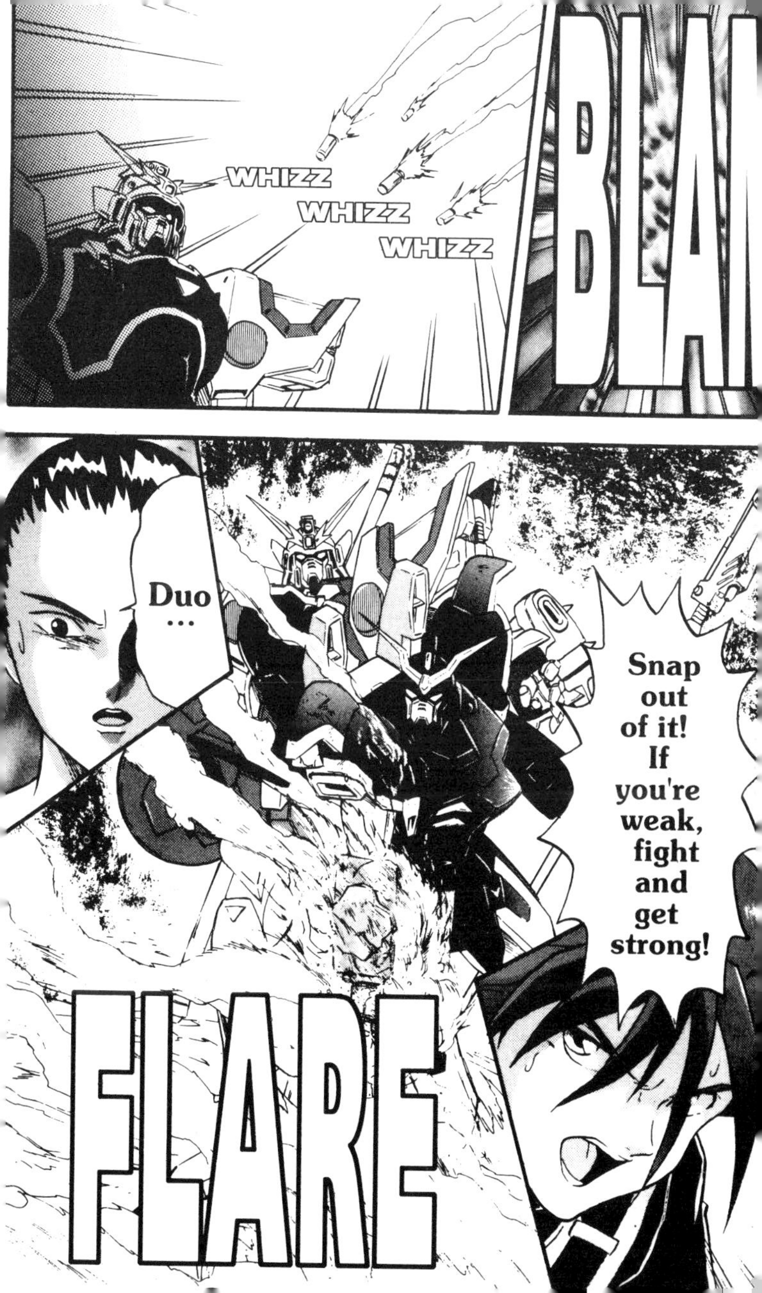
WHIZZ
WHIZZ
WHIZZ
BLAM
Duo ...
Snap out of it! If you're weak, fight and get strong!
FLARE

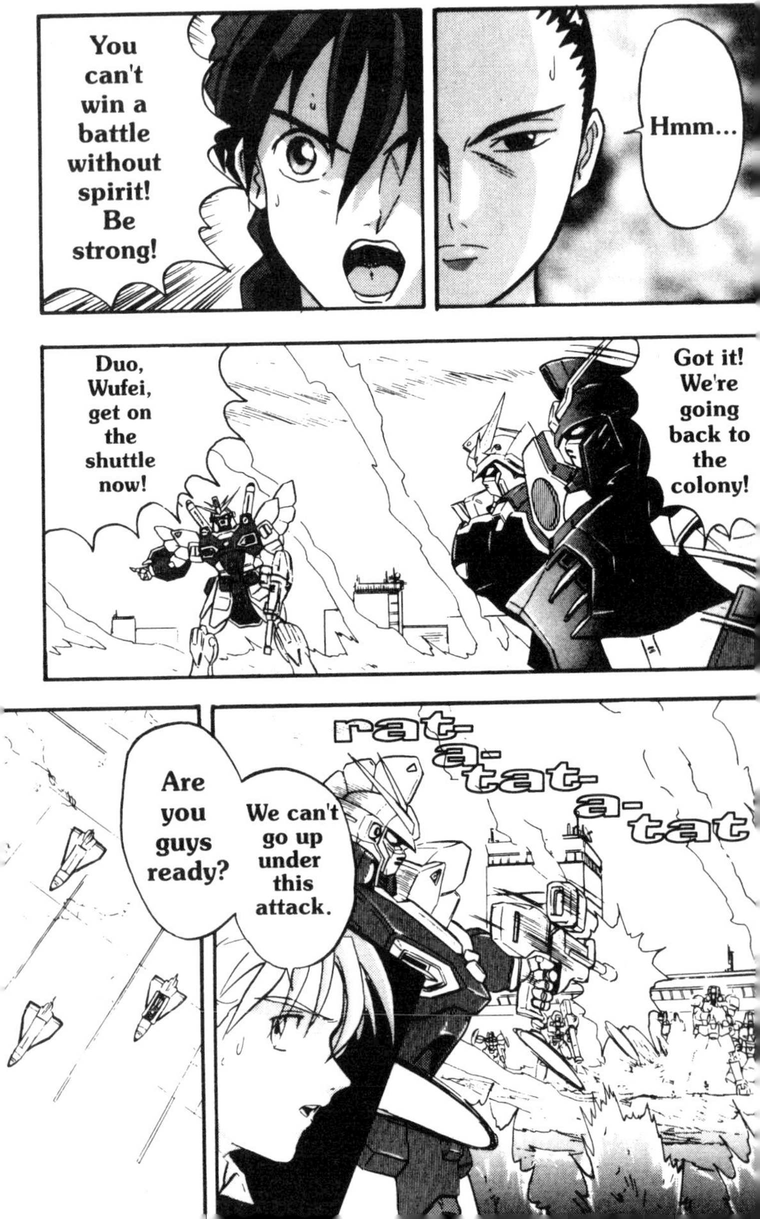
You can't win a battle without spirit! Be strong!
Hmm...
Duo, Wufei, get on the shuttle now!
Got it! We're going back to the colony!
Are you guys ready?
We can't go up under this attack.
rat-a-tat-a-tat

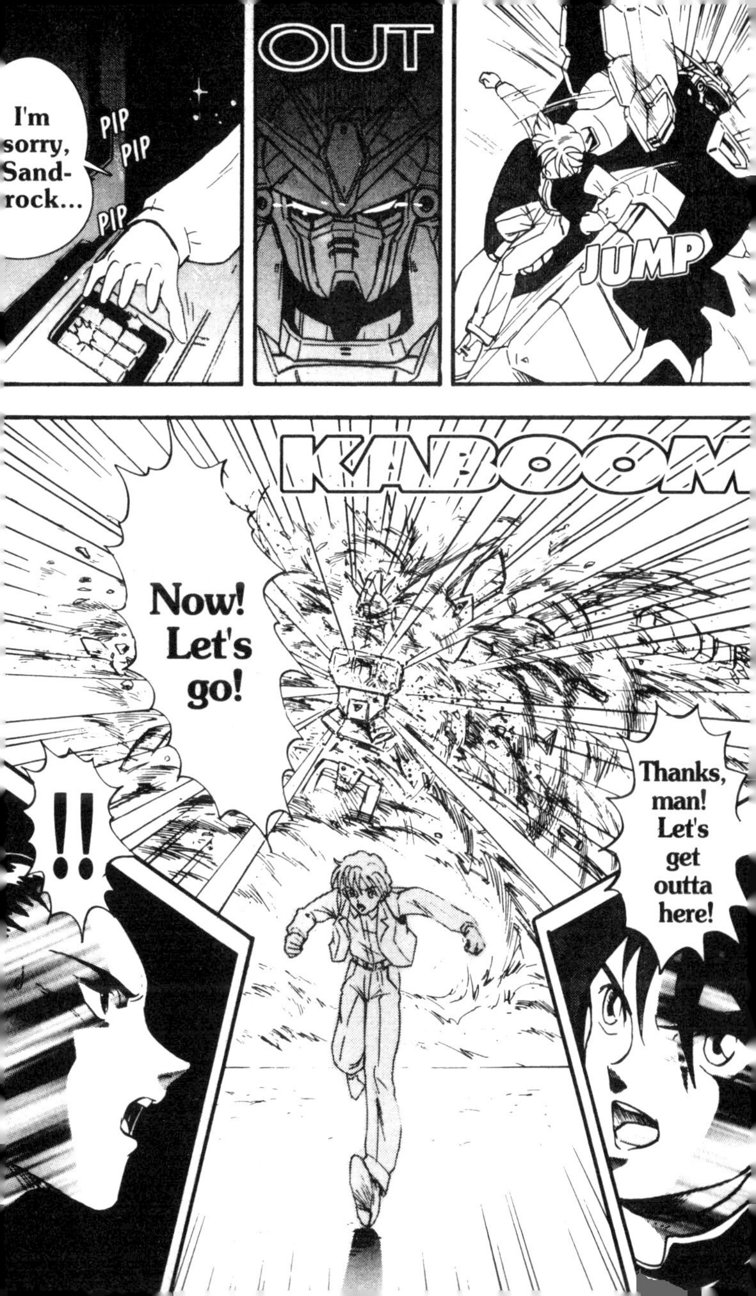
I'm sorry, Sand-rock...
PIP
PIP
PIP
OUT
JUMP
KABOOM
Now! Let's go!
!!
Thanks, man! Let's get outta here!

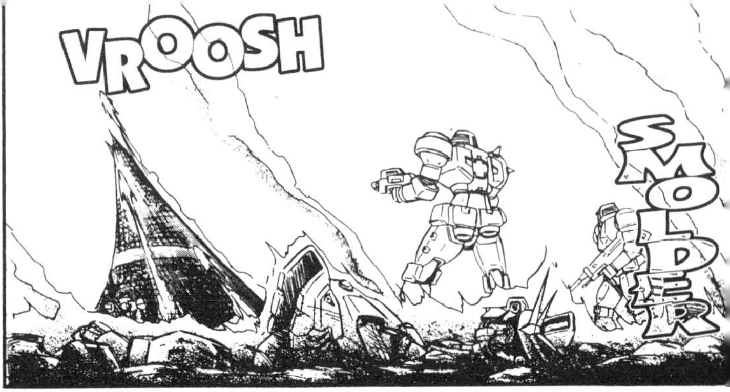
VROOSH
SMOLDER

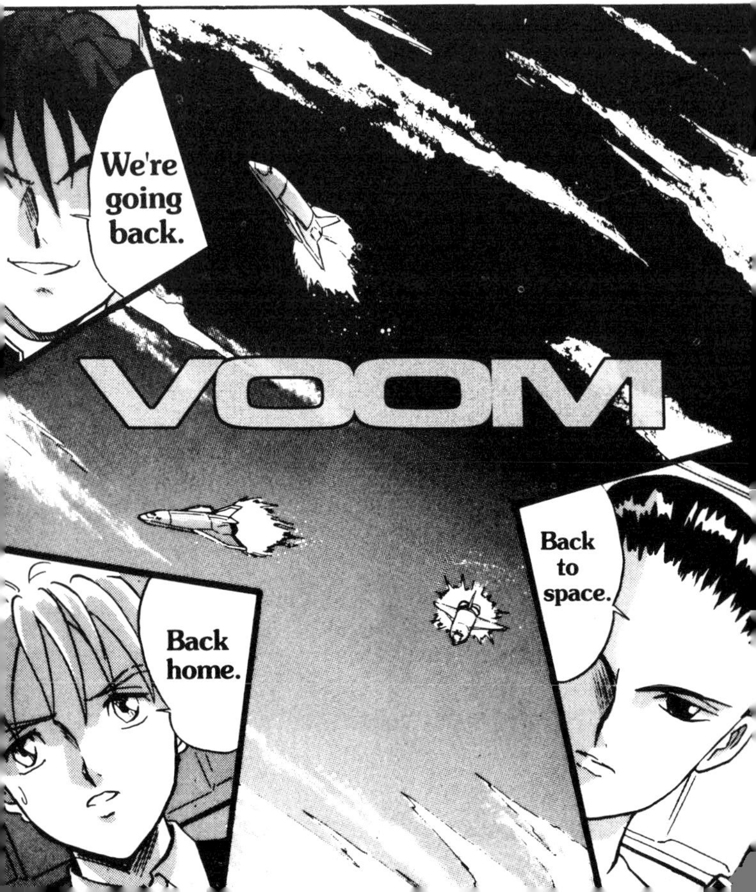
We're going back.
VOOM
Back home.
Back to space.

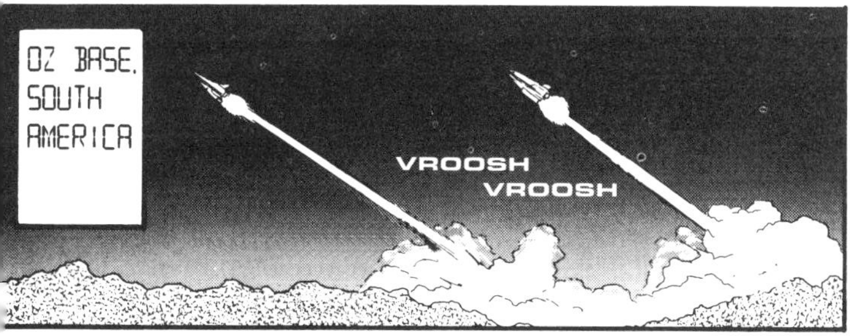
OZ BASE, SOUTH AMERICA
VROOSH
VROOSH

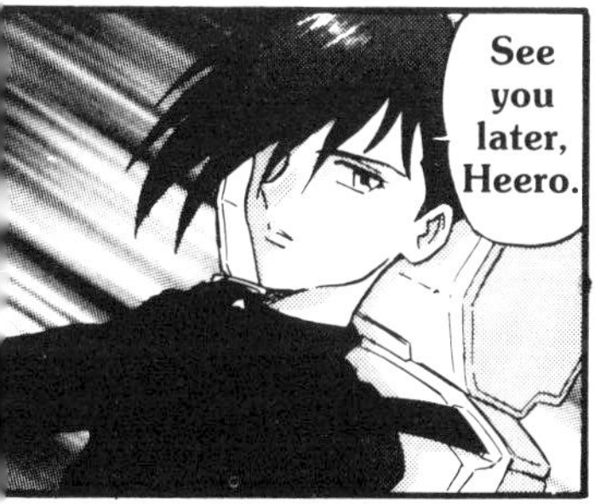
See you later, Heero.

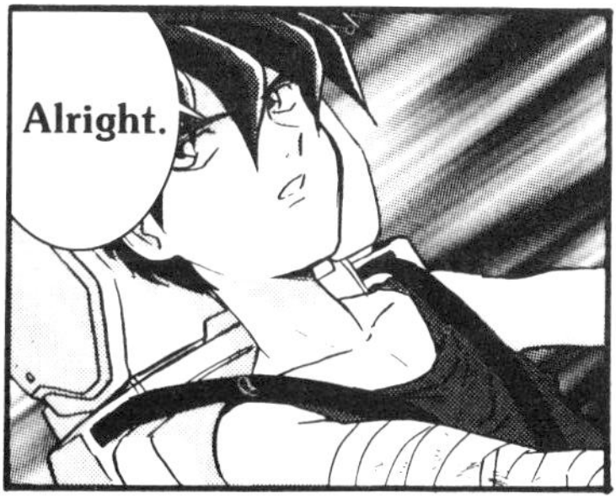
Alright.

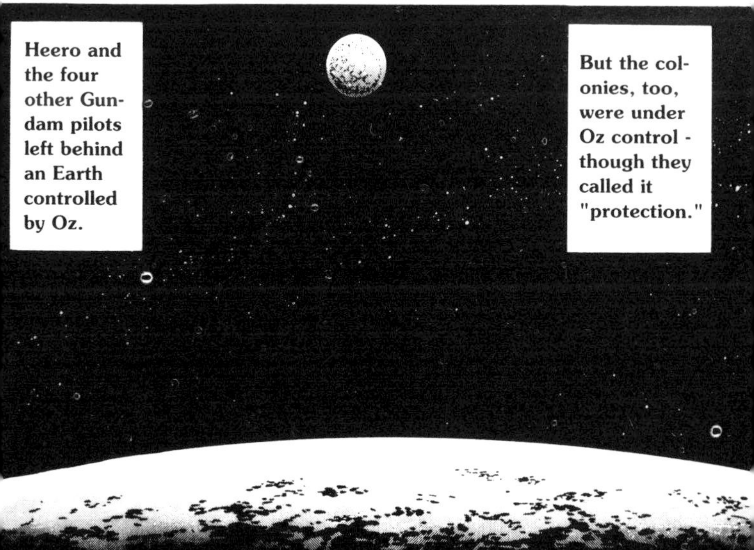
Heero and the four other Gundam pilots left behind an Earth controlled by Oz.
But the colonies, too, were under Oz control - though they called it "protection."

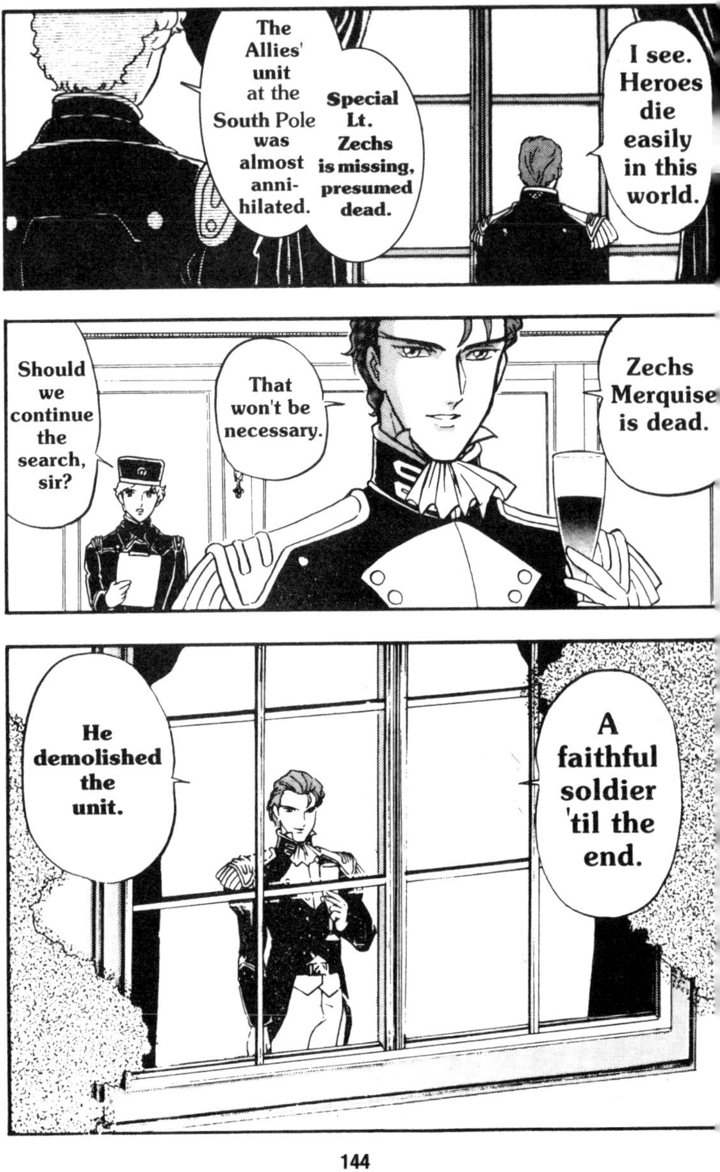

The Allies' unit at the South Pole was almost anni-hilated.
Special Lt. Zechs is missing, presumed dead.
I see. Heroes die easily in this world.
Should we continue the search, sir?
That won't be necessary.
Zechs Merquise is dead.
He demolished the unit.
A faithful soldier 'til the end.

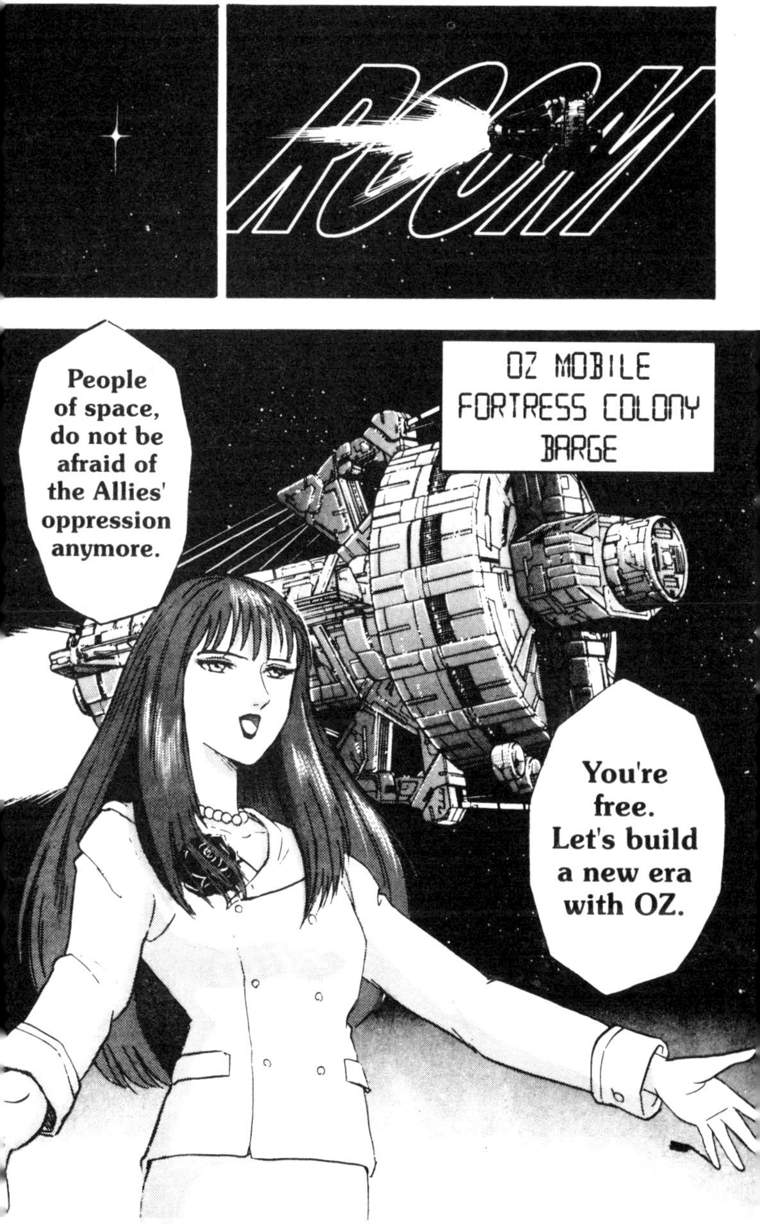
People of space, do not be afraid of the Allies' oppression anymore.
OZ MOBILE FORTRESS COLONY BARGE
You're free. Let's build a new era with OZ.

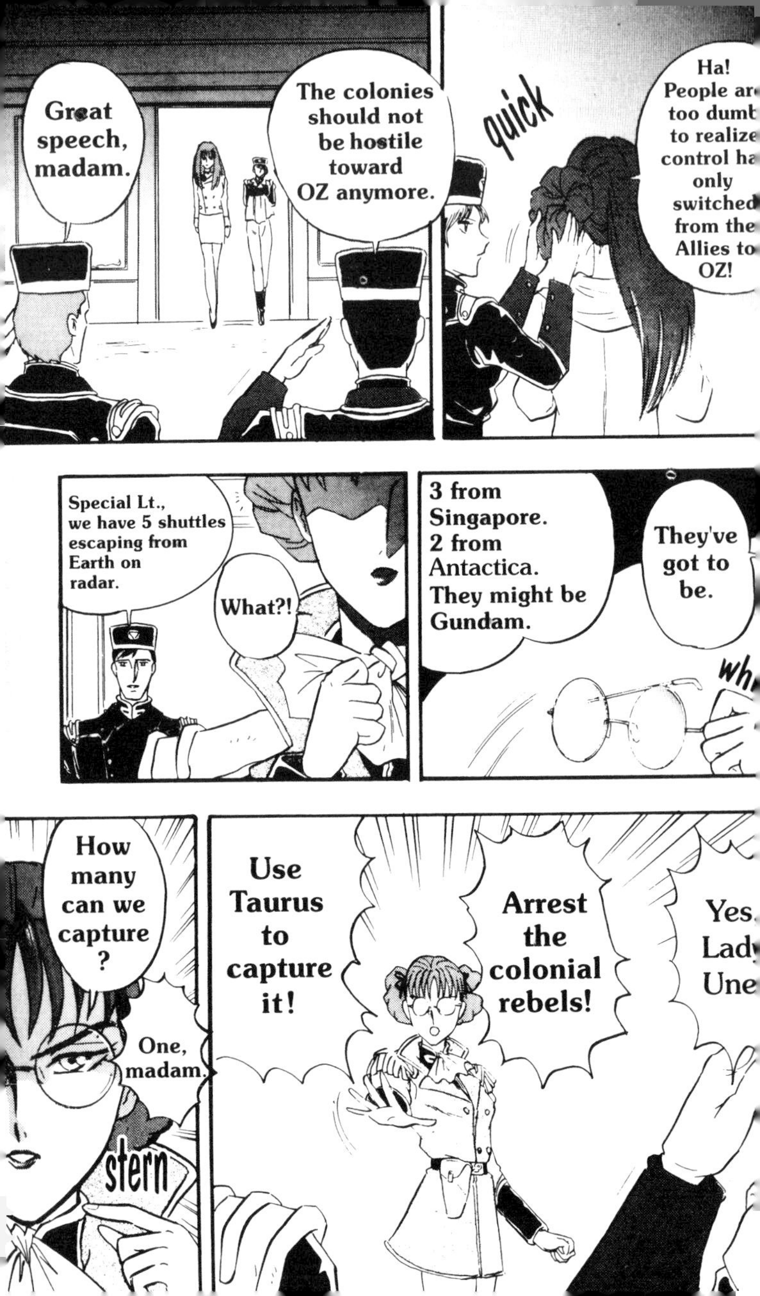

Great speech, madam.
The colonies should not be hostile toward OZ anymore.
quick
Ha! People ar too dumb to realize control ha only switched from the Allies to OZ!
Special Lt., we have 5 shuttles escaping from Earth on radar.
What?!
3 from Singapore. 2 from Antactica. They might be Gundam.
They've got to be.
How many can we capture?
One, madam.
stern
Use Taurus to capture it!
Arrest the colonial rebels!
Yes. Lady Une

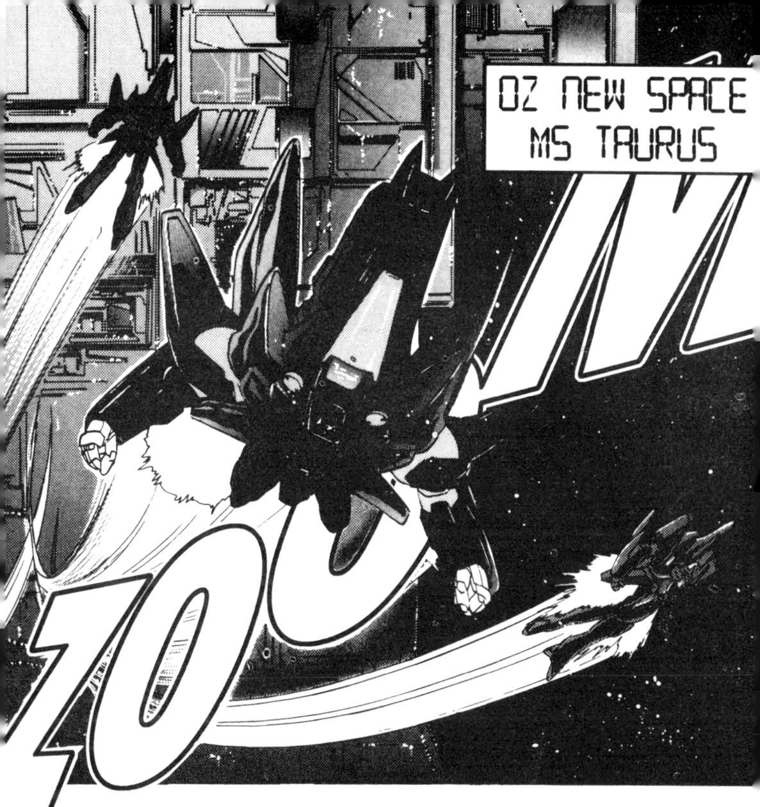
OZ NEW SPACE MS TAURUS

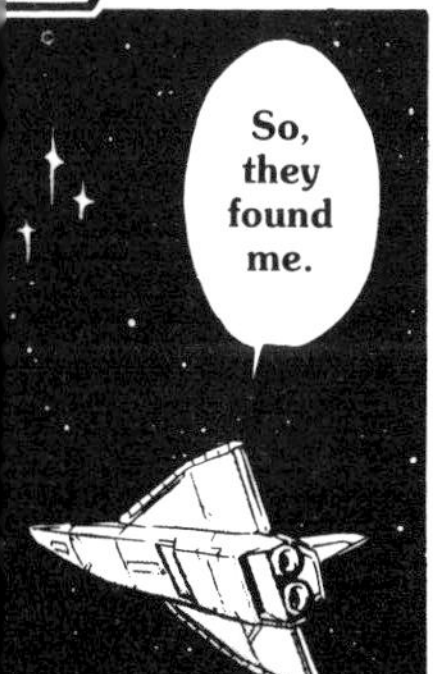
So, they found me.

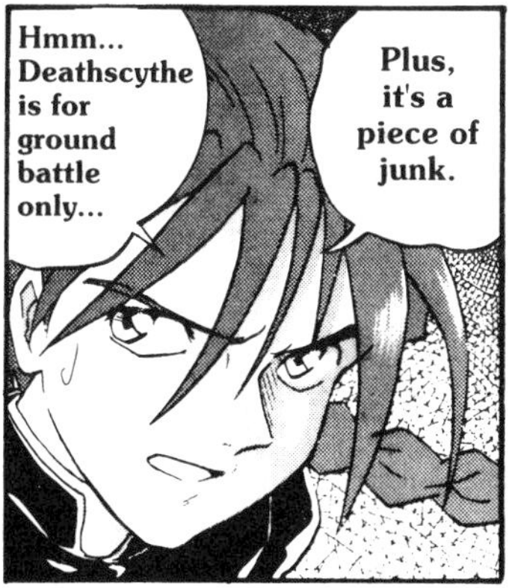
Hmm... Deathscythe is for ground battle only...
Plus, it's a piece of junk.

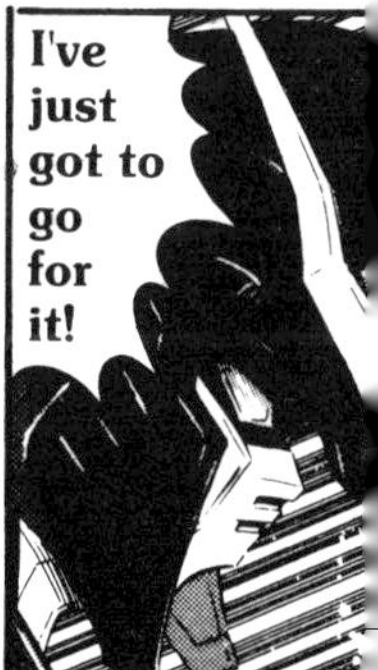
I've just got to go for it!

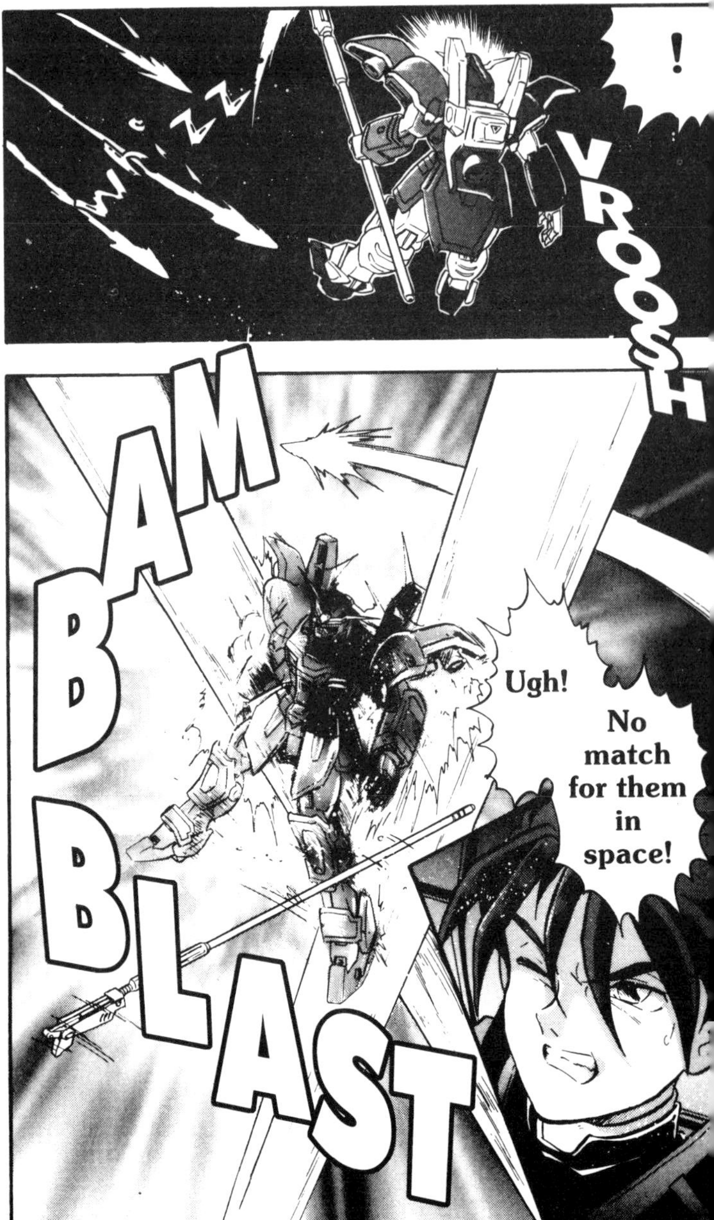
!
VROOSH
BAM
BLAST
Ugh!
No match for them in space!

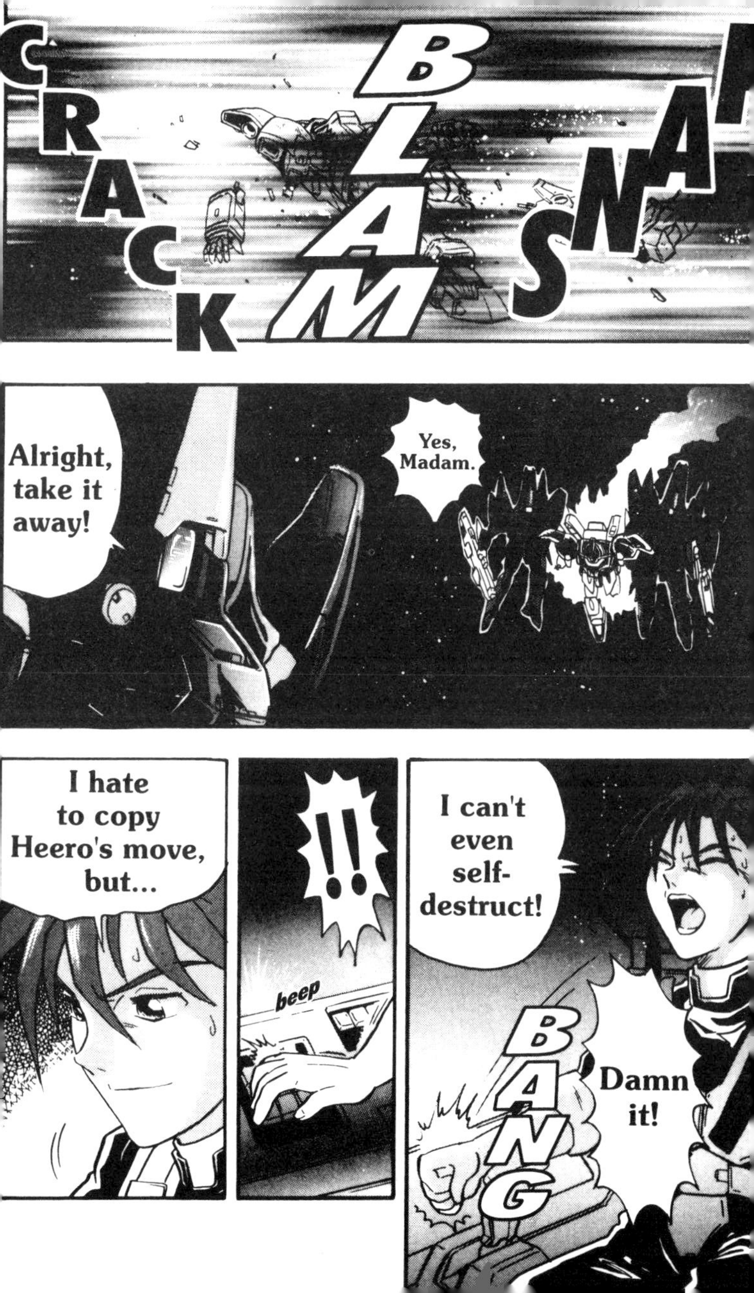
CRACK
BLAM
SNA
Alright, take it away!
Yes, Madam.
I hate to copy Heero's move, but...
!!
beep
I can't even self-destruct!
BANG
Damn it!

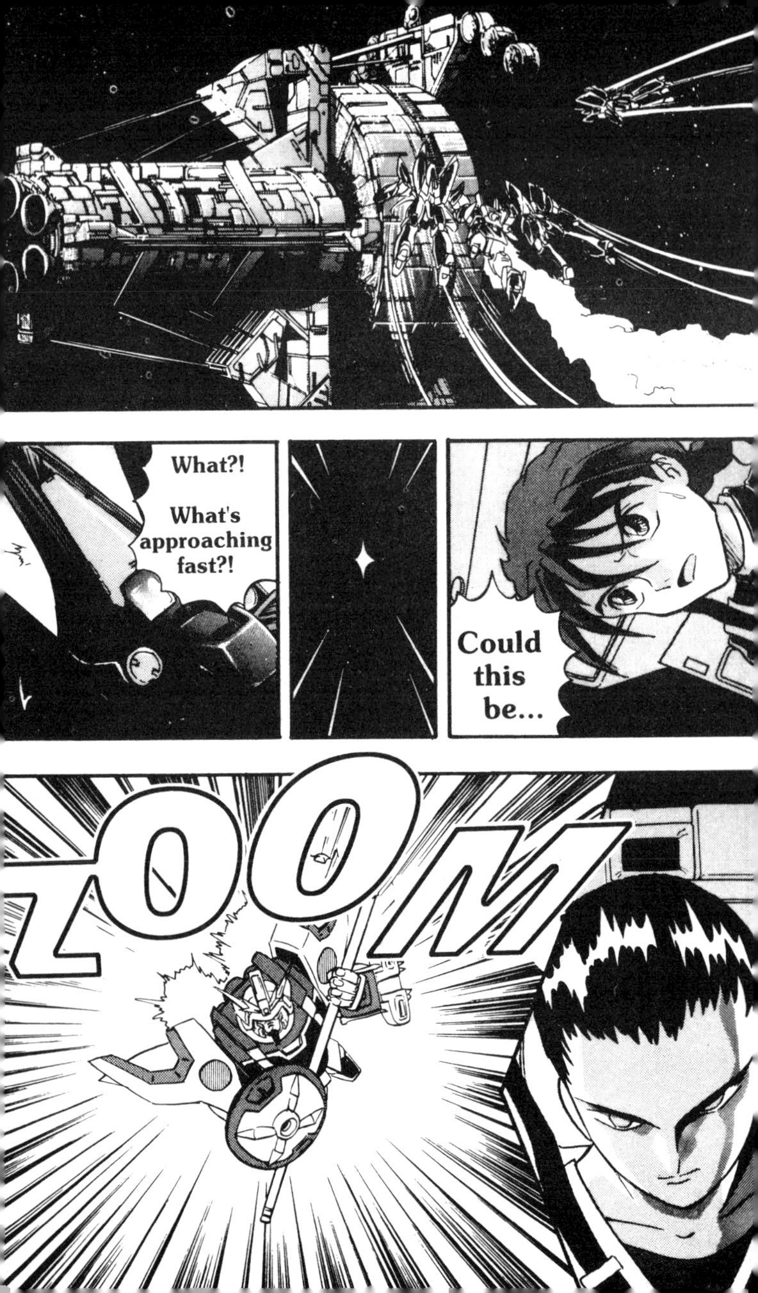
What?!
What's approaching fast?!
Could this be...
ZOOM

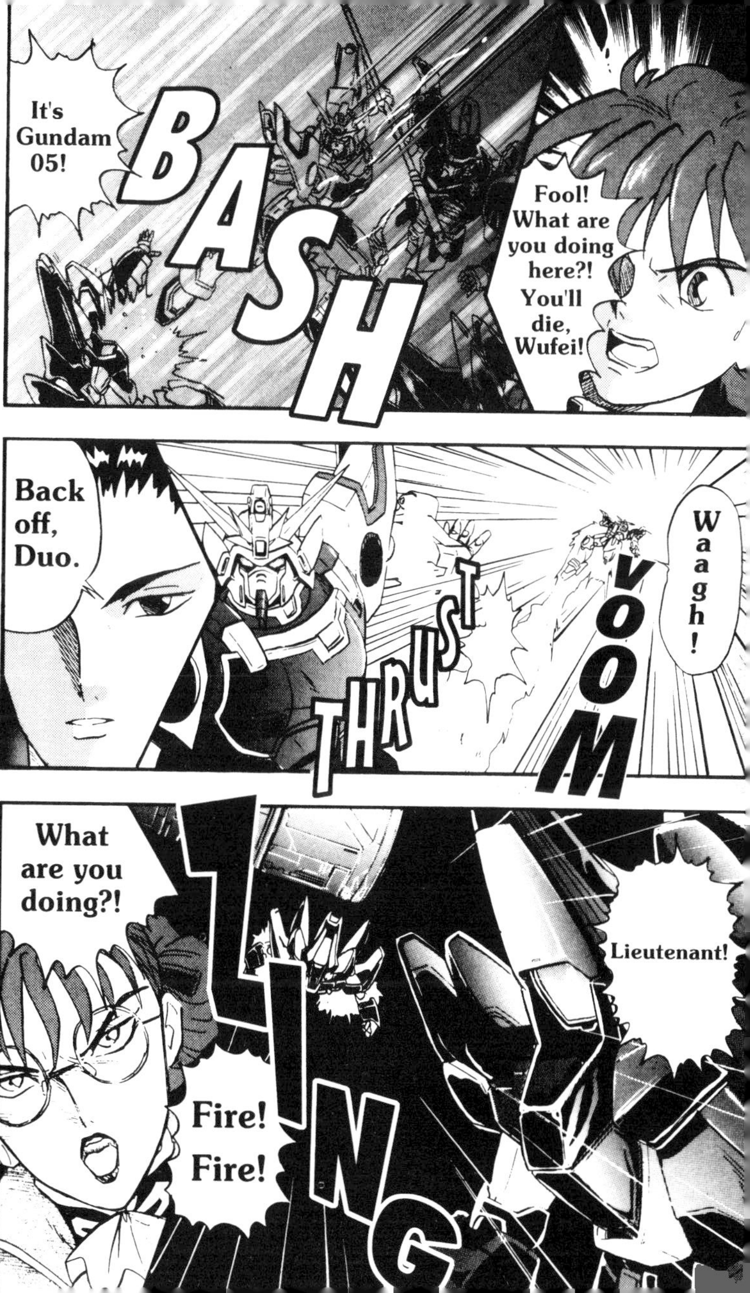
It's Gundam 05!
BASH
Fool! What are you doing here?! You'll die, Wufei!
Back off, Duo.
THRUST
VOOM
Waagh!
What are you doing?!
LING
Lieutenant!
Fire! Fire!
NG

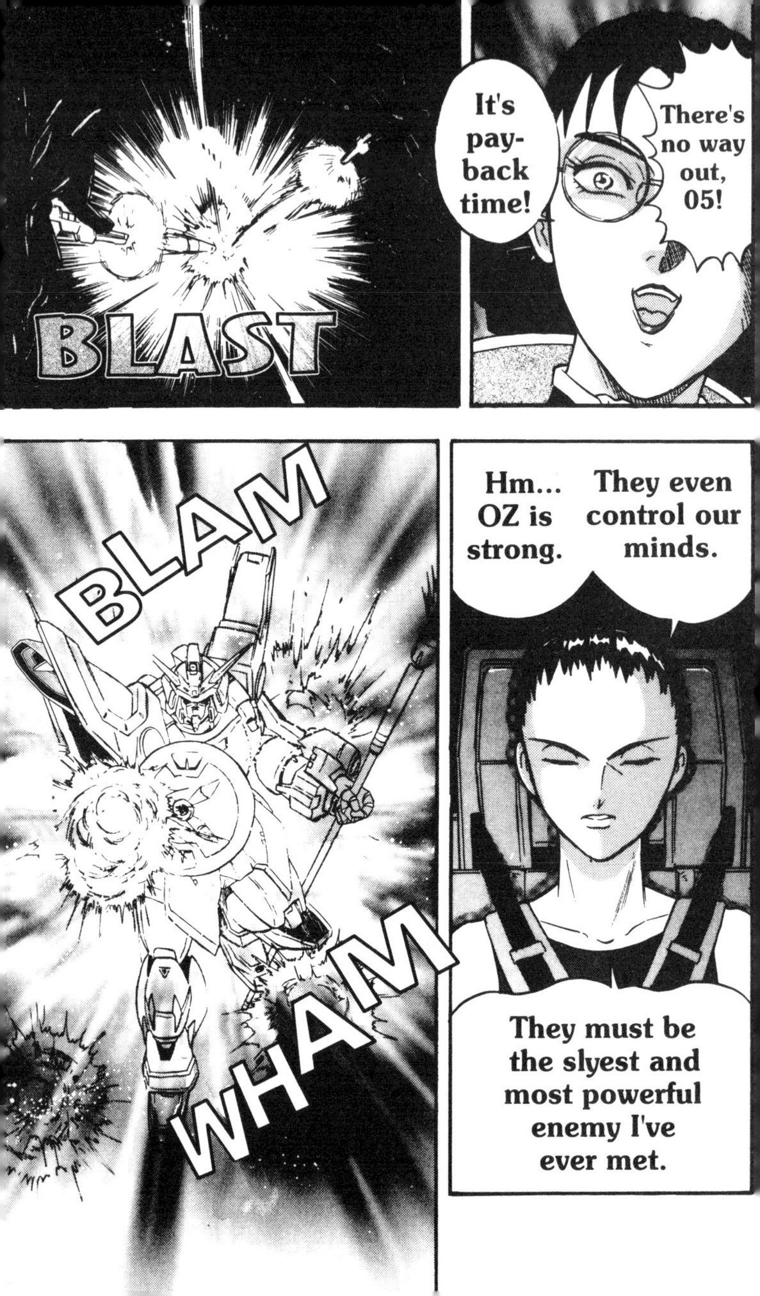
BLAST
It's pay-back time!
There's no way out, 05!
BLAM
WHAM
Hm... OZ is strong.
They even control our minds.
They must be the slyest and most powerful enemy I've ever met.

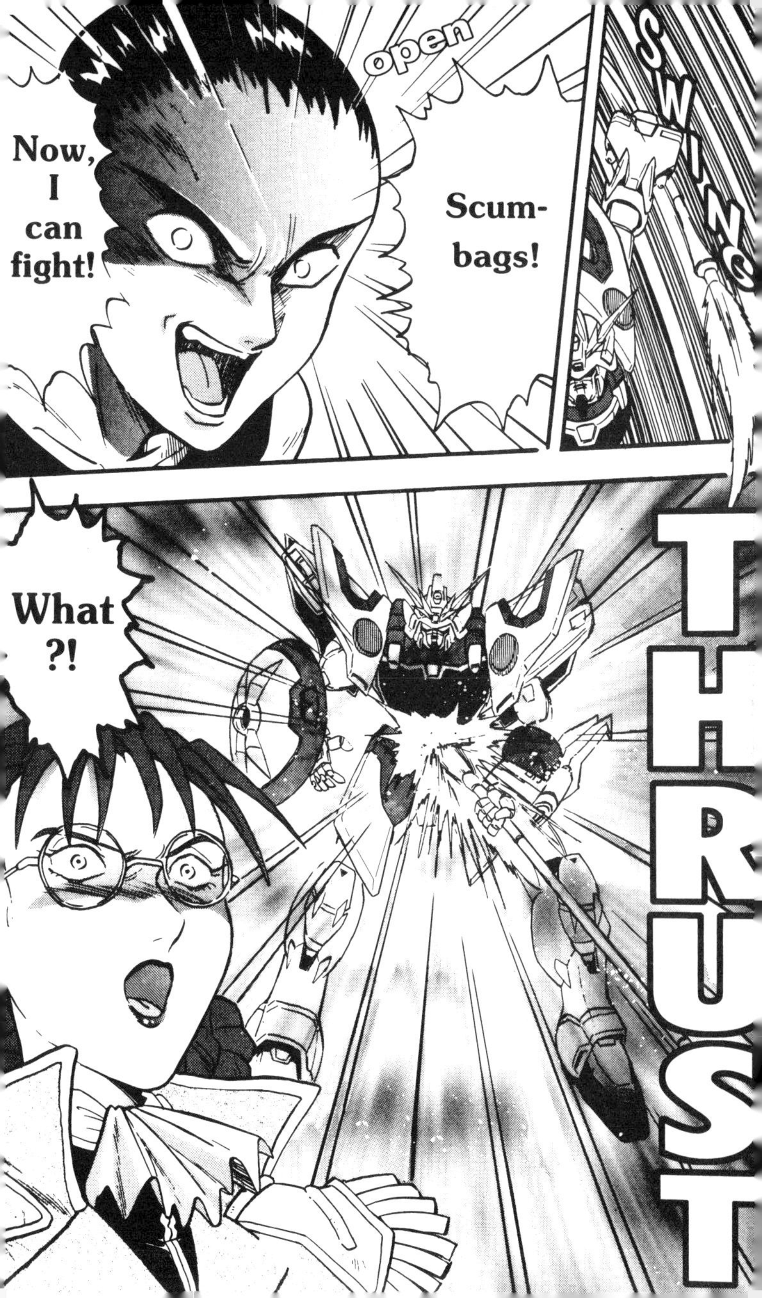

Now, I can fight!
open
Scum-bags!
SWING
What ?!
THRUST

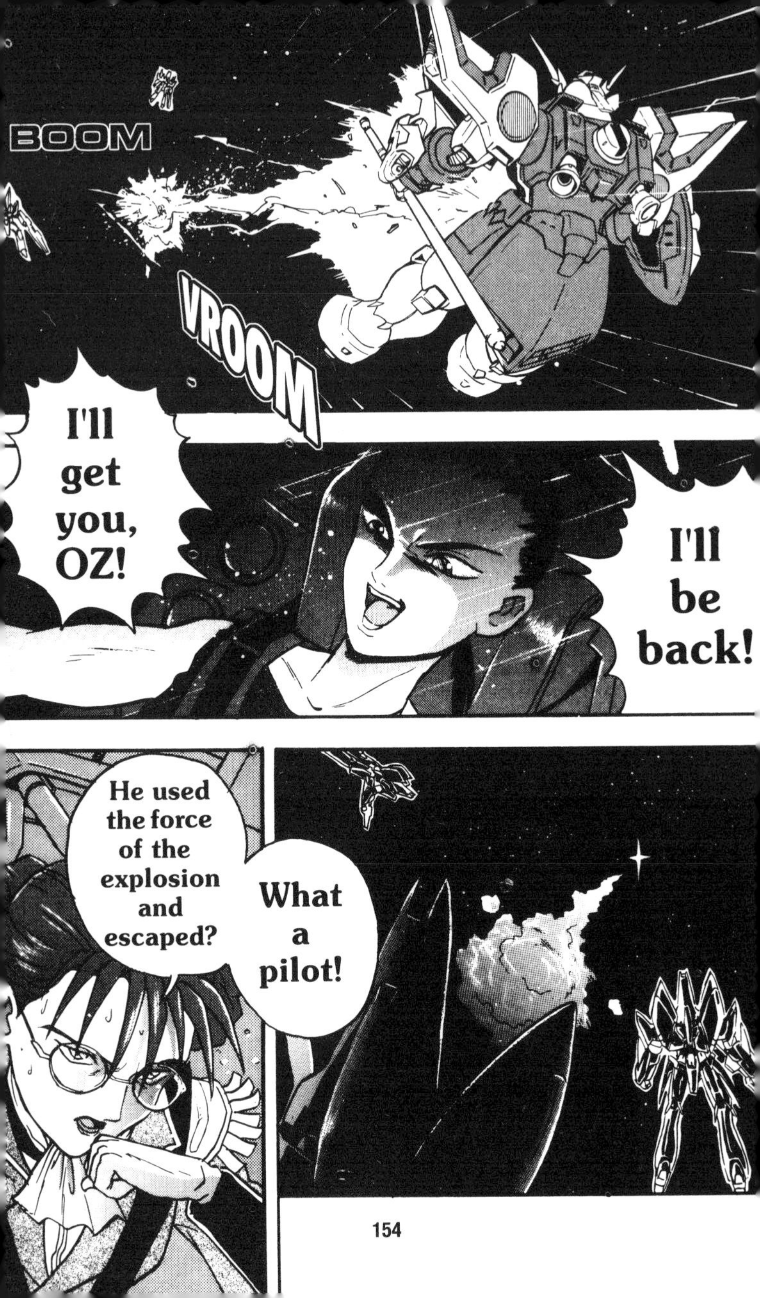
BOOM
VROOM
I'll get you, OZ!
I'll be back!
He used the force of the explosion and escaped?
What a pilot!

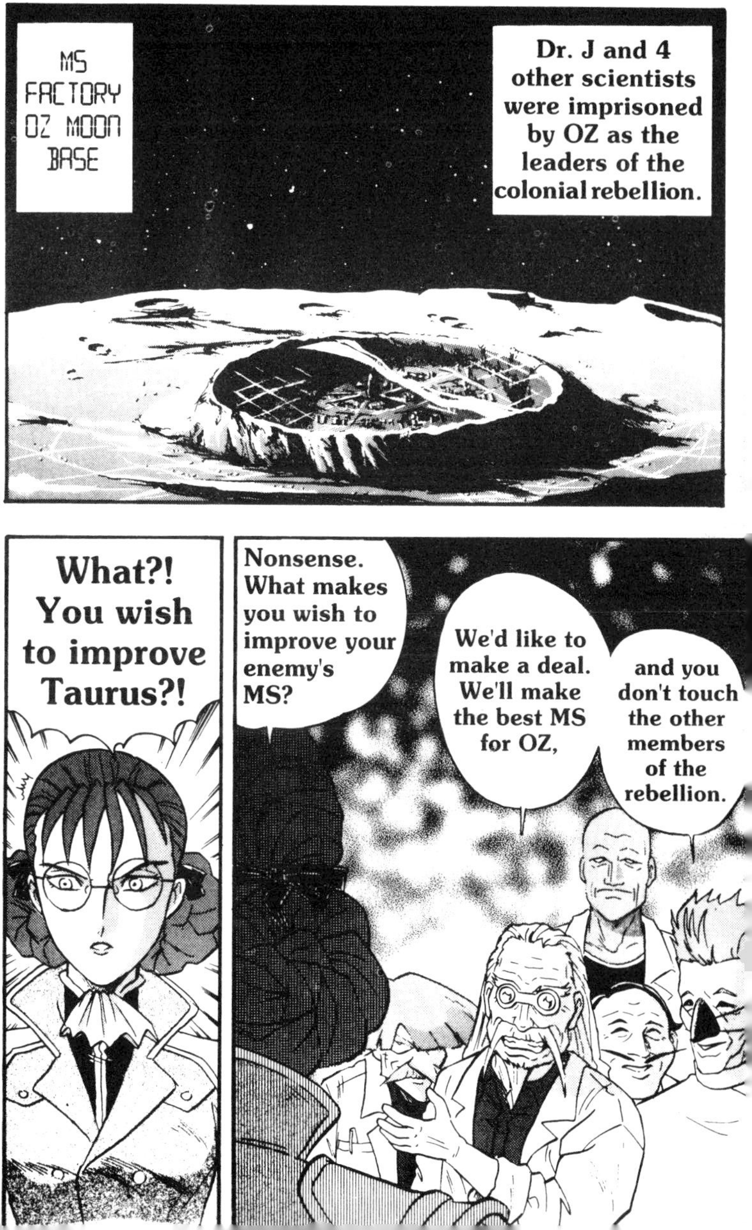
MS FACTORY OZ MOON BASE
Dr. J and 4 other scientists were imprisoned by OZ as the leaders of the colonial rebellion.
What?! You wish to improve Taurus?!
Nonsense. What makes you wish to improve your enemy's MS?
We'd like to make a deal. We'll make the best MS for OZ,
and you don't touch the other members of the rebellion.

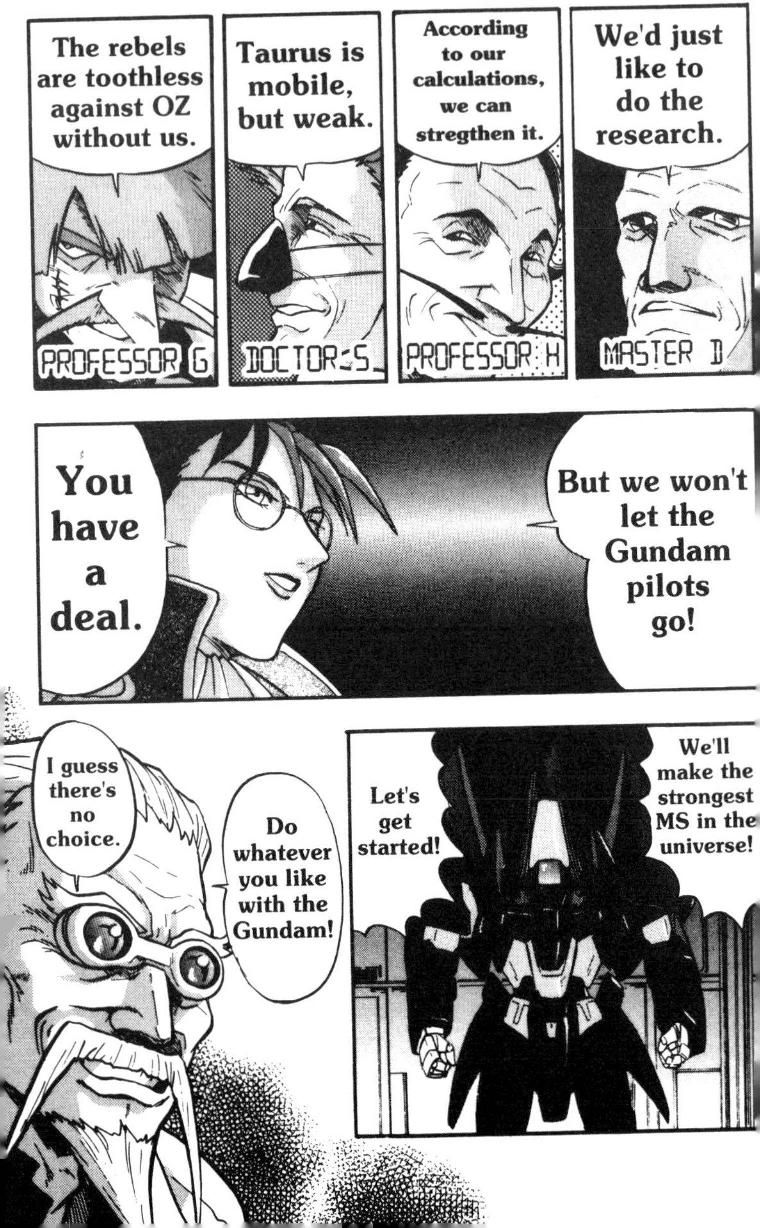
The rebels are toothless against OZ without us.
PROFESSOR G
Taurus is mobile, but weak.
DOCTOR S
According to our calculations, we can stregthen it.
PROFESSOR H
We'd just like to do the research.
MASTER D
You have a deal.
But we won't let the Gundam pilots go!
I guess there's no choice.
Do whatever you like with the Gundam!
Let's get started!
We'll make the strongest MS in the universe!

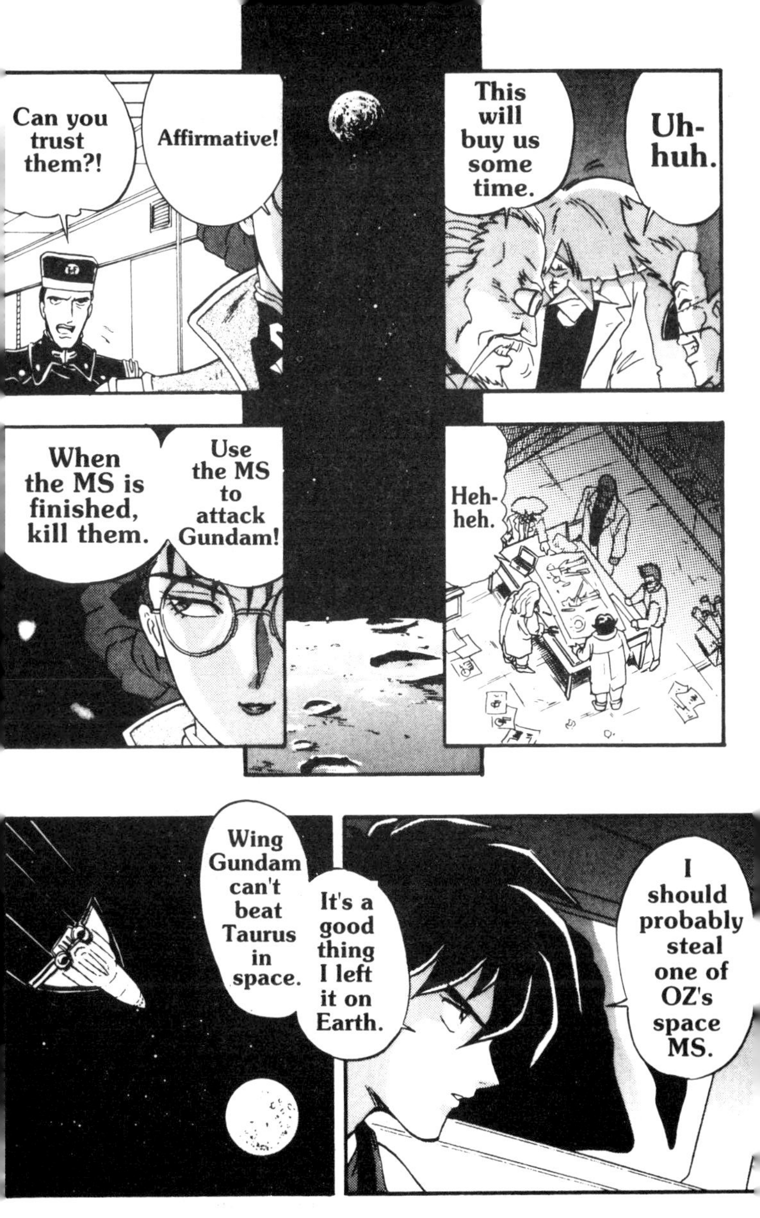
Can you trust them?!
Affirmative!
When the MS is finished, kill them.
Use the MS to attack Gundam!
This will buy us some time.
Uh-huh.
Heh-heh.
Wing Gundam can't beat Taurus in space.
It's a good thing I left it on Earth.
I should probably steal one of OZ's space MS.

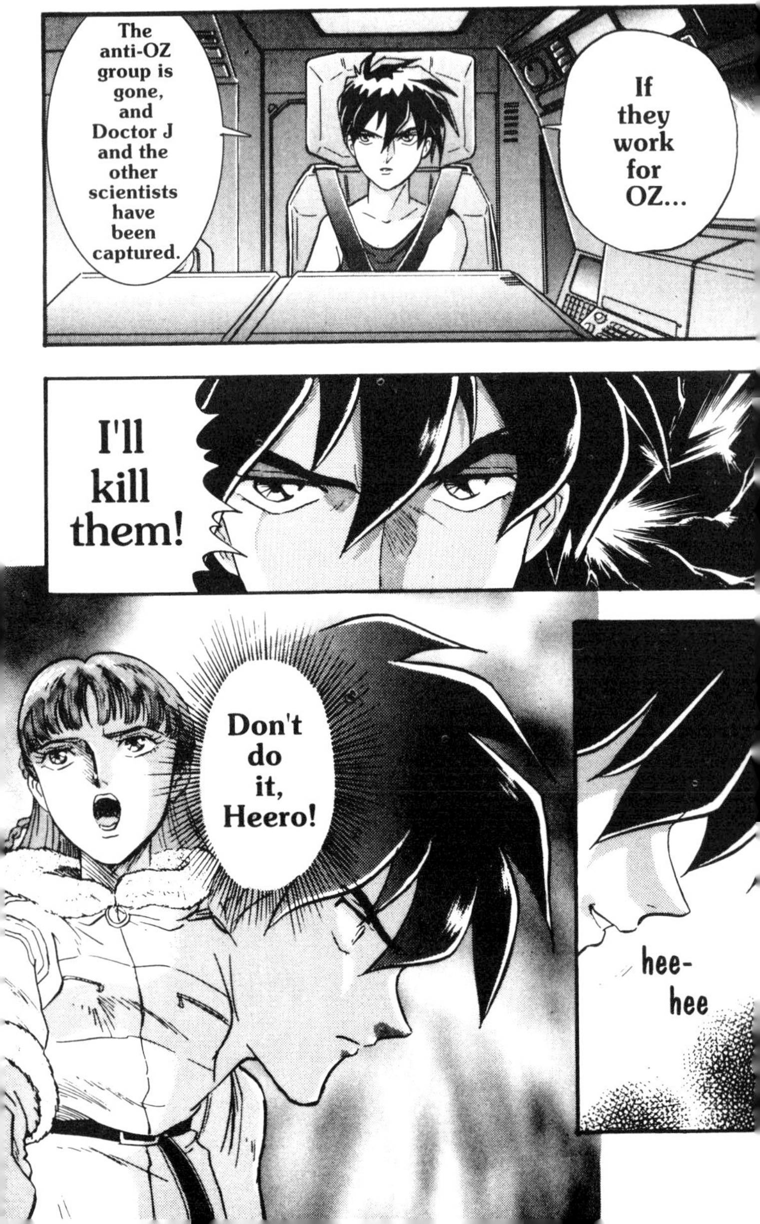
The anti-OZ group is gone, and Doctor J and the other scientists have been captured.
If they work for OZ...
I'll kill them!
Don't do it, Heero!
hee-hee

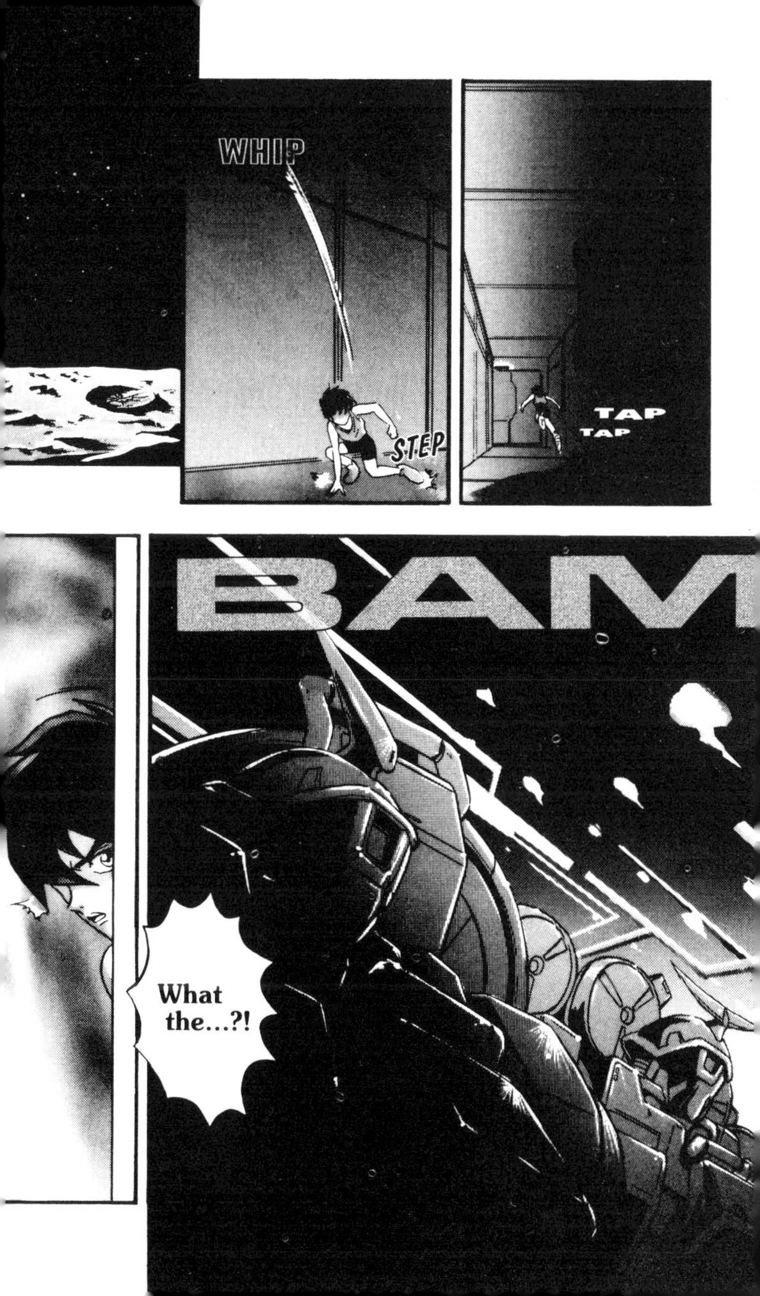
WHIP
STEP
TAP
TAP
BAM
What the...?!

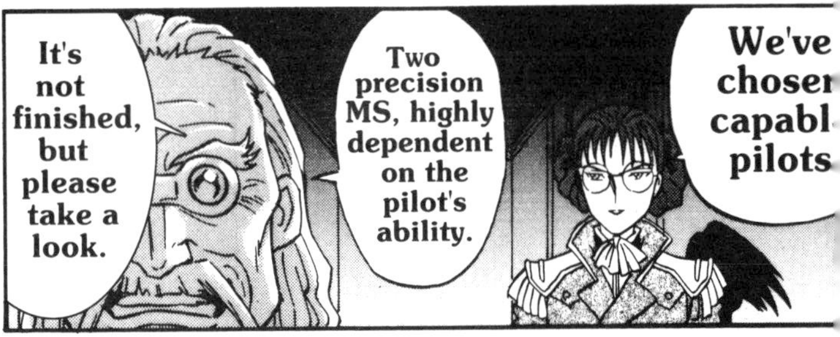
It's not finished, but please take a look.
Two precision MS, highly dependent on the pilot's ability.
We've choser capabl pilots

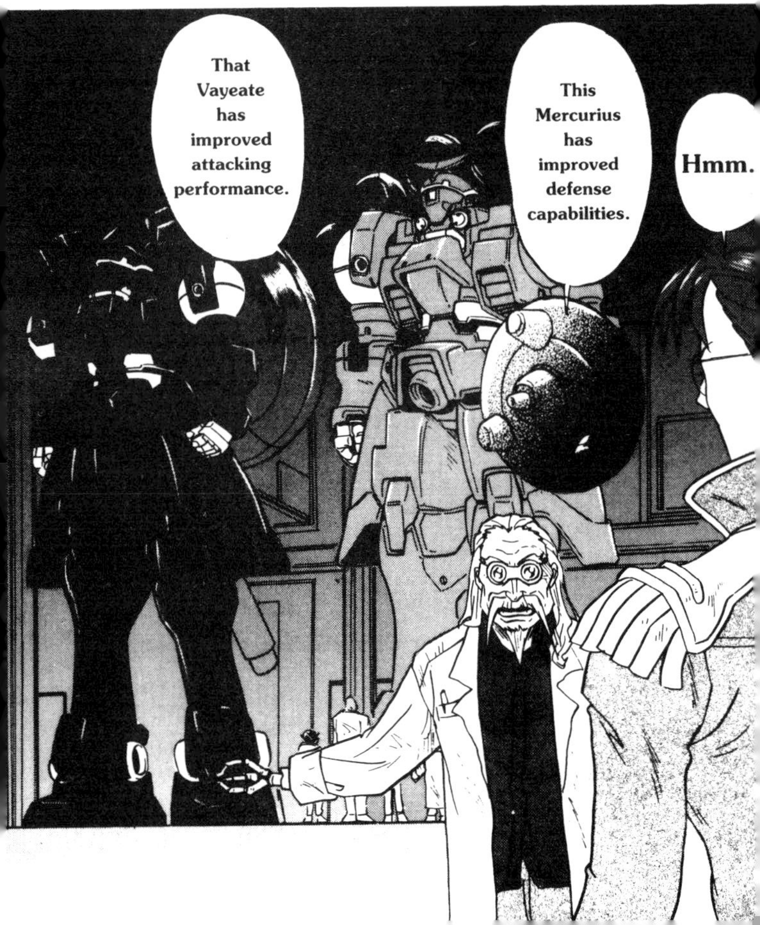
That Vayeate has improved attacking performance.
This Mercurius has improved defense capabilities.
Hmm.

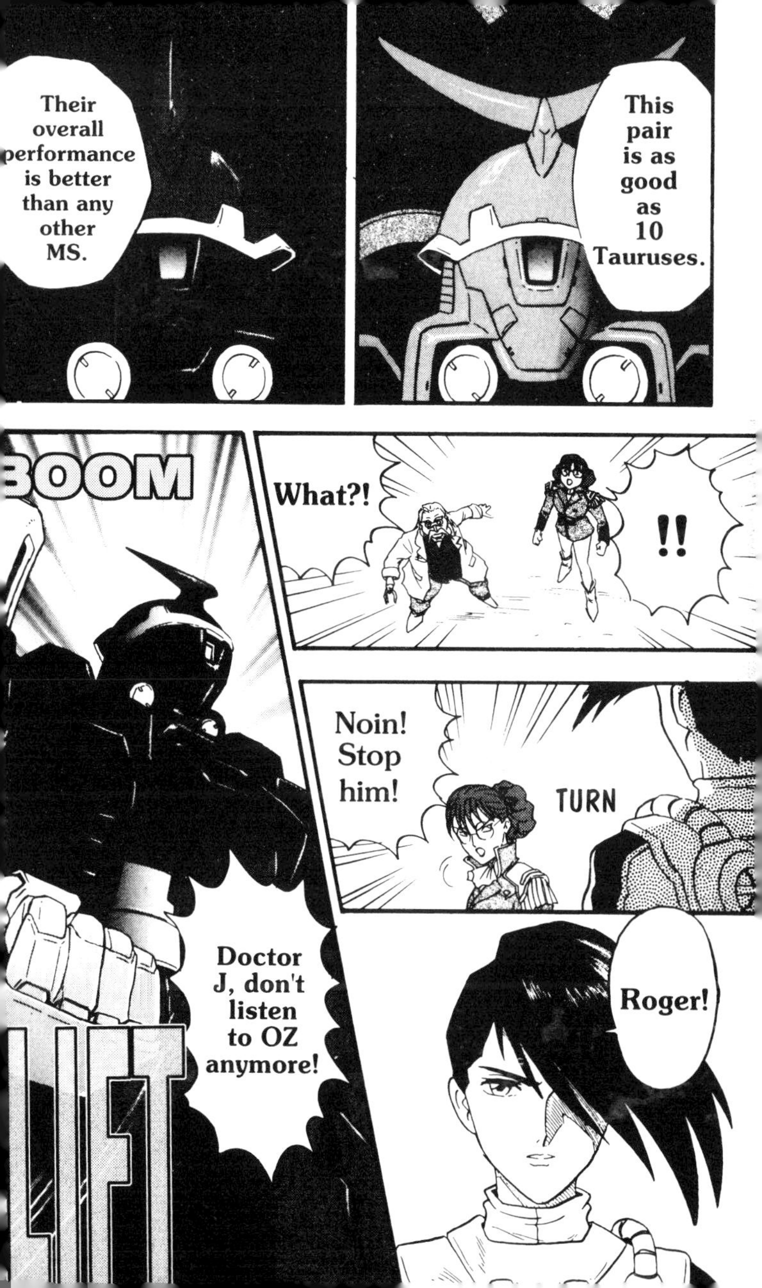
Their overall performance is better than any other MS.
This pair is as good as 10 Tauruses.
BOOM
What?!
!!
Noin! Stop him!
TURN
Doctor J, don't listen to OZ anymore!
LIFT
Roger!

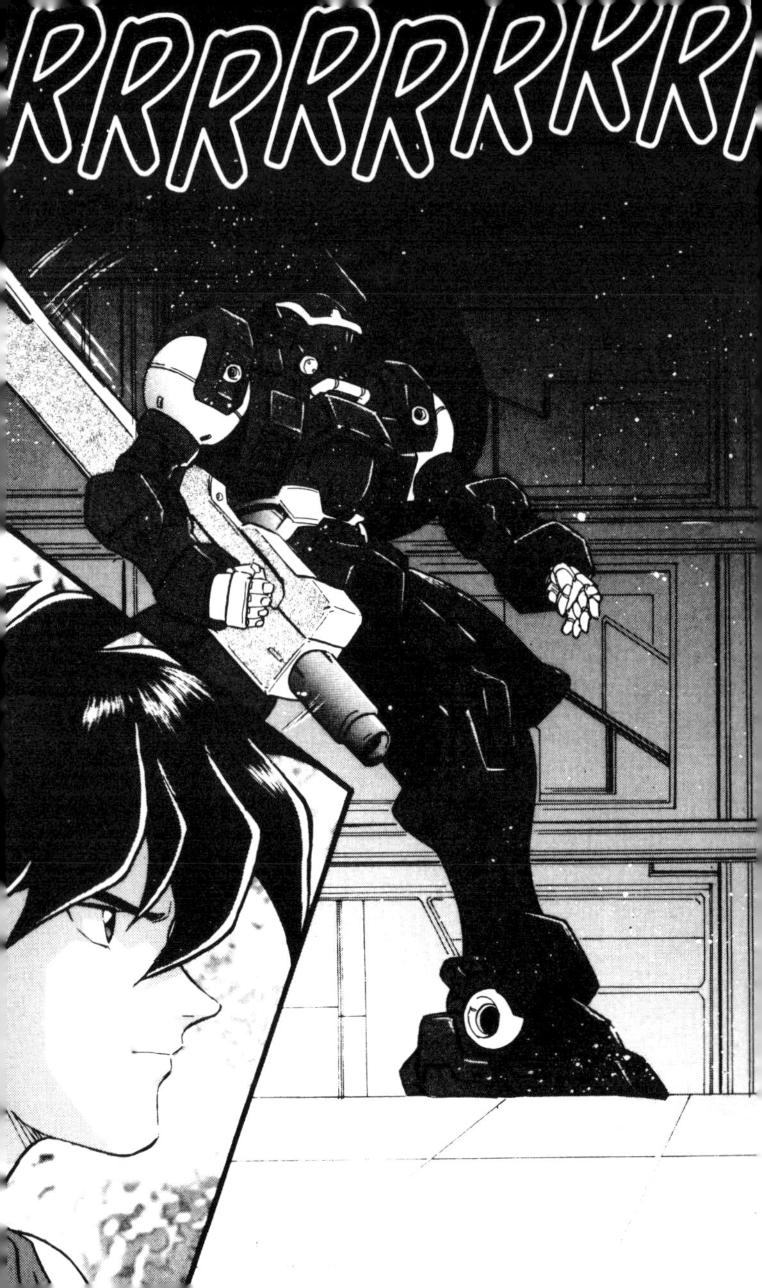
RRRRRRKRI

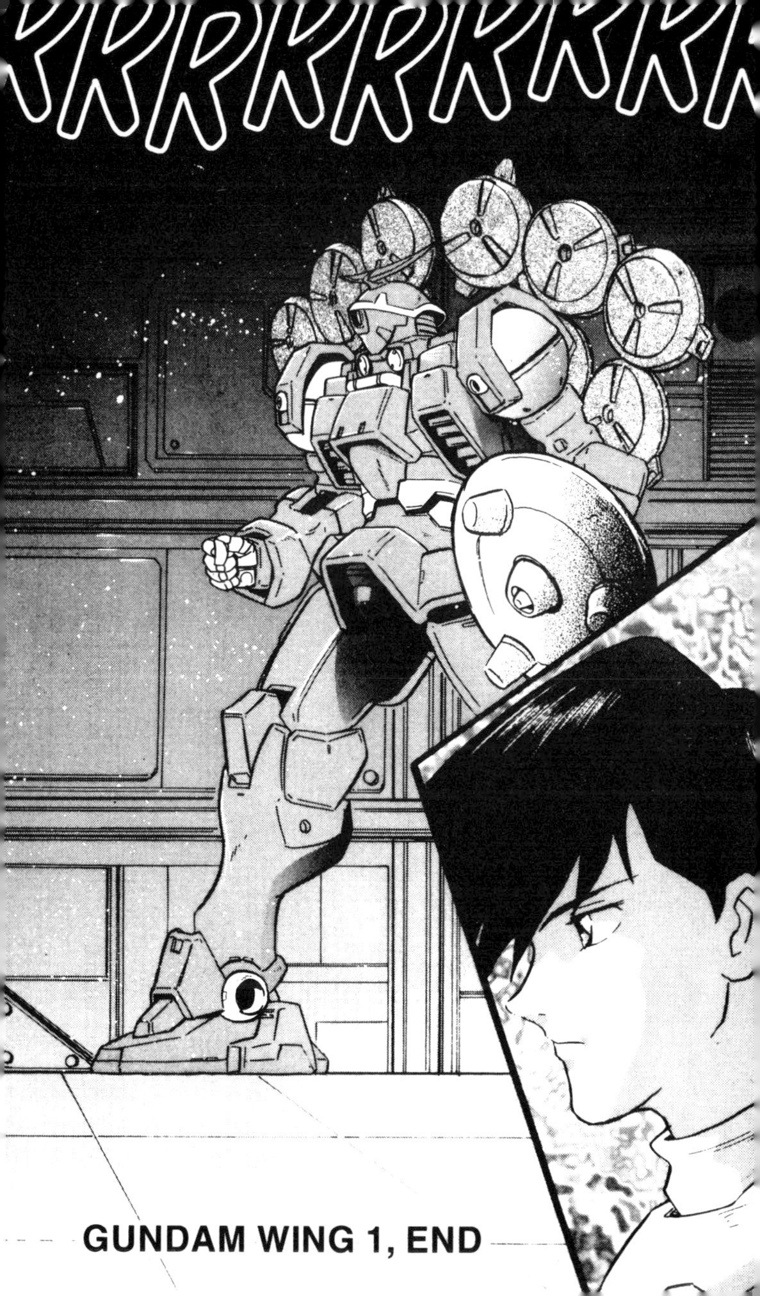
RRRRRRRRR

GUNDAM WING 1, END

Mobile Battle Chronicle G Gundam & New Mobile Battle Chronicle Gundam Wing

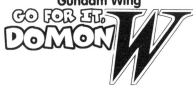

GO FOR IT, DOMON W

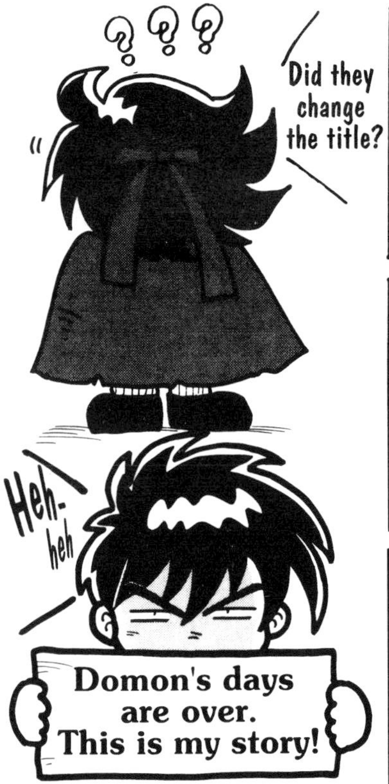

Did they change the title?
Heh-heh
Domon's days are over. This is my story!

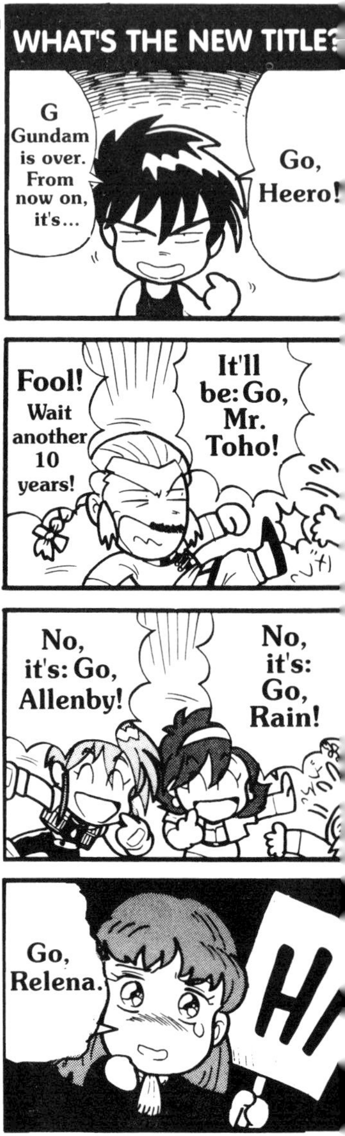

WHAT'S THE NEW TITLE?
G Gundam is over. From now on, it's...
Go, Heero!
Fool! Wait another 10 years!
It'll be: Go, Mr. Toho!
No, it's: Go, Allenby!
No, it's: Go, Rain!
Go, Relena.

ONE MORE TIME ON VIDEO

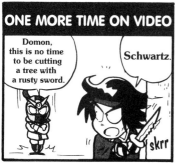

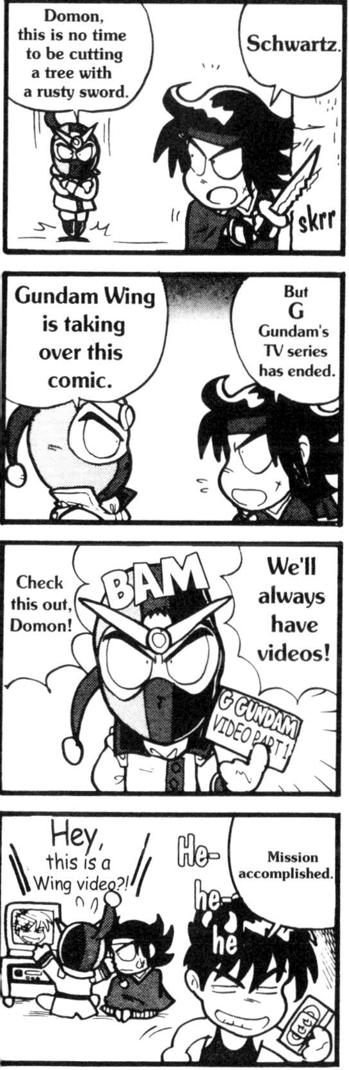
Domon, this is no time to be cutting a tree with a rusty sword.
Schwartz.
skrr
Gundam Wing is taking over this comic.
But G Gundam's TV series has ended.
Check this out, Domon!
BAM
We'll always have videos!
G GUNDAM VIDEO PART 1
Hey, this is a Wing video?!
He- he- he
Mission accomplished.

HEERO'S MISSION

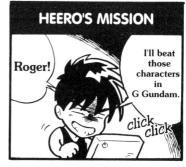

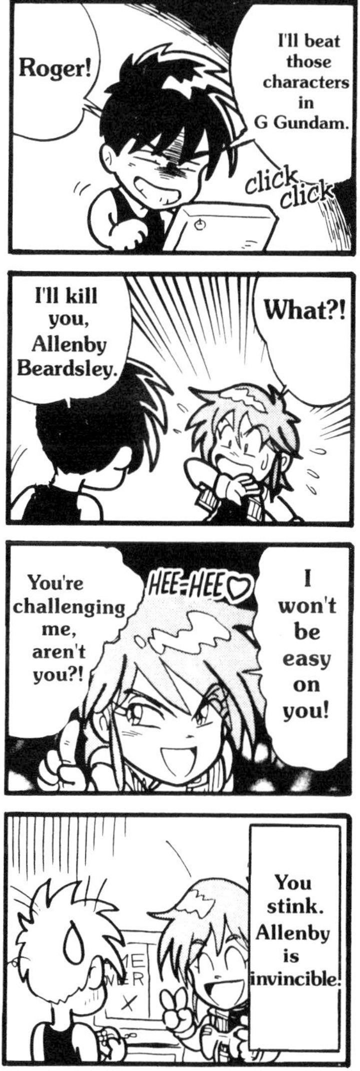
Roger!
I'll beat those characters in G Gundam.
click click
I'll kill you, Allenby Beardsley.
What?!
You're challenging me, aren't you?!
HEE-HEE♡
I won't be easy on you!
You stink. Allenby is invincible.

NEW SONG RELEASE

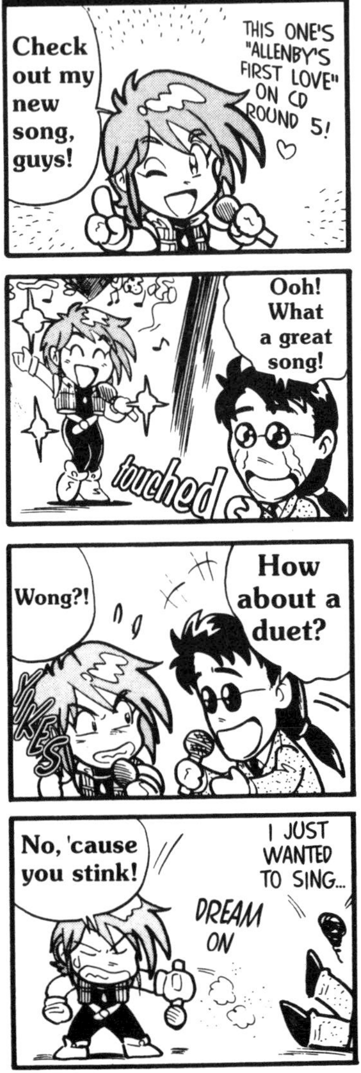
Check out my new song, guys!
THIS ONE'S "ALLENBY'S FIRST LOVE" ON CD ROUND 5! ♡
Ooh! What a great song!
touched
Wong?!
How about a duet?
YIKES
No, 'cause you stink!
I JUST WANTED TO SING...
DREAM ON

SELF-INTRODUCTION

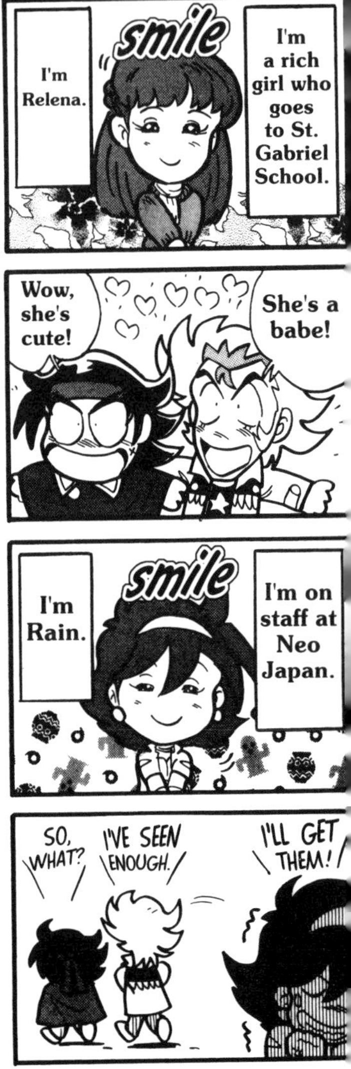
smile
I'm Relena.
I'm a rich girl who goes to St. Gabriel School.
Wow, she's cute!
She's a babe!
smile
I'm Rain.
I'm on staff at Neo Japan.
SO, WHAT?
I'VE SEEN ENOUGH.
I'LL GET THEM!

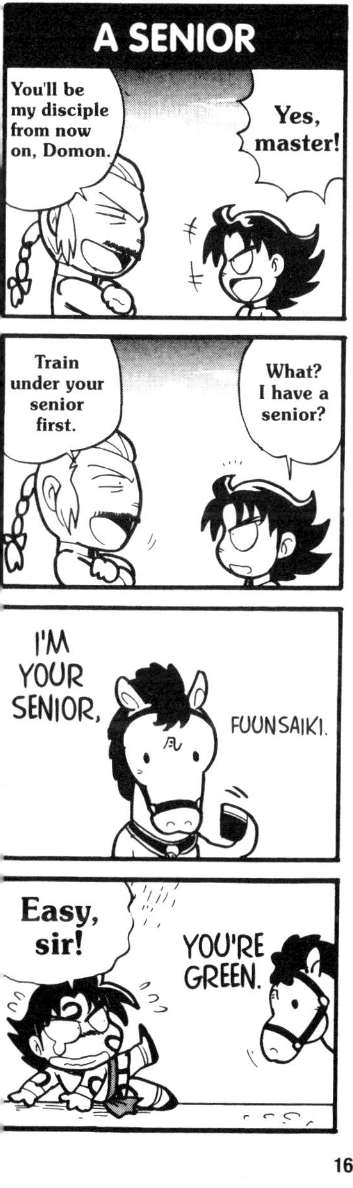
A SENIOR
You'll be my disciple from now on, Domon.
Yes, master!
Train under your senior first.
What? I have a senior?
I'M YOUR SENIOR,
FUUNSAIKI.
Easy, sir!
YOU'RE GREEN.

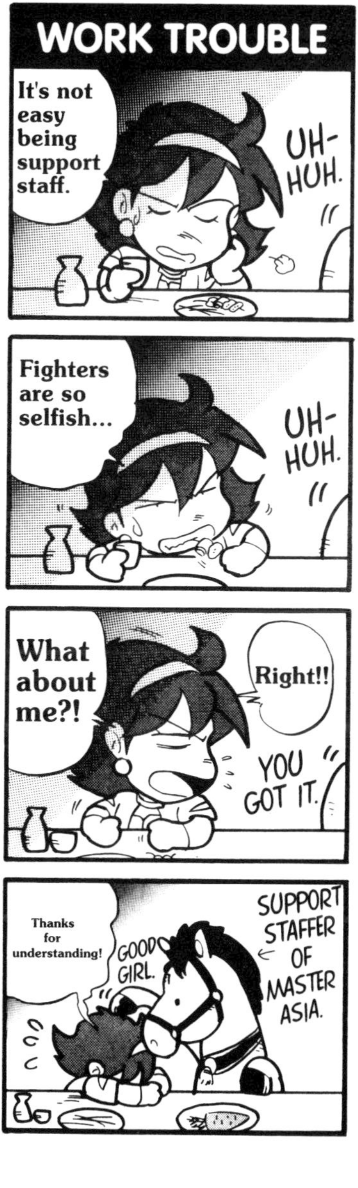
WORK TROUBLE
It's not easy being support staff.
UH-HUH.
Fighters are so selfish...
UH-HUH.
What about me?!
Right!!
YOU GOT IT.
Thanks for understanding!
GOOD GIRL.
SUPPORT STAFFER OF MASTER ASIA.

GO NETHER BROTHERS

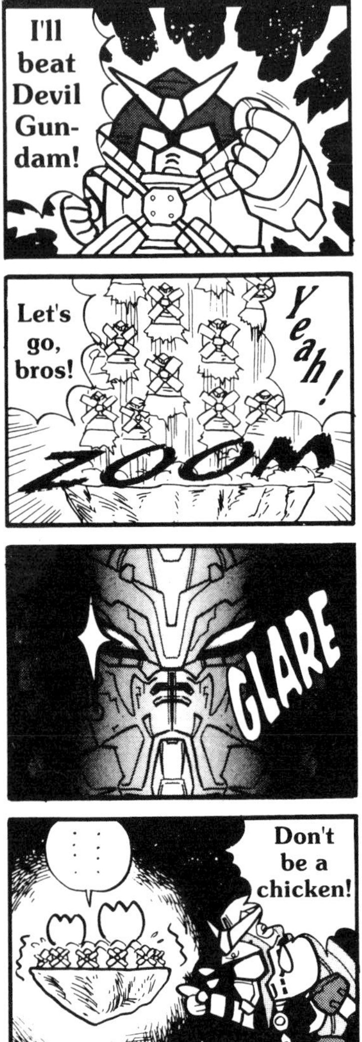
I'll beat Devil Gun-dam!
Let's go, bros!
Yeah!
ZOOM
GLARE
. . . . . .
Don't be a chicken!

GIRLS' POPULARITY CONTEST

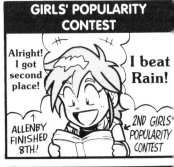

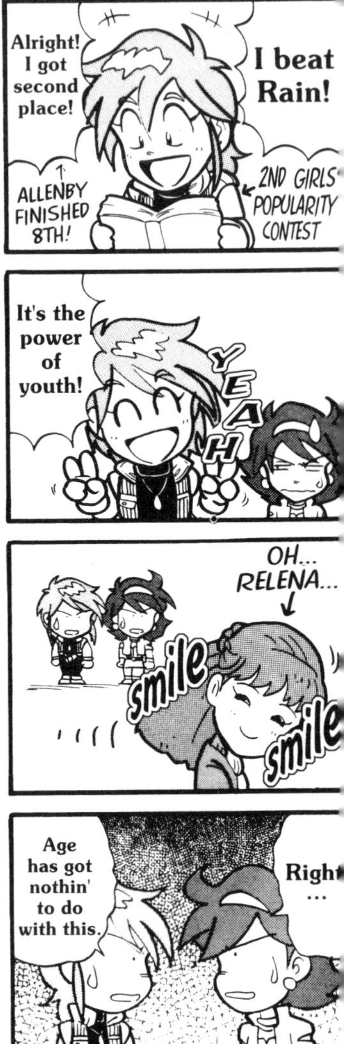
Alright! I got second place!
I beat Rain!
ALLENBY FINISHED 8TH!
2ND GIRLS' POPULARITY CONTEST
It's the power of youth!
YEAH
OH... RELENA...
smile
smile
Age has got nothin' to do with this.
Right ...

Mobile Battle Chronicle G Gundam & New Mobile Battle Chronicle Gundam Wing

GO FOR IT, DOMON W

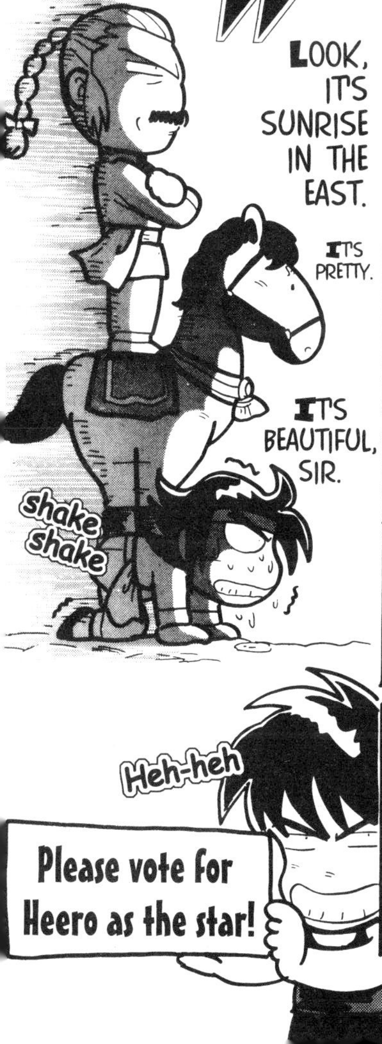
LOOK, IT'S SUNRISE IN THE EAST.
IT'S PRETTY.
IT'S BEAUTIFUL, SIR.
shake shake
Heh-heh
Please vote for Heero as the star!

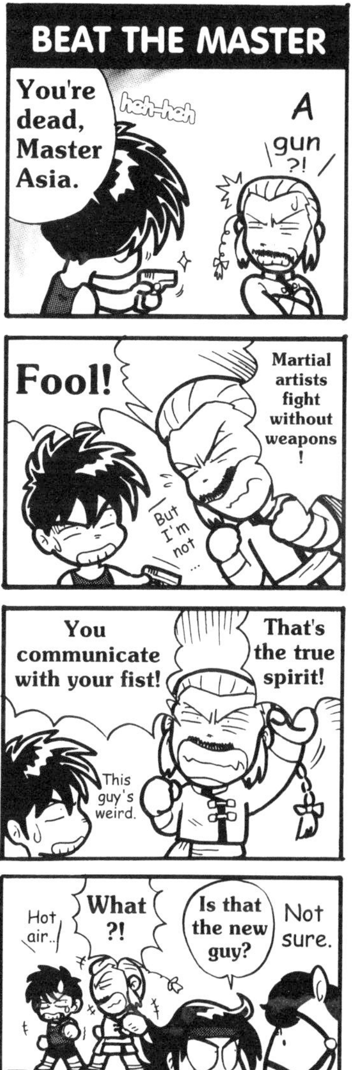
BEAT THE MASTER
You're dead, Master Asia.
heh-heh
A gun ?!
Fool!
Martial artists fight without weapons!
But I'm not ...
You communicate with your fist!
That's the true spirit!
This guy's weird.
Hot air..
What ?!
Is that the new guy?
Not sure.

PRACTICE JOURNEY

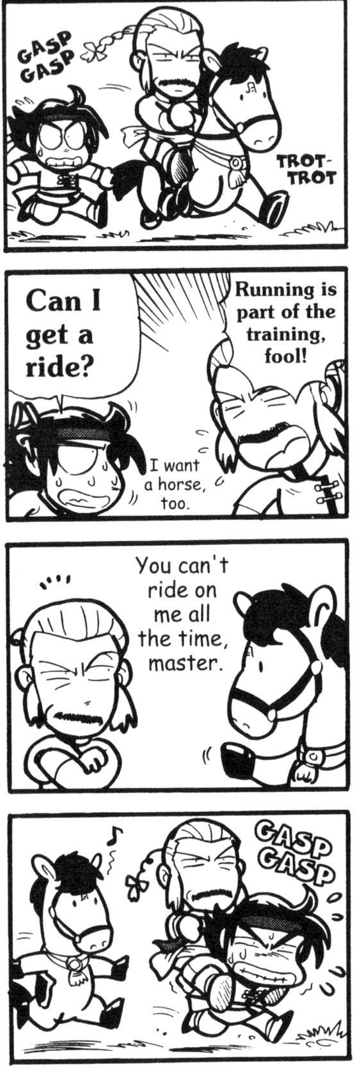
GASP GASP
TROT-TROT
Can I get a ride?
Running is part of the training, fool!
I want a horse, too.
You can't ride on me all the time, master.
GASP GASP

X'S SECRET

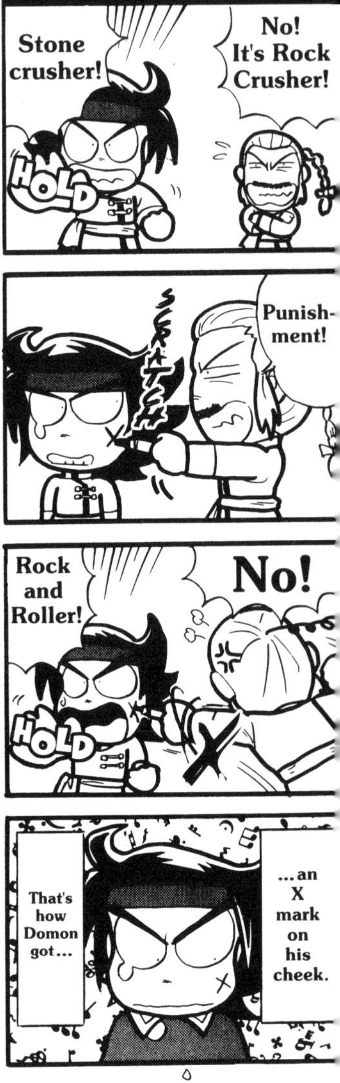
Stone crusher!
No! It's Rock Crusher!
HOLD
SCRATCH
Punish-ment!
Rock and Roller!
No!
HOLD
That's how Domon got...
...an X mark on his cheek.

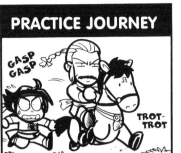

ULTIMATE TECHNIQUE

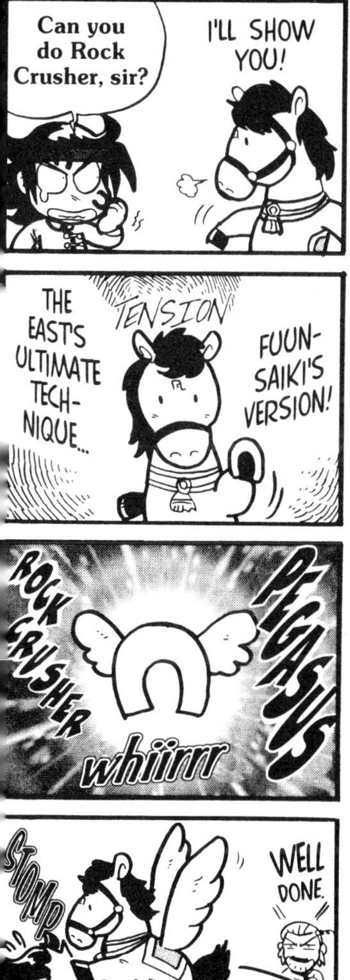
Can you do Rock Crusher, sir?
I'LL SHOW YOU!
THE EAST'S ULTIMATE TECH-NIQUE...
TENSION
FUUN-SAIKI'S VERSION!
ROCK CRUSHER
PEGASUS
whiirrr
STOMP
WELL DONE.
<—blow

LOVE PEGASUS

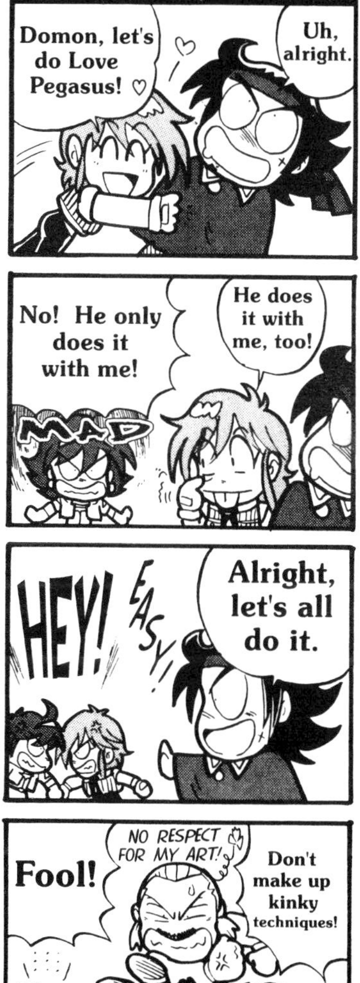
Domon, let's do Love Pegasus! ♡
Uh, alright.
No! He only does it with me!
He does it with me, too!
MAD
HEY!
EASY!
Alright, let's all do it.
NO RESPECT FOR MY ART!
Fool!
Don't make up kinky techniques!

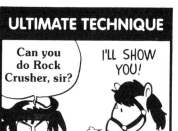

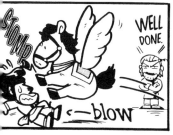

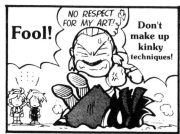

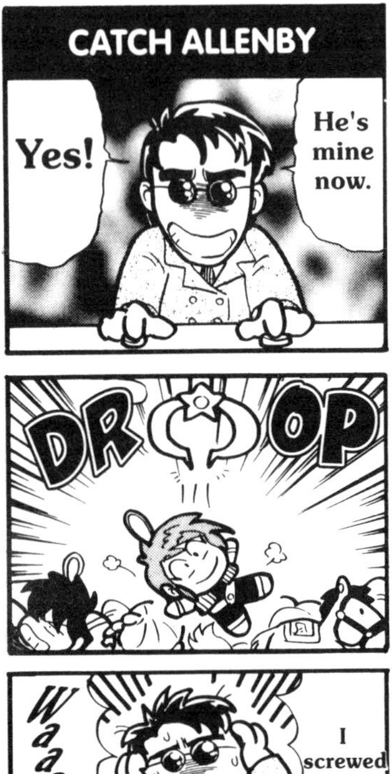
CATCH ALLENBY
Yes!
He's mine now.
DROP
Waaaagh!
I screwed up again!
Another quarter.
WHEE
Just buy the whole arcade, rich guy.

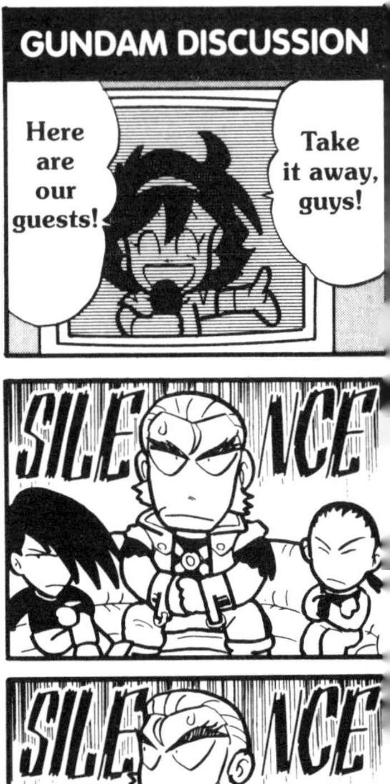
GUNDAM DISCUSSION
Here are our guests!
Take it away, guys!
SILENCE
SILENCE
Who booked those guys?!
THEY'RE ALL DUMB!
HEE-HEE

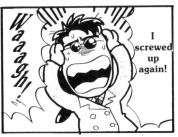

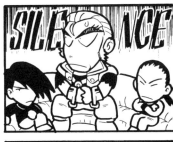

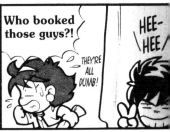

TRANSFER STUDENTS

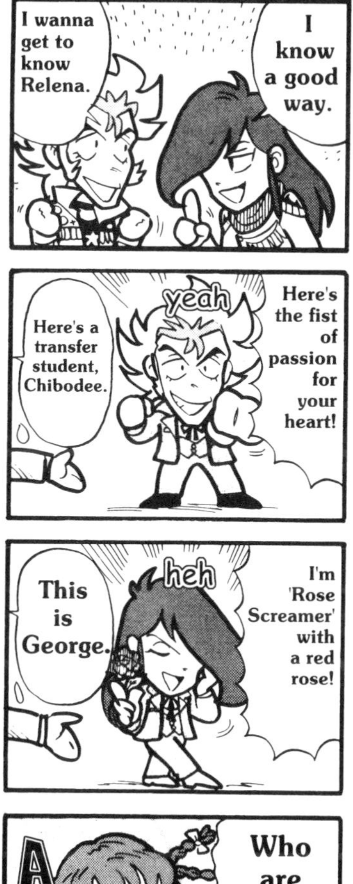
I wanna get to know Relena.
I know a good way.
yeah
Here's a transfer student, Chibodee.
Here's the fist of passion for your heart!
heh
This is George.
I'm 'Rose Screamer' with a red rose!
AIEEE
Who are these freaks?!
A bunch of weirdos.

PRINCE OF THE STAR

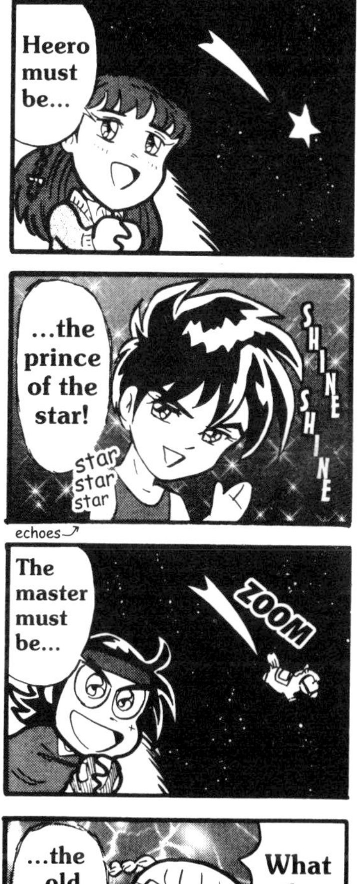
Heero must be...
...the prince of the star!
SHINE SHINE
star star star
echoes
The master must be...
ZOOM
...the old man of the star!
What the heck?!
old man old man old man

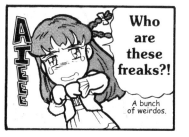

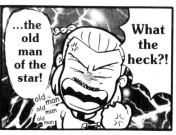

Mobile Battle Chronicle G Gundam
&
New Mobile Battle Chronicle Gundam Wing

GO FOR IT, DOMON W

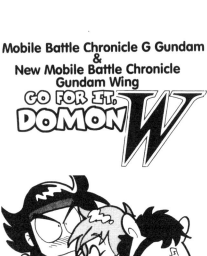

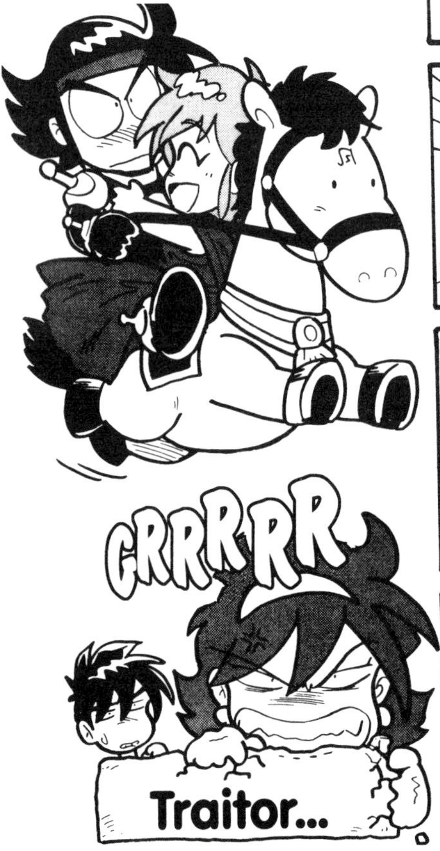
GRRRRR
Traitor...

BLOOPER OF THE MONTH

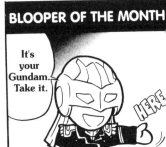

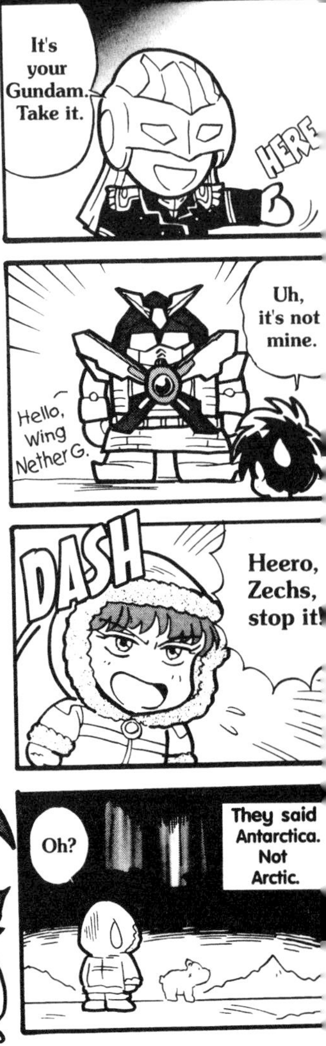
It's your Gundam. Take it.
HERE
Hello, Wing Nether G.
Uh, it's not mine.
DASH
Heero, Zechs, stop it!
Oh?
They said Antarctica. Not Arctic.

TRANSFORM! BIRD-MODE!

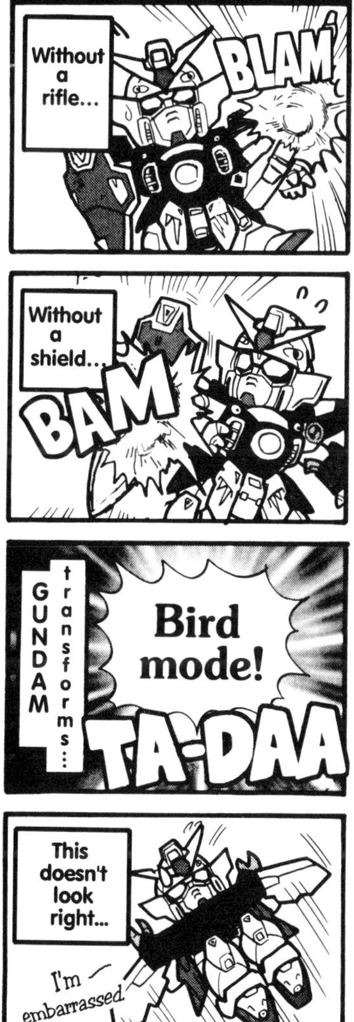
Without a rifle...
BLAM
Without a shield...
BAM
GUNDAM transforms...
Bird mode!
TA-DAA
This doesn't look right...
I'm embarrassed

BEAT SCHWARTZ

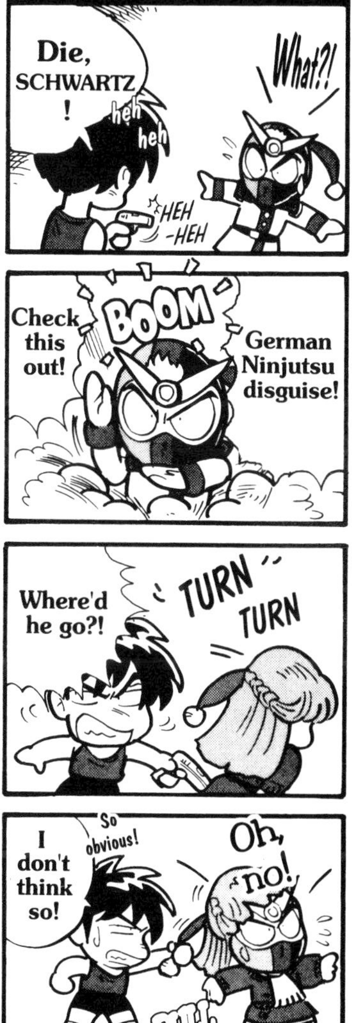
Die, SCHWARTZ!
heh heh
What?!
HEH -HEH
Check this out!
BOOM
German Ninjutsu disguise!
Where'd he go?!
TURN TURN
I don't think so!
So obvious!
Oh, no!
PULL

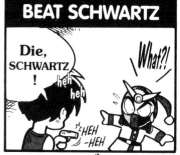

WRONG COCKPIT

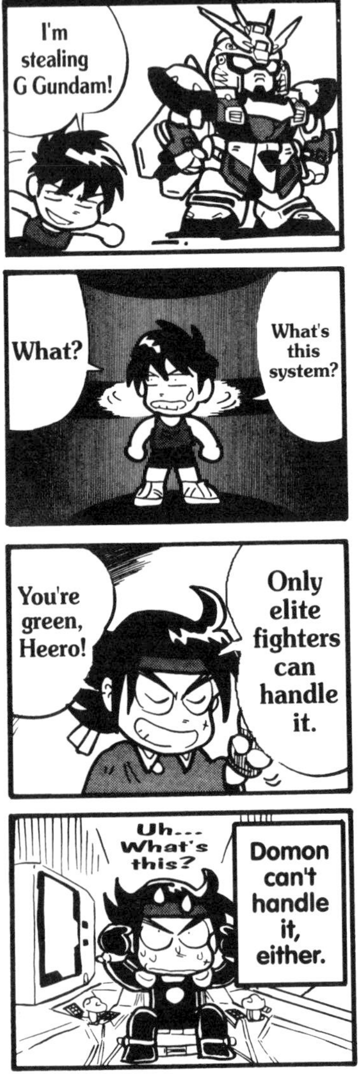
I'm stealing G Gundam!
What?
What's this system?
You're green, Heero!
Only elite fighters can handle it.
Uh... What's this?
Domon can't handle it, either.

HAPPY DUO

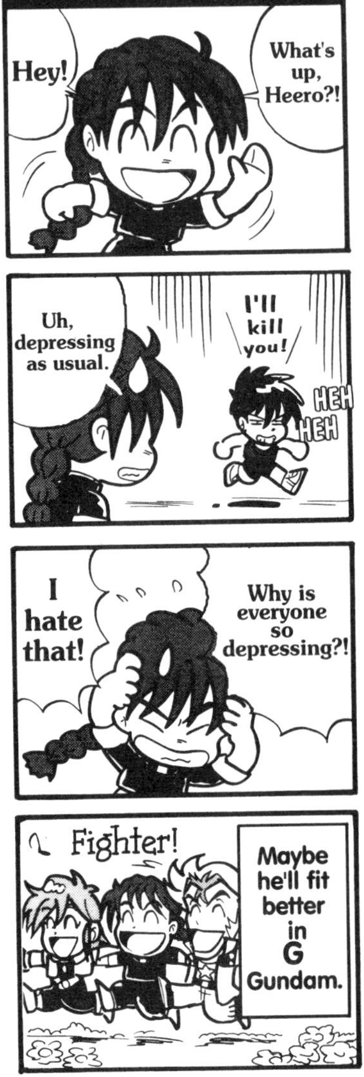
Hey!
What's up, Heero?!
Uh, depressing as usual.
I'll kill you!
HEH HEH
I hate that!
Why is everyone so depressing?!
Fighter!
Maybe he'll fit better in G Gundam.

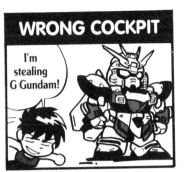

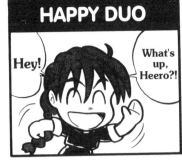

KIND RELENA

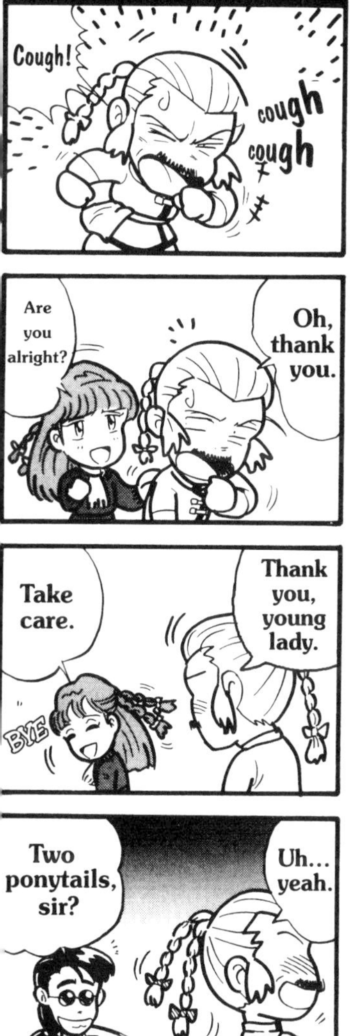
Cough!
cough
cough
Are you alright?
Oh, thank you.
Take care.
BYE
Thank you, young lady.
Two ponytails, sir?
Uh... yeah.

SUPER KING ELECTRIC

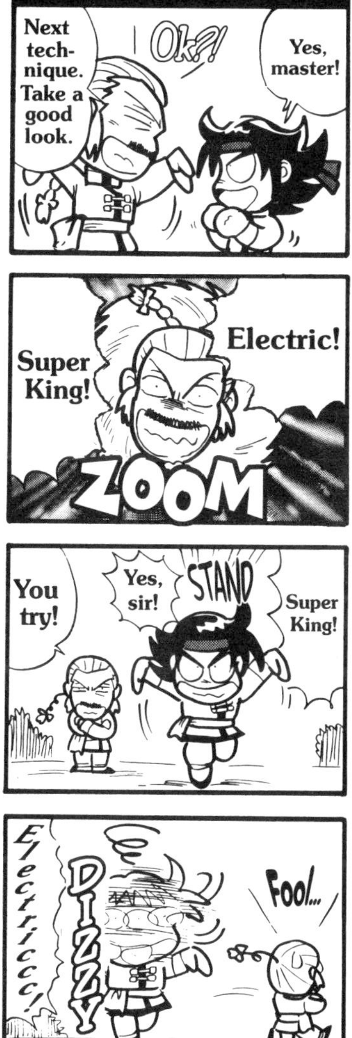
Next technique. Take a good look.
OK?!
Yes, master!
Super King!
Electric!
ZOOM
You try!
Yes, sir!
STAND
Super King!
Electriccc!
DIZZY
Fool...

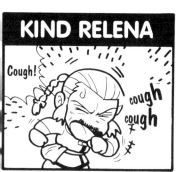

Mobile Battle Chronicle G Gundam
&
New Mobile Battle Chronicle
Gundam Wing

GO FOR IT, DOMON W

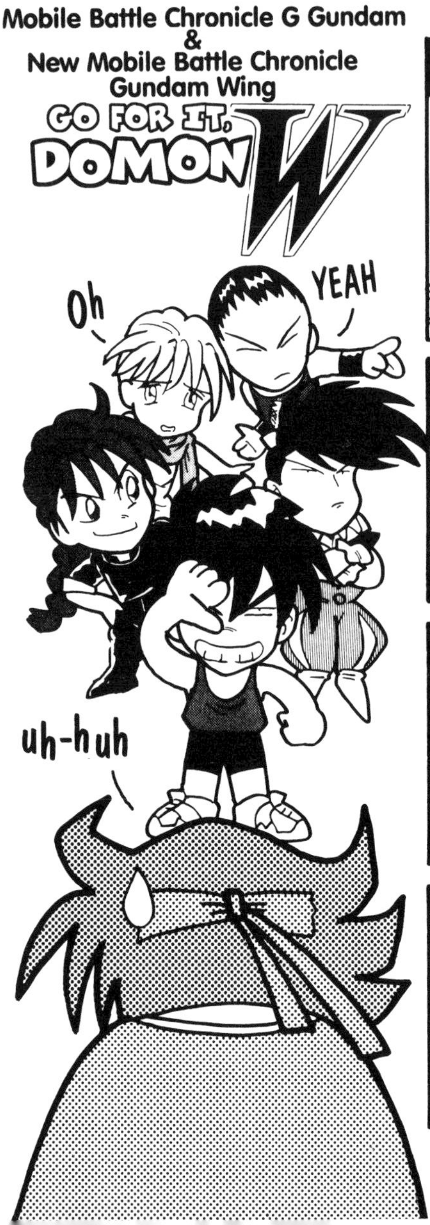
Oh
YEAH
uh-huh

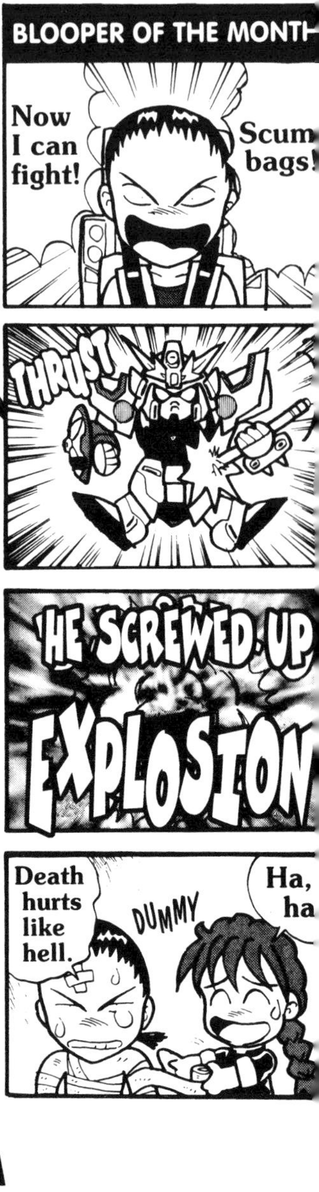
BLOOPER OF THE MONTH
Now I can fight!
Scum bags!
THRUST
HE SCREWED UP
EXPLOSION
Death hurts like hell.
DUMMY
Ha, ha

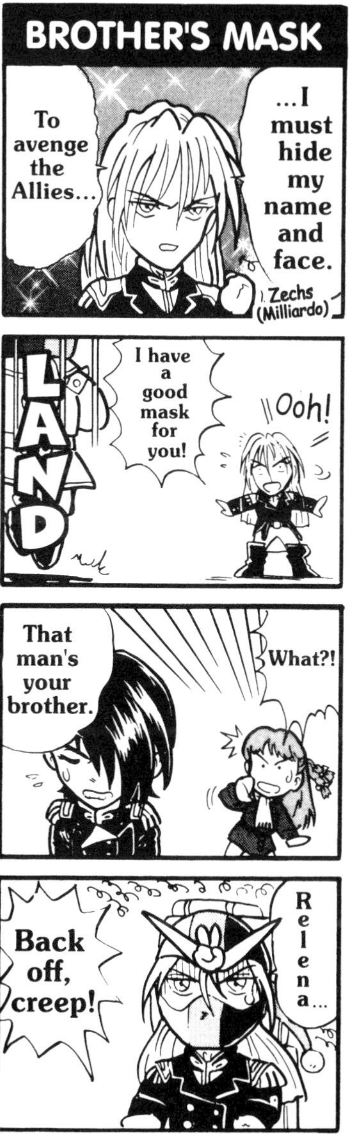
BROTHER'S MASK
To avenge the Allies...
...I must hide my name and face.
Zechs (Milliardo)
LAND
I have a good mask for you!
Ooh!
That man's your brother.
What?!
Back off, creep!
Relena...

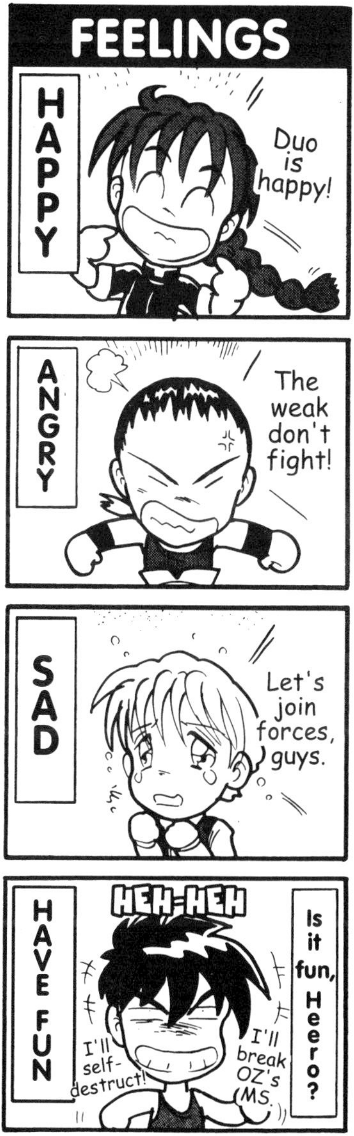
FEELINGS
HAPPY
Duo is happy!
ANGRY
The weak don't fight!
SAD
Let's join forces, guys.
HAVE FUN
HEH-HEH
Is it fun, Heero?
I'll self-destruct!
I'll break OZ's MS.

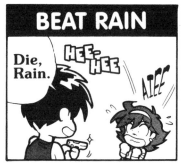

BEAT RAIN

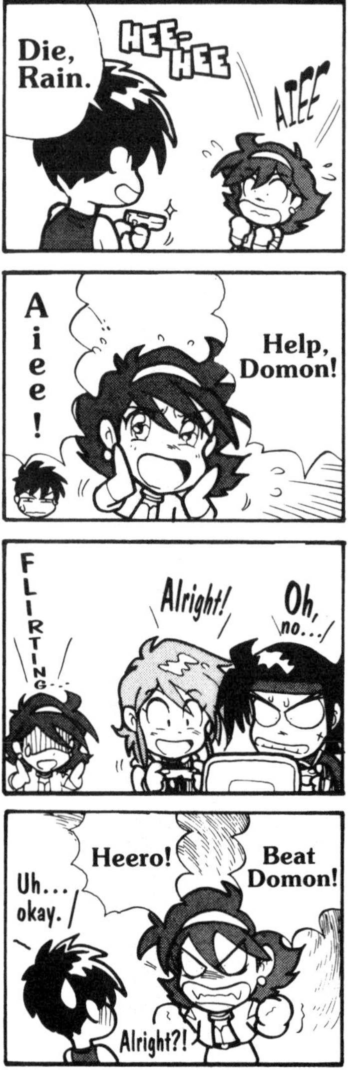
Die, Rain.
HEE-HEE
AIEE
Aiee!
Help, Domon!
FLIRTING
Alright!
Oh, no...
Heero!
Beat Domon!
Uh... okay.
Alright?!

COMBAT TECHNIQUE

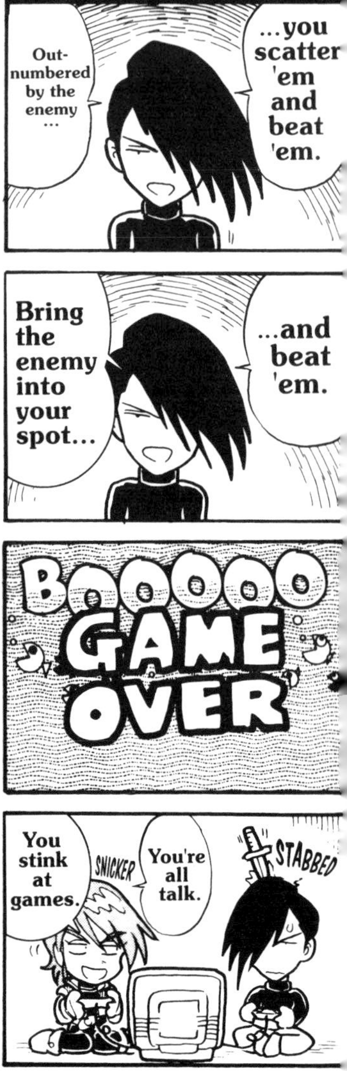
Outnumbered by the enemy...
...you scatter 'em and beat 'em.
Bring the enemy into your spot...
...and beat 'em.
BOOOOO
GAME OVER
You stink at games.
SNICKER
You're all talk.
STABBED

PACIFISM

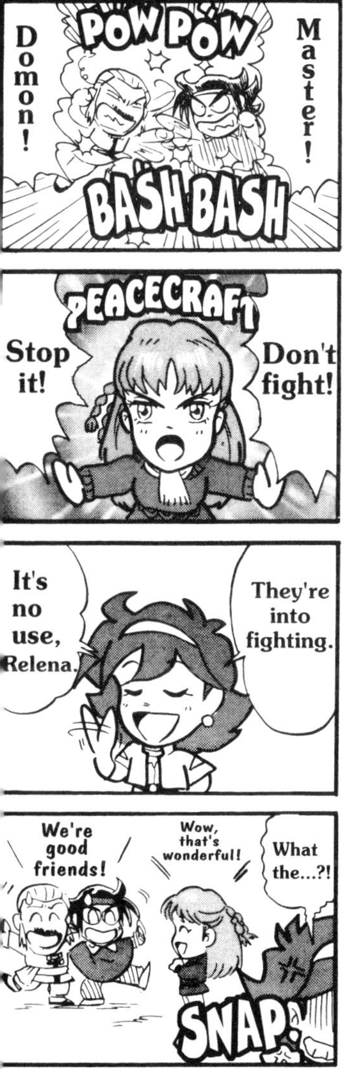
Domon!
POW POW
Master!
BASH BASH
Stop it!
PEACECRAFT
Don't fight!
It's no use, Relena.
They're into fighting.
We're good friends!
Wow, that's wonderful!
What the...?!
SNAP!

KIND RAIN

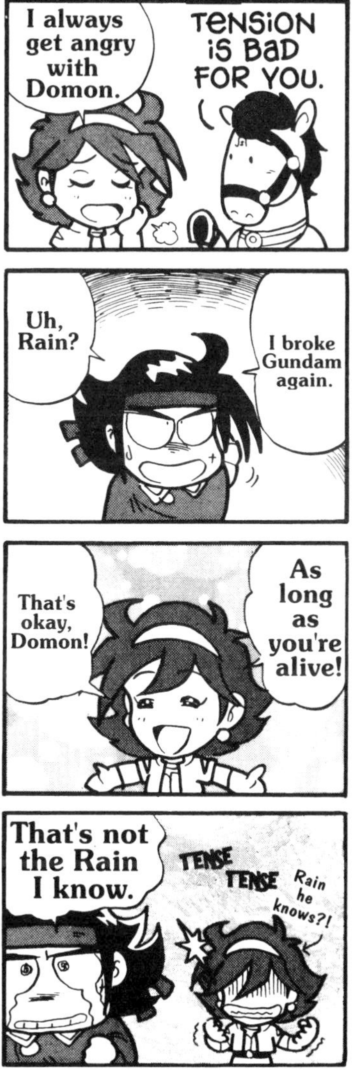
I always get angry with Domon.
TENSION IS BAD FOR YOU.
Uh, Rain?
I broke Gundam again.
That's okay, Domon!
As long as you're alive!
That's not the Rain I know.
TENSE
TENSE
Rain he knows?!

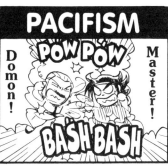

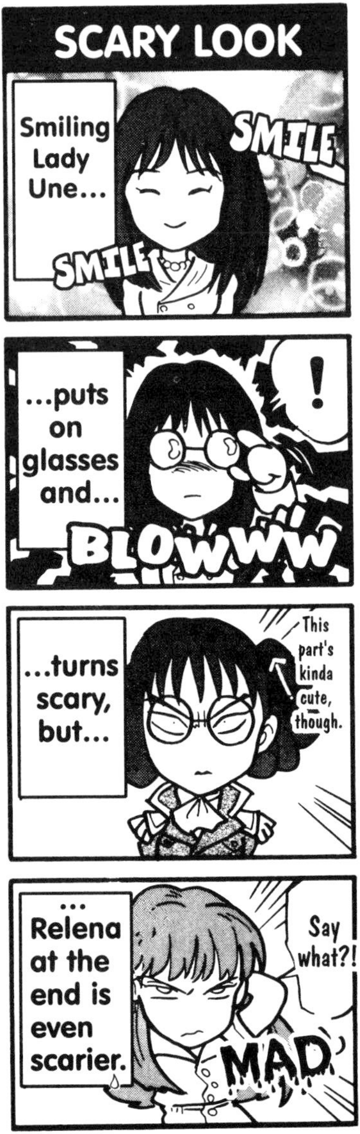
SCARY LOOK
Smiling Lady Une...
SMILE
SMILE
...puts on glasses and...
!
BLOWWW
...turns scary, but...
This part's kinda cute, though.
...Relena at the end is even scarier.
Say what?!
MAD

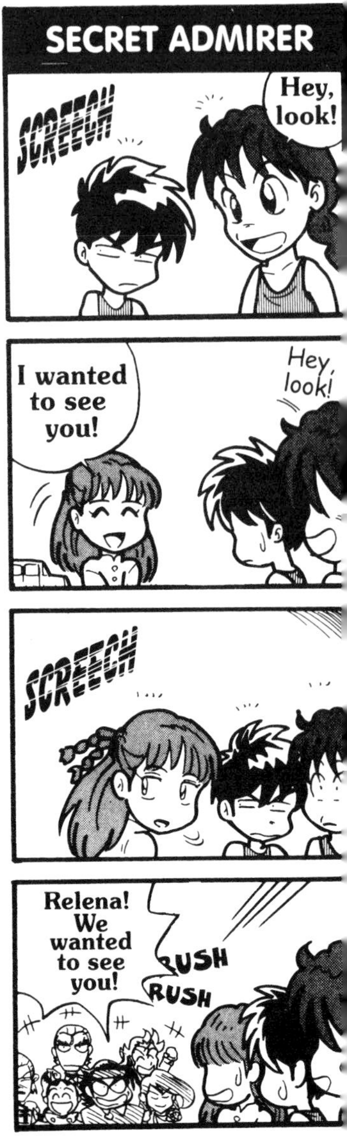
SECRET ADMIRER
SCREECH
Hey, look!
I wanted to see you!
Hey, look!
SCREECH
Relena! We wanted to see you!
RUSH
RUSH

(GO, DOMON W, END)